BRANDIES & LIQUEURS OF THE WORLD

Brandies & Liqueurs of the World

By HURST HANNUM
and ROBERT S. BLUMBERG

1976

DOUBLEDAY & COMPANY, INC.
GARDEN CITY, NEW YORK

Library of Congress Cataloging in Publication Data

Hannum, Hurst.
 Brandies & liqueurs of the world.

 Includes index.
  1. Brandy. 2. Liqueurs. I. Blumberg,
Robert S., joint author. II. Title.
TP599.H28   641.2'53
ISBN 0-385-09615-1
Library of Congress Catalog Card Number 74–2504

PREFACE

It has been our goal to write as comprehensive and useful a guide as possible to the delightful world of brandies and liqueurs, but we should state that it has not been our intention to provide a complete listing of every brandy and liqueur produced in the world. Such an undertaking would be nearly impossible due to the numbers involved, but we have included virtually all the best known of these spirits, pausing along the way to mention enough of the lesser known, more esoteric products to satisfy (we hope) the curiosity of even the most ardent spirit fancier.

We have tried to unearth the true stories of brandies and liqueurs—their history, production, traditions, and character—and not merely to repeat publicity handouts. Wherever possible, we actually visited the distilleries, monasteries, and regions where the spirits are made, hoping to grasp not only the techniques of production but also the attitudes of those who make them. These visits led us along ten thousand miles of European roads, to the large corporations of New York, and on extensive trips through the brandy-producing country in California. The result is a work that we hope you will find both interesting and informative, a work that treats the intriguing world of brandies, *eaux-de-vie,* and liqueurs in the detail it so spiritedly deserves.

Special thanks are due to many people who, if not exactly encouraging, at least put up with us during the lengthy and somewhat sporadic writing of this book. First, of course, is Marion Blumberg, who sustained us both spiritually and gastronomically and who is responsible for the section on recipes. Mary Blumberg handled the typing (and our writing) superbly, and Hurst's special thanks to Caitriona MacReynolds and others in Belfast for helping him through the schizophrenia of trying to practice law and to write books on brandy at the same time.

Our gratitude also goes out to Michael Giovonniello for his excellent illustrations; Irene and Jay Aleck, on whose kitchen table much of this book was written; Richard Leland, who struggled through many tastings; Terri and Jim Olsen, for providing reviving 1963 Taylor when needed; David Bottles, for the cheerful way in which he abandoned his work to guide our week in Alsace; Gustave Lorentz, for his gracious Alsatian hospitality; Susan Shain and her excellent Chinese interpreting; and Robert Finigan, who offered us several interesting bottles.

There are a number of people whose helpfulness greatly facilitated our task, whom we would like to especially acknowledge. These include Bob Flynn, Cesare Gentile, Dr. James Guymon, Jim Lucas, James McManus, Eli Skofis, and Gérard Sturm.

While nearly all those whom we contacted for information were friendly and helpful, the kindness and assistance of some went well beyond the call of duty. Among those to whom personal thanks are due are Mr. and Mrs. Frank Brastaad, Colin Campbell, Jean-Paul Camus, Jacques Canton, Nicolò Luxardo di Franchi, Jacques Firino Martell, and Phillippe Mitterand. We would also like to thank Bénédictine, Chartreuse, the Christian Brothers of California, Luxardo, Stock, the California Brandy Board, and the Bureau National du Cognac for supplying us with photographs.

CONTENTS

PART ONE

Brandies

THE SCIENCE AND THE ART

The Spirit

The cultivation of the vine and the production of wine have been known for thousands of years—virtually since the beginning of recorded history. But while the process of distillation has also been known at least since the time of the ancient Egyptians, the distillation of wine into its spirit, brandy, dates back only a comparatively few centuries.

History does not well record who first discovered the principle of "distillation," which comes from the Latin word *distillare,* meaning to drop or trickle down. This refers to the physical principle that a liquid, when heated to a temperature called its boiling point, will vaporize, and when the vapor is subsequently cooled below the boiling point, it will recondense into drops of liquid. It is thought that by 800 B.C. the Chinese were distilling a spirit from a rice-and-sugar wine, and the Egyptians practiced the art of distillation to capture the essences of herbs, plants, and flowers. Greek writings describe the production of turpentine through cooling the vapors of heated pine resin, and Aristotle wrote in the fourth century before Christ that sea water, after being heated and changed into vapor, returned as sweet water. The science of distillation continued under the Romans, and was introduced from the Middle East by the Moors as they spread their influence across northern Africa and into southern Europe during the early Middle Ages. In Europe, distillation became one of the major tools of the alchemists in their search for a process to turn base metals into precious ones.

In the late thirteenth century, Arnold de Vila Nova taught alchemy in what is now Spain and France, and to him is attributed the first written word on the subject of the distillation of wine into a spirit. He was so excited by the restorative and curative powers ascribed to his liquid that he called it *"aqua vitae"*—the water of life. The Catalan scholar and missionary Raymond Lully was a pupil of Vila Nova, and he maintained that *aqua vitae* must have been divinely inspired.

Whether it was actually Vila Nova or an earlier unknown who discovered that wine can be distilled into a powerful and fiery spirit does not matter. What is important is that by the fourteenth century, as Europe moved into the Renaissance, the distillation of wine began to spread throughout the southern part of the continent, and in the chilly climates farther north the distillation of grain spirits may even have preceded this.

The first mention of the distillation of wine in the Armagnac region is contained in a legal document dated 1411 and conserved today in the offices of the French *département* of Haute-Garonne. In the early 1500s wine was being distilled into *eau-de-vie* in Alsace, and in 1514 a Parisian corporation was formed which included sauce, lemonade, and vinegar makers and distillers of *eau-de-vie*. By 1559 the lawmakers of Bordeaux thought it necessary to forbid distillation within the city for fear that a disastrous fire would occur. From its secret, alchemical origins, distillation of brandy or *eau-de-vie* had progressed until by the mid-seventeenth century it was being sold from pushcarts on the streets of Paris.

The English word "brandy" is said to have derived from the Dutch term *brandewijn,* or burnt wine, referring to the fire applied to wine to heat it and vaporize the alcohol.

The simplest and oldest way of making brandy is in a pot still. This consists of a container, or pot, in which the liquid to be distilled is placed. Originally, the pot was heated by a wood fire, though today natural gas is the most common heating agent. There is a collecting system attached to the top of the still to catch the vapors, which are condensed on their way down to a receiving vessel. The basic pot still is still used in many areas of the world, most notably in Cognac, although modern refinements have made it much more complicated than the above simple description might suggest.

Though the pot still is a well-tried, traditional means of producing some complex and delicious brandies, it is a relatively slow and inefficient means of distillation. So, in the early 1800s several new designs came forth, the most practical of which was invented by an Irishman named Aeneas Coffey. This so-called Coffey still consists of a large column with a source of heat, usually steam, at the bottom. The wine or other liquid material to be distilled is added about halfway up the column. The heat of the steam rising from below vaporizes the falling wine, and the volatile elements, including ethyl alcohol, rise to varying heights before condensing into liquid. The upper part of the column contains a number of perforated plates upon which the liquid collects and from which it may be withdrawn. The water and nonvolatile compounds pass in large part to the bottom of the column, where they can be removed as waste. This type of still has the economic advantage that it can distill large quantities of material continuously, without having to be cleaned and recharged the way a pot still does. Additionally, this new still could be modified to yield a neutral, high-proof spirit whose quality could be more easily regulated than with the pot still. Named for its shape or mode of operation, the column, or continuous, still is in wide use throughout the world today for the production of all types of spirits.

Distillation

Like any other liquid, wine will boil, or vaporize, when sufficiently heated. Since ethyl alcohol boils at 78.3° Celsius (173° Fahrenheit) and water does not boil until 100° C (212° F), it is possible to vaporize nearly all the ethyl alcohol by heating wine to an appropriate temperature. When condensed, the liquid becomes a powerful, concentrated spirit.

When a pot still is used for distillation, brandy is usually taken off after the second distillation, at about 65–70% alcohol. With a continuous still, the strength of the distillate depends on the height of the column and the level at which the product is withdrawn. In Armagnac the column stills are relatively small and the brandy is taken off at 60–70% alcohol; with a large continuous still like those used in California, the brandy is withdrawn at about 85% alcohol. A column still can also be run to produce very-high-proof neutral spirits, at close to 97% alcohol, the point at which ethyl alcohol forms a constant-boiling-point mixture with water and can no longer be separated out.

Throughout much of the world, the alcohol content of a spirit is labeled as a simple volume percentage, certainly the most rational system of measurement. In France the term degrees Gay Lussac is used; thus a 40% alcohol spirit is labeled 40° G.L. In that part of the world under English influence, however, the term "proof" is used. But just as English and American are two different languages, so are English and American proofs different. Proof is an old English term stemming from the days when the strength of a spirit was measured by mixing it with a small quantity of black powder. If the mixture exploded when ignited, this was "proof" of its strong alcoholic content. Later it was found that the minimum strength necessary for this reaction is slightly above fifty per cent ethyl alcohol by volume, and alcoholic proof in Britain is now fixed so that 100 British proof equals 57.1% ethyl alcohol by volume. The American system has the benefit of simplicity: "proof" is twice the alcohol content by volume. Thus a brandy marketed at 40% alcohol would be labeled 70 proof in Britain, 80 proof in the United States, and 40° Gay Lussac in France.

High-proof ethyl alcohol is referred to as a silent or neutral spirit. Though strong and fiery, it has little in the way of aroma or flavor. Distillates that contain only high-proof ethyl alcohol cut with distilled water are also neutral spirits; a good example of this is the vodka that has swept the United States in popularity in recent years. Produced mainly from high-proof grain spirits and not aged in any vessel that would impart flavor, such vodka is so light that one manufacturer coined the slogan "leaves you breathless." "Tasteless" might as well be added, since such a spirit relies on the fruit juice or mixer to which it is added for flavor.

Just as wine is much more than a simple mixture of ethyl alcohol and water, brandy is also a very complex substance, in which alcohol simply plays a larger part. Many of the highly aromatic and flavorful compounds present in wine are carried over by distillation and contribute much of the fruitiness and complexity in a good brandy. These organic compounds are usually present in only very small quantities and are referred to as "congeners." Congeners are found naturally in grapes and other fruit used to make wine. They also are produced as by-products of yeast-induced alcoholic fermentation and can be formed during the aging of wine, in the distillation process itself, and during the aging of brandy in wood.

Certain of these organic compounds have boiling points lower than that of ethyl alcohol, and when wine is heated they thus vaporize rather easily and quickly. In a pot still they are present primarily in the initial phase of distillation, in what is called the "foreshots" or "heads" section of the distillate. In a continuous still their volatility causes them to pass to the very top of the column, where they can be removed from the main product and reprocessed.

Aldehydes are a major component of distillate heads. Acetaldehyde is present in small amounts in all wines, and if excess amounts pass into the distillate the spirit will smell and taste unpleasantly hot and harsh. Other highly volatile substances include acetate, present in wines that have started to vinegarize, and various gaseous forms of sulfur. While sulfur is often applied to vineyards and wines to inhibit the growth of undesirable bacteria, yeasts, and molds, its presence in wine that is to be distilled is undesirable, for it can easily taint the aroma of brandy. Other off aromas or flavors in wine may also pass easily into the distillate, and good brandy can thus be made only from fresh, sound, unspoiled base wine.

Ethyl alcohol, which has two carbon atoms per molecule, is but one of a number of alcohols formed during the fermentation by yeast of grape juice into wine. Other alcohols, with more than two carbons, also present in wine and brandy are called higher alcohols. During distillation these can be concentrated to a sufficient degree so that the higher-alcohol fraction, when added to water, will separate into an oil phase, or oil layer. This oil phase is called fusel oil, and since the higher alcohols are the major component of fusel oil, they may also be referred to as fusel alcohols.

All distilled spirits whose flavor reflects their base fruit or grain have certain levels of higher alcohols. In small quantities these compounds are highly desirable, for they add complexity, flavor, body, and aroma to the product, and they may also enhance the spirit's aging potential. With time, certain fusel alcohols will change into the intriguing aromatic compounds known to chemists as esters. However, when present in excess, fusel alcohols impart an unpleasant, overly pungent smell reminiscent of a cross between very grapy, freshly fermented wine and bubbling tar. Since the total elimination of higher alcohols would rob a spirit of much of its character, the maintenance of fusel alcohols at a desirable level is one of the major challenges to the distiller.

In their pure form higher alcohols have a boiling temperature higher than that of water. However, due to their chemical properties, when mixed with water or dilute solutions of ethyl alcohol the volatility of higher alcohols is enhanced and they will boil off at lower temperatures. In continuous stills fusel alcohols tend to concentrate at a level on the column where the alcohol is around 65%; both above and below this level the concentration gradually decreases. Since in California "beverage brandy" is usually removed from a continuous still at close to 85% ethyl alcohol, such a distillate is relatively low in fusel alcohol content and correspondingly relatively light in flavor. The final product of a pot still, however, is usually 65–70% alcohol, and thus pot-still brandy tends to have a higher concentration of fusel alcohols, to be more flavorful and aromatic, and to require longer aging for full development. The same is true for whiskies: single malt Scotch whisky is distilled in a pot still and is a full-flavored and pungent beverage; blended scotch contains a large proportion of more-neutral spirits from continuous stills, making it lighter and less flavorful than a single-malt.

During the fermentation of wine, certain highly aromatic compounds called ethyl esters are formed. Chemically, they behave in a manner similar to that of the higher alcohols during distillation; that is, they are more volatile in mixtures of water and ethyl alcohol than they are in their pure form. In a continuous still they concentrate at a level slightly below fusel alcohols. In a pot still they tend to come off rather quickly in the heads fraction. These compounds are desirable in small quantities for the complexity they add to the aroma of a brandy, and it is a challenge to the distiller to capture enough of them without also including excessive quantities of undesirable odorous elements from the heads fraction.

The least volatile chemicals will volatize late in distillation, in what is called the "tails," or "feints," of a pot distillate; in a continuous still they will tend to fall to the lowest parts of the column. This fraction is discarded both because it is low in ethyl alcohol and because it contains heavy, undesirable odors and flavors. It is normally redistilled in order to extract as much alcohol as possible.

This has been but a brief, simplified description of a complex science. Over one hundred different compounds have been identified as contributing to the aroma and flavor of brandy, and many more are probably waiting to be discovered. Modern technology, through the design and operation of stills, can control to a great degree the composition of brandy. But science alone cannot make a great brandy. Much still depends on the skill of the distiller—his nose and palate and his experience—to decide which raw young spirit will mature beautifully, which will not, and what blends must be made to produce a flavorful and high-quality product.

Aging

Brandy fresh from the still is water-clear in color, fiery and raw in flavor. Except for a few pomace brandies, which are bottled in this condition—*grappa* from Italy, *pisco* from Peru—all great brandies of the world must be aged to permit the subtle formation of smoothness, delicacy, and complexity.

The most suitable aging vessel for brandy is wood, for several reasons. Wood is a porous substance that allows air to combine with the brandy in the slow oxidation and esterification process that is responsible for imparting intriguing new flavors and rounding off the fiery young spirit. Wood also imparts tannin and flavors of its own to the brandy, as well as a natural color that ranges from pale yellow to a deep amber. Brandy aged in non-porous containers such as glass or stainless steel can undergo only minimal oxidation and will remain as colorless and rough as the day it came from the still.

"Wood" embraces a vast range of substances, and the question of which type of wood is best for aging brandy is a lively one. Oak is by far the most widely used aging vessel. Each variety has its own particular character and flavor, which is imparted to the spirit, and most brandy-producing areas of the world are rather chauvinistic about their own type. While it would be nice to believe that each region has over the years sought out the one variety of wood whose flavor best married with their product, the truth of the matter is that whatever was most available and least expensive was probably used. Thus cognac is aged in Limousin oak, armagnac in the black oak of the local forests, and California brandy in American oak from the hills of Arkansas and Tennessee.

Color is extracted from oak at a rather slow rate. New oak imparts more color than will a previously used cask, and of course very old barrels will impart little color other than that acquired through oxidation. Brandy must be aged in oak at least ten years to obtain what we would consider the typical golden color of a commercial brandy. This time could be shortened by leaving the spirit in new wood exclusively, but this would also extract a great deal of astringent tannin and strong wood flavors. Since 90 per cent of the commercial brandy sold throughout the world today is aged far less than ten years, it has become standard practice everywhere to add caramel syrup for darker color. Caramel is used in both whiskey and brandy, the result being a uniformly colored spirit that meets the public's preconceived idea of what color a good whiskey or brandy should be. The small amount of caramel necessary for such coloration does not impart any significant flavor of its own, so the essential quality of the spirit is preserved.

The amount of time a brandy is left in wood depends on the desires of the brandy maker, of course taking into account the commercial marketing factors with which he must deal. The longer a brandy is left in wood, the greater its cost in terms of untaken profits, tied-up capital, losses from evaporation, etc. The larger the stock of aging brandies a producer has, the more aging cellars and warehouse space he will require. In a few areas of the world, most notably Cognac and Armagnac, the finest young brandies may be selected for prolonged aging in casks. But, as always, the judgment of the maker is all-important, for even the best brandy cannot be left in wood indefinitely. As a general rule, the finest cognacs reach their peak after about fifty years; beyond this they may become excessively dark and woody and lose any fruit or elegance they had in their youth. Armagnacs seem to have an optimum age of twenty to thirty years, while California brandies may peak at only ten to fifteen years. Of course, exceptional brandies do exist; we have tasted from cask brandies far older than this in both Cognac and Armagnac and found them to be magnificent.

The quality of a young brandy plays a major role in its aging potential, and no producer would waste his time aging a poor distillate for a long time. The newness of wood selected is also important. A young brandy can spend only a relatively short time—several months to a maximum of a few years—in new oak before it obtains too much wood flavor and becomes bitter and unbalanced. A short time in new oak, followed by progressively longer periods in older oak, will produce a complex brandy, in which the gradually obtained wood character is well balanced by the developing complexity of the brandy itself. A brandy placed only in older casks from its youth can remain in the barrel even longer without becoming excessively woody.

But economics prevents us from buying (and most producers from offering) great quantities of twenty-to-fifty-year-old brandies; most brandy sold and consumed in the world is quite young. Some 80 per cent of bottled cognac is little more than three years old; the average age of California brandy is four years, and many bottles squeak out of the warehouse when only two or three. In an attempt to make up for smoothness that might otherwise have been obtained by age, it has become common practice nearly everywhere to add certain smoothening or softening agents to brandy. The most common of these is sugar, for 1–2 per cent of sweetness will soften the harshness of a young brandy just as it may often be used to mellow a rough wine. In some countries rather strong flavoring elements such as vanilla, dessert wines, or fruit and citrus flavor may be added. If this appears reminiscent of the late Middle Ages, when herbs and spices were added to cover the taste of bad brandies, it may not be without reason. The modern problem, however, is often the opposite, as flavors may be added to enhance neutral spirits.

One of the true skills of the brandy maker is the art of blending. While the quality of newly distilled brandy varies less from year to year than does that of wine, each distillate does have its own particular character. Each producer has a distinctive style, and the brandy maker will set out to balance the pungency of one young distillate with the delicacy of another, the fullness of one barrel with the lightness of a different batch. Almost all young blends will also be enhanced by the addition of small quantities of aged stock. Some brandy makers prefer to blend shortly before bottling, allowing the final batch a few months to marry in large holding tanks. Others think it best to blend very young brandies so that they will have the longest time possible to develop and integrate their flavors.

Brandy is usually bottled and sold at 40–45° G.L., the alcohol level at which most experts feel the best balance is struck between alcohol and flavors. However, as we have seen, brandy comes off a still at anywhere from 60% to 85% alcohol. Before being bottled it is cut to the appropriate level with purified or distilled water.

Brandy aging in cask loses a certain part of its volume to evaporation through the pores of the barrel. This averages between 3 and 5 per cent each year, depending primarily on the climate. In a very dry climate both water and alcohol will be lost, and the alcoholic strength may remain nearly the same or even rise significantly. In most climates more alcohol than water will be lost and the proof of the brandy will gradually drop. Brandy stored in barrel in a moist climate for forty to fifty years may even drop low enough in alcohol to be bottled directly from the barrel at about 40%. Ordinarily, the strength of newly distilled brandy is cut with distilled water, at the time of barreling, to 50–55% alcohol, and then again, at the time of bottling, to the desired level.

It is usual practice to filter brandy prior to bottling, after the brandy has been chilled for a day or two to precipitate out certain inorganic salts. Before this was done, it was found that some bottles would turn cloudy when passing through cold climates or if refrigerated. While this did not affect the flavor of the brandy, its appearance was ruined. Today cold-stabilization and filtration remove these precipitating compounds before the brandy is bottled.

Brandy does essentially all of its aging during its time in wood. Once bottled no further significant transformation will occur. Brandy will remain stable in an unopened bottle for many years, tasting as fresh when opened as it did when bottled. Care must be taken to store the bottle upright, however, as the high alcohol content of the spirit will slowly attack the cork or other closure material and may impart off flavors to the brandy.

While an opened bottle of brandy will remain in perfect condition for many months, eventually it will begin to slowly oxidize and to lose some of its freshness and aroma. This is particularly true when only a small amount of brandy is left in the bottle for a long period of time. If your own consumption of brandy is limited, you would probably do better to buy small bottles as needed rather than leaving larger sizes partially full for months at a time.

Since brandy ages only in the cask, it makes sense to pay a premium for a recently bottled old brandy, but not to pay for an old bottle containing brandy of unknown quality. The bottles of so-called Napoleon brandy, supposedly bottled during the reign of Napoleon I in the early years of the nineteenth century, are an example. Most of the time, the authenticity of such bottles is difficult to verify, but even if they were legitimate their contents would be no better, and by now probably less good, than when bottled. While, occasionally, dusty old "Napoleon" cognacs will surface and be offered by an enterprising merchant at high prices, such bottles are rarely worth much even as collector's items. If you are intrigued by the prospects of a truly old brandy, try one of the commercially available Extras or Hors d'Âge from a respected shipper of cognac or armagnac.

Tasting, Serving, and Appreciating Brandy

Evaluating a number of brandies at once is a difficult task, for the high alcohol content quickly overwhelms nose and palate. For this reason, professional tasters, who must constantly evaluate young brandies and compare their own product with that of their competitors, generally choose to dilute brandy samples to be tasted with an equal amount of distilled water. This reduces the alcohol content to that of a fortified wine and allows the taster to discern subtle nuances of aroma and taste that would otherwise be masked by the strength of the ethyl alcohol. Dilution is particularly important for spotting off odors and flavors in freshly distilled brandies.

Colors can be compared, but of course this is meaningless if the samples have been adjusted with caramel. The glass should then be gently swirled, as if smelling a wine, and the aroma evaluated. This is by far the most important part of the sensory examination of brandy, and professional "tasters" do much more sniffing than actual drinking. Look for bad qualities first, such as excessive harshness, traces of vinegar or sulfur, or a cooked quality from a too-hot distillation. A good distillate should retain an identifiable character imparted by its base product; brandy should thus retain a certain grapiness in both aroma and flavor, just as calvados should smell of apple and kirsch of cherries.

With some experience it is possible to estimate the amount of fusel alcohols present in a brandy from the nature of the aroma. This is best seen by comparing brandies of known differences: *grappa* or other pomace brandies will have very high levels of strong, oily fusel alcohols; cognac an intermediate amount; and continuous-still California brandies will be relatively light in fusels. Wood character can also be judged from the aroma: is it pleasant and round, or does it seem harsh, artificial, or unbalanced?

When tasting, a small sip of brandy should be swished around the mouth so that it reaches all the taste buds on tongue and palate. Notice any sweetness or other flavoring elements present, whether the brandy is light or full-bodied, its smoothness and balance, and the presence or absence of harsh or unpleasant flavors. The complexity of the flavors and the spiciness and astringency of oak will give an indication of the brandy's age.

When evaluating several brandies at a time it is mandatory to spit out each sample without swallowing and to clear the palate with bread or neutral crackers and water between tastes. Otherwise, the flavors of one will linger over into the next and make judgment difficult. After the brandy is expectorated, subtle changes in the flavors should linger and continue to fill the palate. A "short" aftertaste indicates a relatively simple, undistinguished distillate.

Learning to critically evaluate and compare brandies is a difficult task; many brandy makers and professional tasters will tell you it is a lifelong one. But knowledge of a few basic chemical facts and tasting guidelines will quickly enable you to distinguish differences among types of brandies and will greatly enhance your appreciation of all distilled spirits.

Brandy should be served simply in clear glasses that fit comfortably into the palm of your hand. The heat of the hand will gently warm the brandy, encouraging aromas to pass from the glass. Medium-sized traditional balloon glasses, tulip-shaped glasses, or small chimney glasses similar to those recommended for sherry are all comfortable and efficient for brandy drinking. It is helpful to have a bowl that permits swirling, and a slight in-curving of the rim of the glass allows concentration of the aromas. The huge balloon-shaped glasses offered in some restaurants are totally unnecessary—unless you plan on taking one home for your goldfish!

Brandy is traditionally served after a meal as what the French call a *"digestif."* The traditional caricature of a brandy drinker is that of an overstuffed businessman with glass in one hand, cigar in the other—a not unpleasant posture, by the way, though its appeal may be limited. So much for tradition.

Many modern brandy producers and marketing executives argue that the relegation of brandy to after-the-meal sipping is pure snobbery. They quite rightly point out that brandy can be a welcome addition to various punches and mixed drinks, and that brandy is the natural apéritif to introduce the flavor of the grape and to complement the wine that will accompany dinner. Of course, brandy used for mixing with other beverages should be a relatively young, light, and inexpensive one, for the complexity of an older brandy may interfere with the other flavors. If bourbon and whiskey drinkers would try brandy in place of their usual spirit in cocktails and highballs they might find themselves pleasantly surprised.

Brandy can also play an important role in the kitchen. Apart from its somewhat spectacular role in the preparation of flaming dishes of all kinds, its clean, subtle grape flavors blend well with most meats and add an interesting complexity to sauces.

While young brandies can be excellent mixers, a well-aged brandy with complex flavors, what the British term a liqueur brandy, belongs at the end of a meal. Here you can fully appreciate the finesse and charm of an old cognac or the fullness of an Hors d'Âge armagnac while relaxing in the quiet hours of the evening. And the French are right in calling brandy a *digestif,* for a fine brandy has amazing restorative powers which help settle the effects of a long and perhaps overly rich meal, as well as prepare you for a good night's sleep and for the morning that inevitably arrives.

COGNAC—MOST FAMOUS OF ALL

THE BRANDIES OF FRANCE

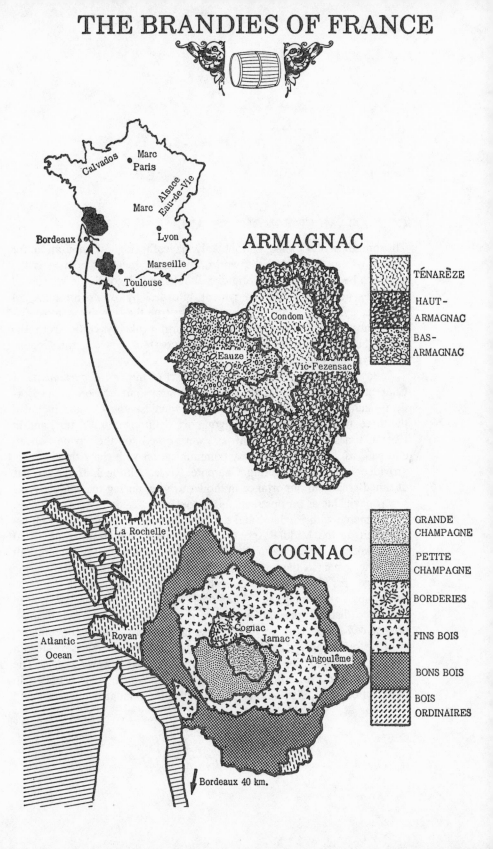

COGNAC—MOST FAMOUS OF ALL

The brandies of Cognac undoubtedly have the highest reputation for quality of any brandy in the world, and many feel that cognac is the standard by which all other brandies should be judged. While we should certainly not ignore the enjoyment afforded by other brandies, of different styles and tastes, it is nevertheless true that the finest, most elegant, most complex brandies in the world probably come from the fewer than 100,000 hectares (250,000 acres) of vines in the Cognac district of southwestern France.

Today, Cognac consists for the most part of the two *départements* of Charente and Charente-Maritime, its southern limit bordering the Bordeaux subregion of Blaye. Historically, what is now Cognac included the three ancient provinces of Angoumois, Saintonge, and Aunis, and in Roman times the three "countries" were noted for their wine, wheat, and salt, as well as for the easy communication with the Atlantic coast provided by the meandering Charente River. Although the river has declined greatly in importance in modern times, during the Middle Ages it was navigable as far upstream as Angoulême.

Commerce with England and the Scandinavian countries was well established by the Middle Ages, opening markets and trade routes that would later provide a natural outlet for the brandies of the region. Salt and wine remained the most important exports at this time, often being exchanged for wood and salted fish from the northern climates.

Perhaps surprisingly, the Charentes region was among the last in France to distill important quantities of wine into brandy. While mention of *eau-de-vie* may be found in some sixteenth-century documents, most historians agree that it was not until the early- or mid-seventeenth century that distillation became widespread in what is now Cognac. The earliest cognac firm still in existence, that of Augier, was founded in 1643. In contrast, distillation was already being regulated in Alsace and

Paris a hundred years earlier, and Armagnac had been producing brandy since the 1400s.

No one agrees precisely on why the growers of the Charentes turned to distillation, but it seems likely that devastation of the vineyards during the religious wars of the fifteenth and sixteenth centuries, subsequent overplanting (perhaps with lesser grapes), and a resulting drop in the quality of the wine all contributed to the rapid and widespread change from wine production to brandy production. Another explanation is that the wines of the Charentes simply did not travel well, but their reputation in preceding centuries contradicts this hypothesis.

In any event, distillation of the relatively thin, acid wine of the Charentes was widespread by the beginning of the eighteenth century, and Diderot's *Encyclopédie* of 1751 mentions Cognac as a town "famous for its *eaux-de-vie*." The brandy was produced in much the same manner as it is today, but it was generally consumed as a raw, fiery spirit which might have been aged only as long as the voyage to its eventual destination required. While Cognac brandy gradually created a name for itself in France, its orientation from the beginning was largely toward exportation—at first to the same markets with which the Charentes farmers, via Dutch merchants, had been trading for centuries. Several shipping houses were established that still exist today, including Martell (1715) and Rémy Martin (1724), and between 1718 and 1736, nearly five hundred thousand barrels of cognac were shipped from the port of La Rochelle.

As the eighteenth century became the nineteenth, distillation of cognac brandy had become an important business whose reputation had spread far beyond the original markets of England and Scandinavia, although both remained major importers of cognac. This trade was interrupted by the Napoleonic Wars, but normalcy quickly returned. Some grape growers (*viticulteurs*) continued to distill and ship their own products; they are called *bouilleurs de cru*. But as distillation expanded, more and more was done by the *bouilleurs de profession,* the professional distillers, who may or may not also own vineyards. But perhaps most important were the shippers (*négociants*), who bought either wine to be distilled or *eau-de-vie* which they then blended and sold. By now it was realized that aging in oak casks greatly improved the character of the young, rough cognac, and it was the *négociants* who began building up stocks of aged cognacs in a systematic way. Courvoisier, Delamain, Denis-Mounié and Hine were all founded in the early-nineteenth century strictly as blending-aging-shipping concerns which did no distilling of their own. Many of the other well-known names on today's bottles of cognac were also introduced in the nineteenth century, although most did some distilling as well as acting as *négociants*.

It was not until the mid-nineteenth century that cognac producers began exporting in bottles; until that time, all *eaux-de-vie* were shipped in cask to their destination. Bottle sales guaranteed that the cognac would not be blended with other products and also made brand names more important, although today a few markets (such as the state monopolies of Scandinavia) continue to receive barreled cognac which is then bottled by the importer.

Before the root louse Phylloxera attacked the Cognac vineyards in 1875–80, there were some 280,000 hectares of vines under cultivation in Charente and Charente-Maritime. By 1890, only 53,000 hectares remained, and little increase was noticeable until new plantings were authorized in 1960. By that time, some 68,000 hectares of vines were providing grapes for cognac production, and a major increase in the authorized plantings in the early 1970s should bring the figures up to 100,000 hectares. Yet, due to modern vineyard techniques and a higher percentage of wine actually being distilled, more wine was distilled in the years 1966–70 than in 1866–70, although the 1970 vineyard acreage was only 40 per cent of that a century earlier.

As one might expect, the augmentation of the Cognac vineyards is a reflection of the steadily increasing sales of cognac throughout the world. This is due to the efforts of both the large cognac houses themselves and also, since its establishment in 1941, to the collective publicity and internal controls exercised by the Bureau National Interprofessionnel du Cognac. The latter is a semipublic body on which both growers' co-operatives and professional distillers-*négociants* have equal representation. Its responsibilities include preparing regulations for the cognac trade; providing technical documentation; encouraging research in viticulture, oenology, and distillation; and publicizing cognac as a whole. The Bureau is also responsible for ensuring the age and origin of all cognac exported.

Since the end of World War II, the cognac industry has been characterized by steadily increasing sales and by the gradual concentration of production in the hands of several large shippers. Sales have passed from 27 million bottles in 1947–48 to 112 million bottles in 1972–73, of which approximately 80 per cent was exported. Primarily because of rising cognac prices, sales in 1973–74 dropped to just under 100 million bottles. The three largest houses, Martell, Hennessy, and Courvoisier, probably account for over half the total exports of cognac, and the top dozen or so firms surely account for 90 per cent of the export market.

The domestic French market remains the single most important sales area; in recent years, Frenchmen have consumed about 20 million bottles annually. The United Kingdom has traditionally been Cognac's most important foreign customer, and "brandy" in England is synonymous with cognac. The Scandinavian monopolies (Finland, Norway, Sweden) are much less important in terms of absolute sales, but have continued to buy more cognac nearly every year. West Germany has been an important market for cognac, in recent years second only to the United Kingdom in exports, but recently the rising price of cognac has contributed to a significant drop in sales in favor of less expensive spirits. Another important market is the Far East, particularly Hong Kong, Singapore, and Japan.

The United States remains an important consumer of cognac, although sales have plummeted since their peak in 1970–71, reflecting increasing competition and consumer resistance to the new, higher price of cognac. The jump in price has been caused by increased costs in France, the devaluation of the dollar, and discriminatory tariffs on cognac stemming from the so-called Chicken War of the early 1960s. (When the exportation of American chicken to Common Market countries was effectively stopped by tariffs, the Americans countered by imposing a tax on cognac.) As a result, the price of a bottle of cognac in the United States rose nearly 50 per cent in two years, and most three-star cognacs now sell for double the price of an average California brandy. Sales since 1972 have remained relatively constant, however, and the United States has now regained its place as the second most important cognac export market due to declining sales in other countries.

In 1909, the traditional geographic limits of the Cognac region were codified by governmental decree, and today only brandy produced from vineyards within the delimited area is entitled to the appellation "cognac." The six major subregions, or *crus,* spread in roughly concentric circles around the town of Cognac, and cognac from vines entirely within one of these *crus* may be labeled with the name of that area.

There are two main variables that determine the quality of the different subregions—climate and soil. The climate of the central districts is least influenced by the extremes of the ocean to the west and the continental weather to the east. It is also here that the chalkiest soil is found, which is considered to be the best medium for the white grapes of Cognac. The two central subregions are known as "champagne," not to imply any kinship with the famous French sparkling-wine district (although the chalky soil of both is quite similar), but, rather, as a historical reference to the countryside; *champagne* in French seems to have originally described plains, meadows, or open country. This is distinguished from the outlying *bois,* or wooded district.

Grande Champagne is situated to the south of the river Charente, below Cognac and the neighboring town of Jarnac, and encompasses about thirty-five thousand hectares of land of which just under twelve thousand hectares is planted in white-grape vines. Due to its very mild climate and the high proportion of carbonate of lime in the soil, it has traditionally been considered the finest of all the Cognac growths. The *eaux-de-vie* of Grande Champagne are above all elegant, often possessing a characteristic violet bouquet when mature. They require more aging than cognacs from the other subregions, but they will remain at their peak for years.

Petite Champagne stretches in a semicircle around Grande Champagne, still to the south of the Charente. Its total area is nearly double that of Grande Champagne, but only about a fourth, or fourteen thousand hectares, of the cultivable area is under vines destined for cognac. Differences between the *eaux-de-vie* of the two subregions are slight, although Petite Champagne does not quite match the finesse of the best Grande Champagne cognacs. The *eaux-de-vie* from around Archiac are considered particularly fine.

Fine Champagne is not actually a separate geographic subregion; it is an appellation for a blended cognac entirely from Grande and Petite Champagne, of which at least 50 per cent is from Grande Champagne. In the 1960s Rémy Martin began to publicize the quality of "Fine Champagne" cognac; others, including the "Big Three" of Courvoisier, Hennessy, and Martell, resisted what they considered the overemphasis on only two of the subregions. The latter group held that a blend that included brandy from other areas, Borderies and Fins Bois, for instance, could be the equal of many "Fine Champagnes," and they probably also felt that insistence on Fine Champagne might be detrimental to sales of young, 3-star cognacs which rely heavily on blends of *eaux-de-vie* from less celebrated districts.

Borderies is the smallest subregion, lying just north of the Charente River, adjacent to Grande and Petite Champagne. While nearly one half of the cultivable land is in cognac vineyards, its thirty-eight hundred hectares still yield less than 5 per cent of the cognac produced in the entire region. The soil contains only half the carbonate of lime of Grande Champagne, and the climate is more influenced by the sea. The resulting *eaux-de-vie* are distinctive, full-bodied, and flowery, with strong, fragrant aromas, and are in great demand for blending. They have the additional advantage of aging fairly rapidly, and can thus add both body and maturity to many blends. Only a few pure Borderies are available, among which is Camus's Château du Plessis.

Fins Bois entirely surrounds the preceding three subregions, and its thirty-four thousand hectares of vines provide nearly 40 per cent of the *eaux-de-vie* produced in Cognac. It is the largest of the subregions and thus more subject to variation, as it is influenced by both the sea and the hills to the east. Good cognacs that reach maturity relatively quickly can be produced here, and Fins Bois provides the foundation of most good, average cognacs.

Bons Bois, in turn, surrounds the circle of Fins Bois, and its vineyards are responsible for approximately 22 per cent of the cognac distilled. Less than 8 per cent of the fairly rich cultivable land produces wine for distillation, and the *eau-de-vie* is somewhat thin and uninteresting. Many of the larger *négociants* claim to scorn the Bons Bois, though its cognacs probably find their way into many less expensive blends.

Bois Ordinaires lie to the west of the Bons Bois, in sandy soil greatly influenced by the coastal climate. The westernmost area, which includes the islands of Ré and Oléron, is sometimes referred to as the *Bois à Terroir,* and it is said that the seaweed sometimes used as fertilizer influences the taste of the *eau-de-vie.* Only thirty-five hundred hectares of vineyards are entitled to be distilled as cognac, while another twenty-six hundred hectares produce a local red wine.

The techniques used in the production of cognac are basic, although the path from vine to barrel to bottle is one that takes great skill and patience to master. Each step is regulated by governmental decrees, which attempt to maintain the traditional methods of Cognac without unnecessarily inhibiting the use of modern techniques where appropriate.

While vineyards are very much in evidence as you travel through the gently rolling hills of Cognac, only rarely will you see unbroken expanses of vines similar to those in California's Central Valley. Less than 15 per cent of the total area of the four subregions from Grande Champagne to Fins Bois are actually planted in vineyards, although the triangle passing through Cognac, Jarnac, and Archiac, in the heart of Grande and Petite Champagne, is dotted with enough vineyards to make that statistic surprising.

The composition of those Cognac vineyards whose grapes are destined for distillation is regulated by a decree of May 15, 1936. It provides that the primary grape varieties must be Saint-Émilion (Ugni Blanc), Folle Blanche, or Colombard, and permits a maximum of 10 per cent to be planted in secondary varieties (Blanc Ramé, Jurançon Blanc, Meslier Saint-Francois, Semillon, Sauvignon Blanc, and Sélect).

In the days when the white wines of Aunis, Saintonge, and Angoumois were being enjoyed by the Scandinavians, Colombard was probably the most important variety. As distillation became common, however, it was replaced by the Folle Blanche, which yielded *eaux-de-vie* of great finesse and aroma. Unfortunately, the Folle Blanche is particularly sensitive to rot (*pourriture grise*), and after the decimation of the Cognac vineyards by Phylloxera in the 1880s and a particularly humid, rot-producing vintage in 1891, it fell into disfavor.

Since the beginning of this century, the most important grape has been the Ugni Blanc, which is locally known as the Saint-Émilion (although it has no relation to the famous Bordeaux region of the same name). Today the Ugni Blanc accounts for perhaps 95 per cent of all the white-grape vineyards in Cognac. A few distillers maintain that the Folle Blanche produced a better *eau-de-vie,* but the Ugni Blanc offers the advantages of greater yield and stronger resistance to both frost and rot, and it too is certainly capable of producing a fine brandy.

None of the secondary varieties are particularly important, although the Sélect, a cross between the Jurançon Blanc and Ugni Blanc, seems to have potential.

The grapes ripen in October and November, late enough so that many of the pickers from Bordeaux can simply follow the harvest northward to Cognac. It is becoming increasingly difficult to get enough labor, however, particularly in a bountiful year like 1973. Many migrant workers, often from Spain, are beginning to stay home as standards of living rise and work becomes more plentiful in their own countries. Growers can rely on members of their families for some help, but many of them are looking seriously at the possibilities of mechanical

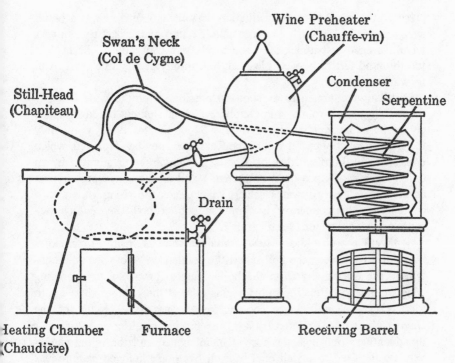

A Cognac Pot Still

harvesters. Even those who dislike the idea admit that it is probably inevitable, although few farmers would have enough capital to buy their own mechanical monster. While the size of the average vineyard has been slowly rising, it is still less than three hectares (seven and a half acres) per grower, although plantings tend to be larger in the higher-quality *crus*.

After picking, the grapes are generally crushed and fermented by the grower, most commonly in large concrete tanks. It is forbidden to use an Archimedes (continuous) press or to add sugar to the must. Contrary to normal wine-making practices, sulfur is not added, as its character could easily carry over into the distilled spirit. Fermentation takes one to two weeks, and as soon as it is finished the fermenting tanks are topped up and sealed to prevent oxidation of the wine. Wine from the Ugni Blanc is relatively high in acid, which is important in helping to preserve the wine prior to distillation as well as contributing to better aging, and it is also fairly low in alcohol. Wines of the past ten vintages have averaged just under 8%, and rarely rise over 10%. The taste is too thin and tart to be very pleasant, but, in any event, little remains in its wine state for very long.

Distillation commences as soon as possible after the wine has fermented, usually around mid-October, and is limited by law to the period between September 1 and May 31 of the following year. Only the traditional copper pot still of the Charentes may be employed, which consists in its simplest form of a boiler (*chaudière*) surmounted by an onion- or olive-shaped head (*chapiteau*) and an elongated pipe known as the *col de cygne* (swan's neck), which leads the rising vapors to a condenser. The condenser is simply a copper coil (*serpentin*) surrounded by cold water (see diagram).

Some stills, both old and new, contain a wine preheater, or *chauffe-vin,* situated between the boiler and the condenser. A copper pipe containing the hot vapors from the boiler passes through a tank holding wine waiting to be distilled; this begins to heat the wine as the wine in turn acts as a preliminary coolant for the vapors. The use of the *chauffe-vin* is not regulated by law, and producers differ as to whether its advantages outweigh the cost of maintenance and the initial capital expense required to install one. Martell has not employed *chauffe-vins* for some time, while Camus feels that the increased efficiency is important and continues to build them into their new stills. The house of Bisquit-Dubouché takes an unusual middle path: their new facilities in Rouillac contain *chauffe-vins* for the first distillation but not for the final one.

Cognac must by law be distilled twice in the traditional Charentes manner; no rectifying columns or precondensers are permitted.[1] The wine is not racked or filtered before distillation, as it is felt that the lees give additional character to the distillate. The first distillation transforms the wine into a rather flat, unpleasant, milky liquid called the *brouillis.* This comes off the still with an alcohol content that gradually declines from an initial 50% to perhaps 2%, yielding an average strength 27–28°. As this is only the first distillation (*chauffe*), most dis-

[1] *"Esprit de cognac"* is a specially prepared, triply distilled spirit which is added in small amounts to champagne as part of the *dosage* (with sugar) which determines whether the sparkling wine will be Brut, Extra Dry, or Doux. The *esprit* must be between 76° and 85° G.L.

tillers do not eliminate the heads and tails fractions, but pass all the *brouillis* along for the second distillation. Distillation of the *brouillis* takes eight to twelve hours, and although modern gas fires need less regulation than did the old wood-burning ones, each still must be kept under constant observation throughout the period of distillation.

The *brouillis* represents about one third the quantity of wine used, and it thus requires two or three loads of wine to produce sufficient *brouillis* to fill the boiler for the second distillation. Some distillers have begun to use larger stills, with a capacity up to one hundred hectoliters, for a more efficient first distillation. The capacity of the still for the second distillation, however, is limited by law to thirty hectoliters.

While the first distillation must be carefully regulated, it is during the course of the second, or *bonne chauffe,* that the skill and art of the distiller truly come into play. He must decide exactly where to separate the unwanted heads and tails fractions of the distillate, retaining only the heart (*coeur*) of the *eau-de-vie.* A *brouillis* at 28% alcohol will normally yield an *eau-de-vie* that would begin to come off the still (after discarding the small heads fraction) at around 75°; the division between heart and tails is generally made at 60°, leaving an average of 70° alcohol, which is just under the maximum permitted of 72%. The volume of the heart, which has now become young cognac, is only one third that of the *brouillis,* though the alcoholic strength has more than doubled.

The remaining fraction, often even larger in volume than the heart, is collected as *secondes,* or tails, for it contains congeners that would contribute undesirable flavors and aroma to the cognac heart. The tails have an alcoholic strength of about 30°, and they are redistilled with a subsequent batch of either *brouillis* or wine to extract as much alcohol as possible.

The heart of the *bonne chauffe* is cognac, colorless and even now with a fairly distinctive, slightly floral aroma. The taste, however, is fiery and powerful, for the 70° alcohol is nearly twice the strength at which we normally drink spirits. Now begins the slow transformation into the complex, elegant brandy we know as cognac, as we pass from the skill of the distiller to the art of the blender and the gradual influence of time.

Cognac can by law be aged only in casks made of oak, and it is from these casks that the young, colorless brandy slowly extracts a deepening yellow-amber color and some of the spicy character and tannic astringency of the oak itself. The cognac also develops complexity due to the minute yet complicated chemical changes that occur through oxidation.

Although the type of oak is not officially regulated by law, traditionally only oak from the Limousin Forest, scattered to the northeast of Cognac, around the city of Limoges, was used for aging cognac. The trees are fairly large, moderately wide-grained, and their wood is rich in tannin. As the need for oak casks increased and transportation became easier, many Cognac shippers turned to the more distant Tronçais forest, which covers perhaps forty square miles in the middle of France. The trees of Tronçais are taller and more slender than those of Limousin, and the close-grained wood may have a slight rose tint. Both Limousin and Tronçais are now in common use in Cognac, and, while some houses do have definite preferences, there seems to be no easily detectable difference in cognacs aged in one or the other oaks.

The oak used in fashioning cognac barrels comes only from the lower trunk of the tree. The tree should ideally be between a hundred and one hundred and fifty years old, though today because of diminishing forest reserves most barrels originate from trees under a century in age. Once the trees are cut, the staves are split, not sawed, so as not to disturb the natural grain of the wood. They are then stacked in the open air, to be seasoned for at least three years (and often much longer) before being formed into barrels. The action of sun, wind, and rain is necessary both to dry the wood and also to remove some of the harsher tannic bitterness and oils.

Although some labor-saving machines have been introduced in the more modern coopering establishments (*tonnelleries*), barrels are still fashioned essentially by hand. Both the normal 300–350-liter casks (*barriques*) and the large blending vats (*tonneaux* or *foudres*) are held together with only wooden pegs and the iron hoops around their outside; nails would impart an off taste to cognac. With the aid of machines, a *barrique* can be made in just under two hours; a man working without the assistance of any machine would take an entire working day. The firm of Taransaud, the largest cooperage in the Cognac region, has an apprenticeship program that lasts from two to five years and requires each man to learn to fashion a barrel entirely by hand. Several of the large cognac houses also have their own *tonnelleries*. Should you find yourself in Cognac, don't fail to visit a cooperage—it is a fascinating trade, and certainly one of the most essential elements to the development of a fine cognac.

New cognac fresh from the still, sometimes cut slightly with distilled water, is generally placed in relatively new oak barrels for a period of several months to a year. To avoid extracting too much tannin from the new barrels, the cognac is then usually transferred to older wood for further aging. Some producers who favor a lighter style, such as Delamain and Camus, prefer to employ older barrels from the beginning, using only as many new ones as are required to replenish their stocks. Such older barrels are sometimes "refreshed" as new staves are added to replace worn-out ones.

All cognac aging houses, or *chais,* are situated above ground, unlike the subterranean caves that are favored for laying down fine wines. The changing temperatures are thought to aid the slow oxidation which is essential to the gradual softening and mellowing of a young cognac, and they also contribute to evaporation. At a rate of around 3 per cent annually, each year the equivalent of over 12 million bottles of cognac are lost through evaporation, which is called *"la part des anges"* (the angels' share). The evaporating cognac is appreciated by more-physical hosts as well: the roofs and walls of cognac *chais* are blackened by a fungus (*Torula compniacensis*) that flourishes in the humidity of the rising cognac vapors.

The traditional cognac *chais* are fairly low, to achieve better insulation and thus avoid excessive evaporation, but modern buildings are likely to be high enough to hold up to eight levels of barrels in metal stands; the *chai* recently completed by Bisquit even has an automatic barrel unloader! But the older, low-ceilinged rooms are still common, often covered with a dark cognac fungus similar to that on the roofs and usually home to a colony of well-kept spider webs. The *paradis,* a special section reserved for the oldest and finest cognacs, may present an almost sepulcher-like aspect as one surveys the rows of silent, cobwebbed barrels—except that as long as the *eau-de-vie* is in wood, it remains very much alive!

Several important changes occur in cognac as it ages: both the volume and alcoholic strength decline (in the climate of southwestern France the more volatile alcohol evaporates faster than water); tannins are absorbed from the oak, giving both color and flavor to the *eau-de-vie;* and complex chemical modifications occur due to oxidation and other interactions. Both the tannin content and acidity of the cognac increase, particularly during the first few years. After five years, the rather yellow cognac already exhibits noticeable tannin and perhaps a slight vanilla bouquet, although the taste is still a bit rough. With further aging, the color deepens to amber, more complex floral-vanilla aromas will appear, and the taste softens. There is also a very gradual augmentation in the sugar content, due to the breakdown of cellulose structures in the oak, which lends a barely perceptible "sweet" finish to cognacs perhaps thirty to fifty years old.

Only the finest cognacs are ever kept to age for such long periods of time, although small proportions of aged cognac may be present even in young blends. Too long in wood may destroy the grapy, fruity character of the cognac, leaving only the astringent harshness of tannin behind. For this reason, most of the cognacs used in the oldest blends are transferred to glass demijohns until they are used, to prevent their becoming excessively woody.

Of course, aging takes time, and in today's world time is money. To obtain the effect of natural aging in wood in a shorter time, one may try putting the wood into the brandy, as well as vice versa. This practice, which is perfectly legal in Cognac, as it is in other parts of the world, consists of adding oak shavings or a liquid infusion or extract of powdered oak to the brandy as it is aging. The latter, known in France as *le boisé,* is by far the most common method of speeding up aging. While such treatment is probably rarely given to an entire lot of cognac, it may be accorded to a particular batch, which then becomes intensely woody and tannic. This batch can then be used for blending, to give some of the characteristics of age to young cognacs.

Use of *le boisé* is self-limiting, for it can give only color, tannin, and oakiness to an *eau-de-vie;* it cannot hasten the gradual development of complexity and smoothness that will come only after years of slow maturation in wood. Since *le boisé* detracts somewhat from the more romantic image of row upon row of barrels slowly imparting their character to young cognacs (which remains an accurate picture nevertheless), information regarding use of *le boisé* is never volunteered by the Cognac firms themselves. Most, however, do admit that the practice exists. An April 1974 article in *Que Choisir?,* a French consumer magazine, was entitled "Sawdust in Cognac" and contained a rather damning scientific challenge to the "naturalness" of the apparent age of most cognacs. The article concludes that the vast majority of cognacs tested had been artificially "aged," and a tasting panel was of the opinion that a woody *boisé* character was too noticeable in ten of the thirty-six cognacs tasted (which included all the major producers).

Certainly there is nothing wrong with the practice of adding naturally derived oak character to a young brandy, and it should be remembered that this is common in most brandy-producing areas of the world. If overdone, however, it may then necessitate a healthy use of sugar or caramel to overcome the bitterness of the *boisé,* and we must wonder whether the unique character of cognac can be maintained under such conditions.

Every cognac is a blend, and it is through the art of blending that each *négociant* creates his own style, his own character, from what at the beginning may have been a very similar selection of distillates. Blending usually begins immediately after distillation, although generally this consists merely of combining young cognacs from the same *crus,* or subregions.

The first blend among different regions and vintages may take place after only one to two years, although this varies greatly according to the producer. During this time, the cognac in cask is tasted regularly, and those which are to be held for long aging may already be identified. The blend is mixed in large vats and then tasted against the standard that the house wishes to maintain. It is usually left to "marry" and acquire a bit more age in large cooperage, of a hundred to three hundred hecto-liters capacity. The *maitre de chai* and, in many cases, the owners of the house must call on all their expertise and experience to decide what must be added to maintain the brand's consistency and style—perhaps a touch of Grande Champagne for more character or some quicker-maturing Fins Bois for more suppleness.

Vintages are never seen on a French-bottled cognac, although they are generally used for reference in the *chais.* The only vintaged cognacs on the market today are the "early landed" cognacs shipped to England in cask and bottled there by the importer. Such cognacs are often lighter-bodied and more delicate than French-bottled cognacs of comparable age, due to the different climatic conditions during aging. In addition to the fact that there is little variation in distillates from year to year, it is almost unanimously felt in France that blends must necessarily combine both young and old cognacs to obtain a proper balance. One notable exception to this practice is the well-respected house of

Salignac, which blends only among different growths of the same year and not among different vintages.

It is illegal to put any indication of age on a bottle of cognac, even a notation such as "10 years old," due to the difficulty of maintaining accurate records of *eaux-de-vie* that might be several decades old and the practice of topping up barrels to replace what is lost by evaporation. The Bureau National du Cognac is responsible, however, for overseeing the age of cognacs up to five years, and this is accomplished by assigning a certain *"compte,"* or index of age, to each cognac. There are seven different indexes assigned: *compte* 00 is reserved for freshly distilled cognacs during the normal distilling period; *compte* 0 includes *eaux-de-vie* during their first year of aging; *compte* 1 is not reached until the following April 1, when the cognac is about 1½ years old (thus cognacs distilled on September 15, 1974, and March 15, 1975, would both attain *compte* 1 on April 1, 1976); *comptes* 2 through 5 are used for cognacs that have, respectively, 2½, 3½, 4½, and 5½ years of age. No further official records are kept once a cognac reaches *compte* 5. No cognac may be sold to the consumer before it has attained *compte* 1.

While specific designations of age are not permitted, the ensemble of Cognac firms has gradually developed a system of designating the relative ages and qualities of their blends. While the words in themselves mean nothing, they (along with the price) do provide a rough guide as to the average age of the cognac inside.

3-star (***) (sometimes labeled *V.S.*) is the youngest blend of almost every Cognac house and accounts for 80–90 per cent of all cognac sold. There were once 1- and 2-star cognacs, perhaps originally designed to commemorate the passing of a comet, a particularly bountiful year, or some other significant happening—depending on which story you listen to. In any event, today's 3-stars are generally between three and five years old, and there seems to be some evidence that the average age has declined somewhat during the past decade or so. Since the total aging stocks in cognac are presently three to four times greater than annual sales, it would be difficult for the "average" 3-star to be any older than four years. These are young, fairly simple, grapy cognacs that do not pretend to have the finesse and complexity of their older brothers, but today carry price tags well above the everyday brandies of Germany, California, or even other regions of France. They are often slightly sweetened, to soften the inherent harshness present in all young brandies or the woody roughness that may result from a bit too much of *le boisé*.

Several firms now offer a slightly higher-quality cognac, usually with a proprietary name, which is priced just above their 3-star. While it is perhaps too early to tell, this may signify the gradual demise of the 3-star.

V.S.O.P. is the next commonly used designation and usually corresponds to a cognac with an average age of seven to ten years. Any cognac labeled "V.S.O.P.," "V.O.," "Réserve," or with similar indications must contain no *eaux-de-vie* inferior to *compte* 4 in age. The letters "V.S.O.P." are said to have originally meant "very superior (or special) old pale," a non-sequitur since cognacs grow darker as they age, not paler. In any event, a V.S.O.P. cognac is certainly a premium blend and should be in every sense a fine "sipping brandy." The aroma should contain some flowery complexity and a bit of oak character in addition to the particular grapy character common to all cognacs. The flavors are generally rounder and smoother than those of most 3-stars, though a few V.S.O.P.s still contain just a touch of sweetness. In the United States, at least, many V.S.O.P.s sell for only 20–25 per cent above the price of 3-stars, and those interested in a good cognac might do well to spend the extra three dollars or so.

Napoléon and higher-quality cognacs represent only a tiny fraction of the commercially available cognacs, though they are handled with great pride by the producers and enjoyed by connoisseurs everywhere. They must legally be of *compte* 5 or above, though this requirement is rather meaningless, as their average age is probably fifteen to twenty-five years. We have already mentioned that dusty old bottles of "Napoléon" cognac have nothing to do with either emperor of that name—and would probably be little good if they did. In addition, the so-called "Napoléon" French brandies produced outside the Cognac region and often seen in supermarkets and duty-free shops are little more than cheap imitations plagiarizing a famous name. This should not, however, detract from the quality of the "Napoléon" cognacs of today, which make no pretense of being bottled in the distant past and which can be very fine brandies indeed. Many producers choose not to use the name, however: Martell's "Cordon Bleu," Hennessy's "Bras d'Or," Monnet's "Anniversaire," or Polignac's "Réserve Prince Hubert" are all roughly equivalent to the "Napoléon" of other producers. These are cognacs that are fully mature, and whose long years in oak have developed vanilla-floral-oak complexity in both bouquet and flavors. Any "sweetness" present should be the natural result of aging, for there is no need to round out the flavors of a twenty-year-old cognac. A few people may find the higher levels of tannin and oak character distracting or unpleasant, but for most drinkers the wood adds a natural complexity to the cognac. Most Napoléon types will include very high proportions of Grande and Petite Champagne, and all will be expensive, often double the price of a V.S.O.P.

Extra, Extra Vieille, Grande Réserve, and similar designations (often referring to some prince or king) represent the pinnacle of cognac, and their scarcity and price ensure that they will remain outside the experience of most brandy lovers. These qualities are not really commercialized by the Cognac houses. Rather, they are showpieces that may be offered to the lucky visitor or reserved for the rich devotee of cognac. Most will be drawn exclusively from the *paradis* of older stocks that every house maintains, and the *eaux-de-vie* employed are likely to be at least fifty years old. Many have been transferred to glass demijohns to protect them from senility, although one does occasionally encounter extraordinary cognacs still in cask after over a century. While the taste of such ancient cognacs and the rare Extras that are produced on a fairly regular basis can rise to great heights of complexity and subtlety, the tannin and wood character in such *eaux-de-vie* is necessarily very strong and may overwhelm the unsuspecting violets and fruit that one hopes to find in a well-aged cognac. Certainly few people (even the Cognac families themselves often prefer their next-to-oldest blend) would enjoy drinking only Extra cognacs—but don't pass up the chance to try one of these stately, if occasionally slightly faded, old gentlemen if the opportunity ever arises!

A 1903 French law prohibits the addition of any substance that is intended to modify the composition or taste of a natural spirit; in addition, a 1921 decree forbids all "manipulations and practices designed to improve and increase the aroma of natural *eaux-de-vie,* in order to deceive the purchaser regarding their substantial qualities, origin, and type." It is nevertheless permitted, according to both judicial and administrative decisions, to add four substances to cognac prior to bottling: distilled water, caramel, sugar, and an infusion of oak.

We have already discussed the use of *le boisé,* and distilled water is usually added gradually throughout the aging period and then adjusted

at the time of bottling to bring the cognac to its normal strength of 40°
G.L.

Caramel, or burnt sugar, is added just before bottling to give the cognac a darker color, a common practice among whiskey and other
brandy distillers as well. The caramel is said to be tasteless in the small
quantities used, and its addition permits the producer to maintain a
consistent color year after year. Without caramel, the average 3-star
would be pale-to-medium yellow in color, rather than amber.

The addition of caramel and sugar is limited to about 2 per cent by
volume, and in some 3-stars the latter substance probably approaches
this amount. Sugar is added to young cognacs to soften their somewhat
harsh flavors, in the same way that it may be added to brandies from
California and other parts of the world. It is most commonly added in
the form of a syrup rather than directly, and may find its way into some
V.S.O.P.s as well as the younger 3-stars.

Like other brandies and whiskies, cognac ages only in wood and not
in the bottle, so a ten-year-old cognac bottled fifty years ago will be no
better (and perhaps not as good) as one bottled yesterday. As with
other spirits, cognac bottles should be stored upright rather than on
their side, to prevent the alcohol from attacking the cork closure. Some
slight deterioration may become noticeable in a bottle that has only a
small amount of cognac left in it, although in general your cognac
should remain at its best for several years.

The general techniques for tasting brandy apply to tasting and appre-
ciating cognac as well. In Cognac itself, the normal tasting glass is chim-
ney-shaped, resembling a sherry *copa* glass, rather than the balloon
affairs often thought to be traditional. Actually, the balloon glasses are
fine for after-dinner sipping, as long as they are moderate in size.
Warming by cupping your hand around the bowl helps to release the
rising scent of the cognac and also seems to soften the flavors. Those
contraptions for warming the glass over an open flame are not only unnecessary, but the burning flame may impart off aromas to the cognac
as well as being dangerous to cognac and glass alike.

Three-star cognacs are often served with water or soda, particularly
in Britain, where several of the larger houses offer a special young blend
designed to be mixed. While cognac and soda is a decent-enough drink,
we find that plain water dilutes and flattens the flavors of even a young
cognac. A 3-star can be pleasant in some mixed drinks although its
complexity and moderate fusel-alcohol content mean that it is best in

the simple mixtures. A young cognac can also be a very successful addition in the kitchen, not only to flame fancy desserts but also to prepare sauces or marinades for most cuts of meat.

But the cognacs of V.S.O.P. quality and above (and even a few of the best 3-stars) are meant to be sipping brandies at home after lunch or dinner, when their complexity can be slowly savored and appreciated. A well-aged cognac is above all elegant, less substantial than the full-bodied armagnacs and lacking the dry-woody-spiciness that characterizes some of California's older straight brandies, but exhibiting a subtle mélange of intriguing flavors that are duplicated nowhere else in the world. Fine cognacs, particularly from Grande Champagne, often have a distinctly floral quality. Violets, plums, and spiced peaches have also appeared during our tastings, complemented by the "sweet," spicy-vanilla oakiness characteristic of Limousin and Tronçais. Every Cognac firm has its own particular style, ranging from light and delicate to full-bodied and tannic, but each retains the unique character of cognac.

Almost every major firm in the Cognac region welcomes visitors, not only with an interesting tour but usually with a bit of tasting at the end. Gracious, though a bit reserved in manner, the people of the Charentes are very hospitable, and you could certainly spend a pleasant few days in the region.

The town of Cognac itself is centered around the Place François I and, apart from an agreeable little park and a small but improving local museum, it must rank as one of the less interesting provincial towns in France. Lacking even the village charm of Éauze, in the Armagnac region, its lifeless cafes and modest shops hold little attraction for the tourist. But while the exterior is unexciting, one does sense the silent vitality of *négociants,* distillers, vineyards, and aging cognac underneath it all.

Jarnac is just fourteen kilometers east of Cognac, and it houses several important cognac firms, including Courvoisier, Hine, Bisquit, and Delamain. Smaller, and even more quiet than Cognac, it nevertheless offers a pleasing vista of the Charente River and the row of *négociants'* buildings along its banks.

Driving through the region is quite enjoyable, as the vineyards, pastures, and occasional thickets of trees create a varied, peaceful landscape. The lesser Cognac towns of Segonzac, Archiac, and Jonzac have a certain interest, and a meandering trip from Cognac to Bordeaux is certainly preferable to the madness that prevails along the main Paris-Bordeaux road, which skirts Angoulême. The tiny village of Bourg-Charente, just east of Cognac, has a gemlike Romanesque church; others may be found in Basac, Gondeville, and Moulidras. Nearby is the impressive château that belongs to Marnier-Lapostelle, of Grand Marnier fame, which is unfortunately not open to visitors.

You may happen upon a typical Charente farmhouse, built in a square facing inwards onto a central courtyard. The entry is marked by large double doors and a big arch, designed for wagons though today more often used by automobiles and tractors, and there is a smaller door to the side that could be opened to admit people without leaving the courtyard defenseless. Many still have slots about six feet above the ground—handy for lookouts and perhaps arrows in the days when religious wars were common in southwestern France.

The coastal area around the lovely port of La Rochelle is well worth a visit, including the famous oyster beds at nearby Marennes. Both Portuguese and the flatter Marennes oysters are cultivated, and they are often served accompanied by a delicious, small hot sausage native to the region. Some excellent seafood restaurants may be found beside the old port of La Rochelle.

Gastronomy in the Cognac region is oriented around the famous Charentes butter and the fresh products of both sea and river, although the dishes are perhaps not as rich and varied as those of neighboring Périgord. A local goat cheese, Chabichou, is delicious, and when in season the large wild mushrooms known as *cèpes* can be found on almost every table. There are no celebrated Michelin-starred restaurants in the immediate area, but several small establishments offer well-prepared, thoughtful dishes. These include La Ribaudière, delightfully situated on the banks of the river in Bourg-Charente; the Moulin de Cierzac, just outside Cognac; and a new country inn-restaurant situated in its own private park near Cognac, on the road to Saintes. In the town itself, the Sens Unique provides good food at reasonable prices and is certainly superior to the *brasseries* that surround the gallant statue of François I in the square.

There are approximately four thousand individual stills in Cognac, ranging from the new 100-hectoliter stills used by Martell and Polignac for the first distillation, to the modern distillery of Bisquit, which houses sixty-four 25-hectoliter stills under one roof, to the small, probably ancient 10-hectoliter still used by a *bouilleur de cru* to distill the produce of his own vineyard. The *bouilleurs de cru* account for about 30 per cent of the cognac distilled; the *bouilleurs de profession,* who can distill both for themselves and for others (co-operatives or growers), provide 63 per cent of the production, while remaining 7 per cent is taken up by Cognac's two dozen or so co-operatives.

The vast majority, perhaps 95 per cent, of all cognac is aged and sold by the shippers, or *négociants,* who may or may not also have their own distilleries. While there are about 250 *négociants* in the Cognac region, each with his own brand or label, only a comparative handful are responsible for most of the cognac we are likely to see on the shelves of our local bottle shop. The three giants of the cognac industry are Martell, Hennessy, and Courvoisier, who among them sell more than half the total amount of cognac consumed world-wide. Rémy Martin is now probably fourth in sales, followed closely by Bisquit-Dubouché. Other important houses whose labels can be found fairly easily in the United States and Great Britain include Camus, Hine, Monnet, Denis-Mounié, Delamain, Polignac, Otard, Gaston de Lagrange, and Salignac.

While certainly not exhaustive (even the Bureau National does not have a readily available list of all the producers in Cognac), the dozen firms discussed in greater detail below probably represent both the largest and best-known Cognac houses. All follow the general pattern for producing cognac described above, but we hope a closer look at some of the differences among the various houses will give you a better idea of the nuances that exist within the world of cognac.

We have included brief tasting notes describing at least the major offerings of the various firms. While we have noted differences in quality among similar types when they were apparent, many of our preferences for one style over another (particularly in the older cognacs) reflect our own personal tastes. In general, we found the higher categories (*Napoléon* and above) almost uniformly excellent; the V.S.O.P.s were also quite good as a class, though somewhat more uneven; the 3-stars differed widely from firm to firm, and their over-all quality was less impressive.

BISQUIT-DUBOUCHÉ

Founded at the end of the Napoleonic era, in 1819, at Jarnac, Bisquit was one of the more important nineteenth-century Cognac firms; in 1899 it ranked as one of the three largest. Its name has not been as famous in the twentieth century, but there are signs that both production and sales at Bisquit have increased since the company was taken over, in 1966, by the giant French spirits group of Ricard. The most obvious result of this infusion of new capital is the new facilities at the 350-hectare Domaine de Lignères in Rouillac, a few miles from Jarnac in the countryside of Fins Bois. Approximately two hundred hectares of vineyards provide perhaps 6–7 per cent of Bisquit's needs, and a new computer-controlled (where possible) distillery was used fully for the first time in 1973. Plans eventually call for eight new *chais* with a total storage capacity of some 700,000 hectoliters (18 million gallons) of cognac.

Bisquit is a major distiller as well as *négociant,* and up to 70 per cent of their requirements are distilled in their own stills. The young cognacs are aged in both Limousin and Tronçais oak for a year, before being blended and transferred to older casks. The final blend is generally left in large *foudres* of 320 hectoliters for ten to twelve months prior to bottling.

The cognacs of Bisquit are on the light side, and the lower grades are noticeably sweet. Over all, they are good, typical cognacs; we found the Napoléon to be the most successful.

3-star—Representing 60 per cent of Bisquit's production, this is a fairly light, neutral cognac with slight vanilla character and a bit too much sweetness for our tastes.

V.S.—Sold only in the United States, and comparable to the 3-star.

V.S.O.P. Fine Champagne—Light-moderate in body, with flavors that are heavier and woodier than the *V.S.O.P.-Napoléon* Fine Champagne, which is a new blend, destined for the United States. The latter is fairly light but much better balanced than the regular V.S.O.P., and is a clean, attractive cognac with good, light oak character.

Napoléon Fine Champagne—A rich, complex cognac with a good balance of oak, fruit, and vanilla character in both nose and flavors.

Extra Vieille—Lighter, woodier, and less fruity than the Napoléon, though characteristic of its type in the oaky complexity that is present.

CAMUS

Camus was originally a consortium that sold cognac under the label "La Grande Marque" from its founding in 1863 until the 1930s. During this period it was sold in barrel to the United Kingdom and

Russia, but the great majority of sales under the "Camus" label (the only one since the 1930s) are now in bottle.

The Camus firm is still entirely owned by descendants of Jean-Baptiste Camus, who own four properties in Grande Champagne and Borderies, including the unusual estate-bottled cognac of Château du Plessis (in the Borderies). They also manage the estate of the Château d'Uffaut, in Grande Champagne. They distill their own wine and buy other *eaux-de-vie* to meet their needs, which are currently based on sales of about 6 million bottles annually. Camus prefers a lighter style of cognac, and for this reason the use of new Limousin and Tronçais oak is kept to a minimum. The various *eaux-de-vie* are aged separately until the blend for a particular grade is made.

Better known in the United Kingdom and the Far East than in the United States, Camus has recently been emphasizing its Napoléon quality, which now accounts for approximately 50 per cent of sales. Up to 90 per cent of Camus's production is exported, much of it sold in duty-free shops, where the price for a Napoléon cognac is more reasonable. Other activities include the marketing of the apéritif Plessis, which resembles the locally produced Pineau des Charentes, and ownership of Prince de Chabot armagnac.

Unevenness characterizes the Camus line, although the qualities they emphasize are at least the equal of similar cognacs from other major houses.

3-star—Only very little of this quality is produced. Fairly light in aroma and flavor, it is an ordinary 3-star with noticeable sweetness and a slightly rough aftertaste.

Célébration—Introduced in 1963 to commemorate Camus's one hundredth anniversary, this has essentially replaced the *3-star* in most markets. It is a fairly nice cognac with hints of both sweetness and oak in the taste and a touch of caramel in the aroma.

V.S.O.P.—Light-moderate in body and less sweet than the above, with disappointingly neutral flavors and slight wood.

Napoléon—A round, smooth cognac whose aroma has a pleasant oak-rose-walnut complexity. In the mouth the fruit and fairly strong tannin-oak character are well balanced.

Hors d'Âge or *Réserve Extra Vieille*—A dry, woody old bachelor that seems past his prime.

Château d'Uffaut Grande Fine Champagne—Only about five thousand cases of this cognac are produced each year, although limited quantities are occasionally available for export. Perhaps less elegant than one might expect from a Grande Champagne, it is nevertheless a pleasant, well-balanced cognac with light-moderate body, little wood, and a fresh, grapy aroma. Like a very good V.S.O.P. in style.

Château du Plessis Fine Borderie—Even less of the Château du Plessis is produced, perhaps one hundred cases per year, and it is often reserved for the family's own use. Delightful in the pronounced floral bouquet for which the Borderies are noted, it is a refined though fairly full-bodied cognac of distinctive character. Aged for about ten years, it has slight oak undertones.

COURVOISIER

Although in 1899 Courvoisier's sales were well down the list of the major producers, today the large building in Jarnac overlooking the Charente River houses one of the top three firms in Cognac, whose sales may soon approach 20 million bottles annually. Courvoisier acts strictly as a *négociant;* they own neither vineyards nor distilleries, but buy primarily young cognacs which are then aged and blended in the Courvoisier *chais*.

The major blending for the 3-star, which accounts for 80 per cent of Courvoisier's sales, is made after one year in small oak barrels; the resulting blend receives the rest of its aging in large, 450-hectoliter vats. *Eaux-de-vie* destined for the higher-quality blends are transferred after a year to older oak barrels for further aging.

The name of Courvoisier is that of a Parisian wine merchant who founded a company in 1790, which was subsequently reorganized in the 1830s. M. Courvoisier is said to have actually been a friend of the emperor's, hence the company's motto of "the brandy of Napoléon." After being in the British Simon family for much of the twentieth century, Courvoisier was bought in the 1960s by the well-known Canadian distilled-spirits firm of Hiram Walker.

Courvoisier's distinctive squat bottles contain on the whole a relatively dry, oaky cognac of moderate body that probably falls between the lighter Martell and woodier Hennessy in style.

3-star (V.S.)—Rather ordinary, with light-moderate body, some covering sweetness, and a slightly bitter taste of wood (*boisé?*) in the finish.

V.S.O.P—Better balanced and more complex than the *3-star,* with medium body and vanilla-woody undertones. Just a bit rough, but not unpleasant.

Napoléon—Perhaps the first of the "Napoléon" brandies to gain widespread recognition, this is a fairly forceful cognac, with moderate body and wood tannin. Good, with a pleasant, complex vanilla-oak aroma.

Extra Vieille—An oaky astringency is the dominant characteristic, but at the same time this remains a complex, elegant old cognac.

DELAMAIN

Although not important in terms of sales when compared to such giants as Courvoisier, the name of Delamain is well known to cognac connoisseurs, particularly through the fame of their "Pale and Dry" Grande Champagne. The great majority of their *eaux-de-vie* (Delamain are strictly *négociants* and do none of their own distilling) come from the Grande Champagne district, and only 10 per cent of their production is devoted to 3-star and V.S.O.P.

The founding family of Delamain was originally French, but emigrated to England in the seventeenth century. William Delamain was named Marshall of Dublin by the then-ruling British crown, and his descendant James Delamain returned to France in 1759, founding an export firm in the Cognac region. The predecessor of the present company in Jarnac was established as Roullet & Delamain in 1824. It is now entirely controlled by Delamain descendants and remains a family operation. The late Robert Delamain was the author of the classic *Histoire du Cognac*, published in 1935.

All of Delamain's cognacs are light and delicate, due in large part to aging in older rather than new oak. In addition to the superior qualities, Delamain offers a *3-star, Liquid Gold V.S.O.P.,* and a young essentially Grande Champagne cognac designed to be drunk with water, the *Long Drink Finalo.*

Pale and Dry Grande Champagne—About thirty years old, this is an elegant, fruity cognac with only light oak flavors and a very smooth finish. We enjoy its fairly complex, yet delicate style, although some may prefer a more robust cognac.

Vesper Très Vieille Fine Champagne—Aged longer, and a bit fuller than the Pale and Dry.

Très Vieux Cognac de Grande Champagne—Again, an elegant, fruity cognac with traces of prune in the aroma. Light-moderate in body, well balanced, with only light oakiness and excellent character.

DENIS-MOUNIÉ

A moderate-sized, family-owned firm of *négociants,* Denis-Mounié is much better known in Britain than in the United States, despite the development of their "Gold Leaf" blend, which is directed primarily at the American market. Founded in 1838, the company presently sells about 1.5 million bottles of cognac annually.

Although they do not distill any *eau-de-vie,* Denis Mounié do maintain their own cooperage. Only Limousin oak is used to age their cognacs, for they feel that the greater porosity and less rapid yield of tannin in Limousin is more appropriate to the light style of cognac the firm wishes to maintain. Denis-Mounié also markets a Pineau des Charentes, which is bought from local producers and then aged and blended at the firm's *chais,* some of which are just off the Place François I in the town of Cognac.

Denis-Mounié's cognacs are quite consistent in style, and most evidence good balance and fairly delicate flavors.

3-star—Light, simple, and slightly sweet; ordinary at best.

Gold Leaf—Better than the above, with light-moderate body, average cognac flavors, and some caramel sweetness in the finish.

V.S.O.P. Vieille Fine Champagne—A typical V.S.O.P., fairly light in oak character, with good fruit. A bit lacking in distinction, but pleasant and well balanced.

Grande Réserve Édouard VII—Named in honor of King Edward VII of England, who reigned from 1901 until his death in 1910, this is a light, well-balanced cognac with a pleasant, spicy-violet character in both aroma and taste. Light in oak character, with a clean finish.

Grande Champagne Extra—A very good, elegant cognac, with light body and soft, violet-like flavors.

HENNESSY

Roughly the same size as Courvoisier and Martell, Hennessy is of Irish origin and overlooks the Charente from the town of Cognac itself.

Founded in 1865 (they still have a barrel of surprisingly distinguished and alive 1865 Borderies in the *paradis*) by Corkman Richard Hennessy, the company is now aligned with the famous French Champagne firm of Moët et Chandon.

While Hennessy does distill wine from its own five hundred hectares of vineyards, the company is primarily a shipper, buying young *eaux-de-vie* for the other 90 per cent of its needs. It claims to have the largest stocks of cognac in the region, with over 125,000 barrels (the equivalent of 58 million bottles) aging in fifteen different *chais*. Four fifths of the firm's production is exported, with the United States leading both Ireland, where Hennessy is not surprisingly the leading brand, and the United Kingdom.

Hennessy also has its own *tonnellerie,* where only Limousin oak is fashioned into barrels. Cognac fresh from the still is always put into new wood if possible, to be transferred to older, less tannic casks after a year or so. Most of the Hennessy cognacs are relatively full-bodied with strong wood character, particularly the younger ones.

Bras Armé—Hennessy's *3-star,* this is a fairly woody, full-bodied cognac with just a hint of sweetness. While short on finesse, it does have quite good character and flavors.

V.S.O.P.—A good V.S.O.P., quite smooth despite its fairly strong oakiness. Not presently sold in the United States, where it has been replaced by the Bras d'Or.

Bras d'Or—A bit older and placed above the V.S.O.P. in price, we have found the Bras d'Or to be a fairly simple yet smooth cognac, with light-moderate body and less wood character than the V.S.O.P.

Bras d'Or Napoléon—A new blend for Hennessy; the use of "Napoléon" is the first break with a long-standing tradition of not using an appellation that has been closely associated with Courvoisier. The taste is smooth, with a bit less wood than one might expect from Hennessy. Clean in the finish, with some complexity and character.

X.O.—A full-bodied, oaky cognac with lots of wood but also good fruit, reminiscent of plums. Complex and full-flavored, though not quite as rich as the Extra.

Extra—A charming nose with light-moderate oakiness and hints of cinnamon and violets introduces this elegant, complex cognac. Long on the palate and in the finish, this is a fine example of the beautiful balance that can be attained by a rare old cognac.

HINE

Thomas Hine, an Englishman from Dorsetshire, first worked for the firm of Ranson & Delamain upon his arrival in the Cognac region in 1792. He ended up marrying one of the Delamain daughters, and in 1817 the firm became Thomas Hine & Co. While the sixth generation of the Hine family are still involved in the direction of the company, since 1971 it has been owned by the large English group of Distillers Company Ltd.

Then and now acting as shippers only, Hine owns neither vineyards nor distillery, but specializes in aging and blending *eaux-de-vie* to their own spicy, fairly elegant style. The young cognacs are reduced with distilled water to 60% alcohol before they begin aging; when transferred out of their homes in new oak barrels after a year, they are further cut to 50%. After the first year, preliminary blends may be made for the different qualities. Like several other producers, Hine offers slightly different blends in the United States than in other markets. Sales at present are about 1.2 million bottles per year, of which 90 per cent are exported.

Hine probably maintains one of the more distinctive and consistent styles throughout its line, not overly delicate but well blended and balanced.

3-star (in the U.S.A., *Sceptre*)—One of the best 3-stars, with light-moderate body and good spicy, slightly oaky flavors. No noticeable sweetness.

V.S.O.P. (not sold in the U.S.A.)—Similar in its spiciness to the *3-star,* although more complex. Well balanced, with good fruit and fairly light wood character.

V.S.O.P. Fine Champagne (only in U.S.A.)—A rather light, dry cognac with slight oak astringency and a very nice spicy-apricot aroma.

Antique Vieille Fine Champagne (France)—A very fine cognac, with an intriguing spicy-apricot-violet bouquet which carries over into the flavor. Light-bodied and elegant, with a lingering aftertaste and excellent balance.

Triomphe Grande Champagne (U.S.A.)—Similar to Antique, but a bit fuller and woodier in character. Still well balanced.

Très Vieille Grande Champagne (France)—An obviously well-aged cognac with typical Hine spiciness and fruit, along with fairly light wood and a touch of floral undertones. Light-bodied, interesting, and complex, but marred by a slight bitterness in the finish.

MARTELL

One of the oldest of the major Cognac houses, Martell was founded in 1715 by a native of the island of Jersey. It is also one of the few houses still entirely owned and directed by descendants—currently the seventh generation—of the founder. Martell has always been one of the most important firms in Cognac, and even in 1809 a letter from a local government official referred to Martell as the "strongest" Cognac house engaged in the commerce of *eaux-de-vie*. In 1971, Martell just outdistanced Hennessy in export sales, and it is also the leading label in France.

Martell not only acts as a *négociant*, but is involved in all phases of cognac production. It controls about fifty distilleries, and its dozen vineyards probably constitute the largest holdings among the major firms. Hundred-hectoliter stills, without *chauffe-vins,* are utilized for the first distillation, and the young cognacs are placed by preference in Tronçais casks, although Limousin is also used.

Martell cognacs are generally fairly light-bodied, dry, and straightforward in character, with excellent fruitiness.

Dry Pale—Limited quantities of this blend are sold primarily in the British market; it is similar to the *3-star,* perhaps a bit younger and with a touch of sweetness.

3-star (*V.S.*)—A good, honest blend, with light body and typical cognac flavors. One of the nicest 3-stars, with a bit of sweetness in the finish.

Médaillon V.S.O.P.—A well-balanced cognac, which we have often enjoyed, showing good fruit and some oak character. Light-medium in body, with a clean finish.

Cordon Bleu—Fairly elegant, with spicy prune-like flavors, light-medium body, and moderate oak tannin. Well balanced and very pleasant.

Cordon Argent—Possessing a pungent, complex aroma of coconut and spice, this is one of the best of the thirty-to-fifty-year-old aristocratic blends. Only light-moderate in body, but full in flavors and with good fruit to balance the oak astringency.

Extra—Again, a cognac with a full, rich oak-coconut-violet bouquet that jumps out of the glass. A bit fuller and older than the Cordon Argent, but still not overburdened with wood, it has a lingering finish of complex spicy flavors.

MONNET

Monnet was organized as a co-operative of growers and distillers in 1838, and takes its name from one of the founders. Now the firm acts primarily as *négociants*, while maintaining close contacts with some four hundred growers in the Cognac region. Scandinavia, one of Cognac's oldest traditional customers, is the primary market for Monnet, but the label can also be found easily in the United States and Britain.

Although Limousin oak is preferred, some aging is done in Tronçais; the first 3-star blend is made after a year in new barrels. Monnet offers the same qualities and labels in all markets, and sells only 6 per cent of its production in France.

Most Monnet cognacs are relatively light and pleasant, although the flavors sometimes tend to be rather simple.

3-star (in the U.S., *Regal*)—Light-bodied and a bit too sweet, this is a rather neutral cognac with no real faults but little to recommend it.

V.S.O.P.—While not overly complex, this is a pleasant V.S.O.P. with light body, fruity flavors, and a nice plum-oak nose.

Anniversaire Fine Champagne—Good spicy-fruit character, with some complexity and light-moderate oak noticeable. A fairly elegant cognac with a pleasant fruity aroma and clean aftertaste.

Joséphine Très Vieille Fine Champagne—A pleasant, plummy nose with moderate oak also defines the moderately complex flavors. The additional aging leaves it less delicate than the Anniversaire, with light-moderate body and a touch of tannic astringency in the finish that is found in many older cognacs.

OTARD

Situated on the banks of the Charente in the Château de Cognac, birthplace of François I in 1494, Otard certainly has the most historic setting of all the Cognac houses. Much still remains of the fifteenth-century château, through which Otard conducts a very interesting tour dwelling on the historic, rather than the cognac-producing, charm of the château, as ghosts of kings and courtiers sound from the yard-thick stone walls.

The château was purchased in 1795 by Baron Otard, a descendant of a Scots family which had followed the Stuart King James II of England into exile after his defeat by William of Orange in 1690. The Ramefort family still controls the firm and also furnishes Otard with about 5 per cent of its *eau-de-vie* requirements from its own vineyards and distillery. Otard is essentially a shipper, selling a third of its cognac in France, 20 per cent to Great Britain, and 15 per cent to the Far East, with total sales on the order of 2.5 million bottles. Aging is in small Limousin-oak barrels, while the larger, 100–250-hectoliter vats used for blending and finishing are fashioned from Tronçais.

3-star—Rather sweet and simple, though the resulting smoothness and slight caramel quality might appeal to some.

V.S.—Designed for the American market, this is a light-bodied, rather neutral cognac with slight sweetness and little character.

Baron Otard V.S.O.P. Fine Champagne—Drier and more complex than the above, this is a pleasant cognac of moderate body, toffee-like aroma and flavors, and slight oakiness.

Princes de Cognac—A premium blend about twenty-five years old, bottled in an attractive, hand-blown glass decanter.

Charles X—Otard's highest quality, although, like the top cognacs of other houses, it is practically unobtainable and is produced more for prestige than for sales.

POLIGNAC-UNICOOP

The *Union coopérative de viticulteurs charentais* (UNICOOP) was created in 1929 to act as middleman between growers and *négociants,* but soon developed its own production and sales capabilities. The youngest of the important houses, it at first offered cognacs under several different labels. In 1949 Prince Hubert de Polignac, member of an old aristocratic French family from Le Puy, offered to let the co-operative use his name, and today "Polignac" is UNICOOP's only label.

UNICOOP is by far the largest of the Cognac co-operatives, with sales amounting to 7–8 per cent of the cognac market. The organization brings together some forty-five hundred growers controlling forty-eight hundred hectares of vineyards, and it operates 125 stills spread over nearly thirty distilleries in the region. Production methods are quite modern, with 100-hectoliter stills for the first distillation, stainless-steel holding tanks, and a new facility including aging *chais,* bottling lines, and a visitor reception center on the main Cognac-Jarnac road. Tronçais oak is preferred for aging, although some Limousin is also used.

The Polignac label has certainly been one of the most successful in recent years, particularly when one considers that it was introduced only some twenty-five years ago. Sales quintupled between 1967 and 1972, and the co-operative has done remarkably well in breaking into a market that remains dominated by the large *négociants.*

The cognacs of Polignac are fairly distinctive, and run counter to the modern trend by tending to be full and oaky rather than light and elegant. At the present time, only the V.S.O.P. is available in the United States, although this situation may alter as production and marketing capabilities increase.

UNICOOP also markets one of the best-selling Pineaux des Charentes, under the "Reynac" label.

3-star—A slightly sweet cognac of fair character, though it is a bit unbalanced and slightly rough in the aftertaste.

Couronne—Similar to the *3-star,* though less sweet, slightly woodier, and offering more cognac character. Presently sold primarily in French supermarkets and shopping centers.

V.S.O.P. Fine Champagne—A medium to full-bodied cognac with a good, coconut-oak aroma. The flavors are full and spicy, though some may find them slightly overpowered by wood.

Réserve Prince Hubert Fine Champagne—A fairly big, tannic cognac that manages to retain just enough fruit to balance the oak astringency in the flavor. The aroma has a nice spicy-cedar character.

Dynastie Grande Fine Champagne—The top of the line, available only in limited quantities.

RÉMY MARTIN

Today Rémy Martin is less noted for its long history, although it was founded by a Frenchman of that name in 1724, than for its more recent successes in producing and marketing its V.S.O.P. Fine Champagne cognac. It is presently owned by two families, including that of Max Cointreau of liqueur fame, who are descendants of one of the original partners.

Rémy Martin is unique in that it does not presently offer a 3-star quality; its lowest grade is a seven-to-eight-year-old cognac that originates exclusively in the *crus* of Grande and Petite Champagne and is always labeled "Fine Champagne." Although this has been the firm's policy since the early-twentieth century, its success with the Fine Champagne appellation in the 1960s caused several other houses, including Martell, Hennessy, and Courvoisier, to be concerned that overemphasis of only the first two growths was unfair to the majority of cognac, which originates outside these regions. While tempers were short for several years, a gentlemen's agreement not to disparage specific brands or regions has now been reached.

Rémy Martin continues to make nothing but Fine (or Grande, in the higher qualities) Champagne, while the Big Three no longer use the designation. The latter three claim to buy 70 per cent of the output of Grande and Petite Champagne, while Rémy Martin states that the twelve hundred growers with whom it has arrangements give it control of 25 per cent of the production of the two *crus*. Both figures are probably somewhat exaggerated, as the rest of the Cognac firms surely account for more than 5 per cent of the two districts.

Rémy Martin's V.S.O.P. is aged for ten to twelve months in new (less than five years old) oak barrels, at which time the first blend is made. Further blending occurs perhaps once a year thereafter, with the final blend achieved after five years. This then receives its final period of aging, for two to three years in very old barrels, which impart little additional tannin or wood character to the cognac.

Sales are currently around 7 million bottles annually, having increased by 36 per cent between 1971 and 1973, and they are by far the largest producers of V.S.O.P.-quality cognac. It is possible that a 3-star Rémy Martin will be developed for sale in selected markets in the future, but no final decisions on this issue have yet been reached. Several labels of an eleven-to-twelve-year-old Grande Champagne quality are now offered, including *Lacet d'Or* (in the U.S.A.), *Grande Réserve, Vieille Réserve* (in a Baccarat decanter), *Âge Inconnu,* and *Napoléon* (sold only in duty-free shops).

Rémy Martin is unusual in Cognac in that it does not have facilities for allowing casual visitors to tour the premises; those who have a particular interest and who make prior arrangements can, however, be assured of a most cordial reception.

V.S.O.P. Fine Champagne—Always a reliable and consistent blend, although it sometimes seems less distinctive than, for example, Hine or Hennessy. It has a pleasant, flowery aroma, moderate body, only light oak character, and just a hint of sweetness. Very well balanced and blended.

Lacet d'Or Grande Champagne—The lively citrus-coconut aroma is very agreeable, and the spicy flavors and finish are very smooth and drinkable. Similar to the V.S.O.P. in style, not very complex, but well balanced.

Louis XIII Grande Champagne—A twenty-year-old blend, sold only in Baccarat crystal decanters.

Of course, this does not exhaust the many fine cognacs that can be found both in France and in export markets, although the products of some of the smaller houses are available only in limited areas. While many of the small firms produce cognacs that are every bit the equal of the major houses, the products of the latter are often more consistent due to their large quantities of blending stocks. The romantic dream of finding a tiny, unknown firm that produces the perfect cognac is unlikely to be fulfilled, but visiting one or two small distillers will certainly complete your tour of Cognac and complement the impression made by the large shippers.

Among the lesser-known houses of interest we should mention A. E. DOR, whose few ancient, unblended cognacs are sold at the prestigious Fauchon's in Paris, and M. RAGNAUD, a small producer at Ambleville, who offers some excellent Grande Fine Champagne, small quantities of which are available in the United States. Other firms of some importance include AUGIER, now owned by Seagram and the producer of some fine, well-balanced cognacs of moderate oak character; BRILLET, a small house that specializes in the production of Petite Champagne cognac; COMANDON, which provides the cognac for Bénédictine's "B AND B"; EXSHAW, unusual in that its *chais* are located in Bordeaux rather than within the Cognac region itself; GASTON DE LAGRANGE, whose typical 3-star cognacs have been the subject of a fairly intensive advertising campaign in both France and the United States; and MARNIER-LAPOSTELLE, produced by the makers of the

celebrated Grand Marnier orange liqueur. Another small producer is
P. FRAPIN, located at Segonzac, which includes among its cognacs a
single vineyard Grande Champagne called Château de Fontpinot. The
scores of other labels may well include some notable cognacs, although these comprise but a tiny fraction of total cognac exports.

Cognac at its best is probably the finest brandy in the world. Gleam-
ing new distilleries, eight-barrel-high aging *chais,* and the inevitable
advent of mechanical harvesters will not change its basic character.
Twice-distilled in the primitive pot-still system, aged in oak, blended as-
siduously to capture the nuances of flavor and style that distinguish one
firm's products from another's, one need only taste a fine V.S.O.P. or
have the great fortune to sample one of the rare old products from the
paradis to agree that cognac is an elegant and inimitable product in the
world of spirits.

ARMAGNAC—SPIRIT OF THE GASCONS

ARMAGNAC—SPIRIT OF THE GASCONS

France is the proud home of two celebrated grape brandies. The first of course is cognac, the standard to which all great brandies of the world are compared. The other, less well known but equally deserving of praise, is the distinctive and aromatic spirit of armagnac.

The Armagnac region lies in the southwestern part of France, about midway between Bordeaux and Toulouse. It is part of Gascony, an ancient French province steeped in history and tradition that at one time stretched from the mountains of the Pyrenees to the Dordogne River, and from near Toulouse on the east to the Atlantic coast. The Gascons have long enjoyed a reputation as warm-hearted people who enjoy life and fine food, and this certainly remains a good description of today's friendly inhabitants of the Armagnac region.

Armagnac consists primarily of charming, peaceful countryside, for it lies away from the main routes from the Atlantic coast to Toulouse and is thus spared the hordes of travelers that crisscross much of France during summer holidays and long weekends. The entire area is very rural, comprising small villages dotted among farms, orchards, and woods. The largest city is Auch, which has twenty thousand inhabitants. More important to the Armagnac trade are Condom, whose population is seven thousand, and Éauze, an even smaller town, of only a few thousand people, in the subregion of Bas-Armagnac.

For the tourist, Armagnac offers many advantages, as the picturesque and historic sites are not overcrowded even during the summer months. A private car is a must, though, for the sparse population means that local transportation is minimal. Distances are not great, and in a few days you could leisurely see and taste much of what the Armagnac region has to offer.

Among the main historic attractions are the fortified villages, called *bastides,* that remain as reminders of the great struggles that were fought throughout Gascony from 1337 to 1453, during the Hundred

Years' War between the English and the French for control of south-western and coastal France. During this time, Éauze is said to have changed hands more than a dozen times. In the second half of the six-teenth century, fighting again erupted in the region, this time during the religious wars between Protestant and Catholic, and once again the fortifications of the *bastides* became important.

The most completely preserved of these fortified villages is Larres-single, just a few kilometers south of Condom; it is complete with high stone walls, a moat (now waterless), and a Romanesque church in the heart of the enclosure which dates from the twelfth century. An impos-ing sight when approached from the direction of Éauze is the town of Montréal, which commands a wide view of the surrounding countryside from its perch on a high bluff. The narrow streets, steep hills, and fortifications were once an English strong point, as was the thirteenth-century tower known as the Tour de la Motte, just to the south. In the fields on the outskirts of Montréal, excavators have uncovered the ruins of a third-century Gallo-Roman villa which contains some beautiful and well-preserved mosaics. Also nearby is the charming village of Fourcès, partially surrounded by the slow-moving Auzoue River and resembling a somewhat sprawling château protected by its moat. The central market place is very unusual in being circular rather than square, and the archways formed by the surrounding clay-and-timber houses are a typically Gascon form of architecture.

Of course, Gascony is most famous as the home of D'Artagnan, the fourth musketeer immortalized by Alexandre Dumas Père. His birth-place, the Château of Castlemore, can be visited about six kilometers south of Vic Fézensac.

Of the towns more or less directly concerned in the production of ar-magnac brandy, Éauze is perhaps the most important. Its major attrac-tions are an early-Gothic cathedral and, across the square, the Café de France, celebrated as the birthplace of the mother of King Henri IV and today serving as a weekly meeting place where growers and *négo-ciants* taste young brandies and haggle over this year's prices. Éauze holds little else to capture the tourist's attention, but its central location and quiet atmosphere make it a pleasant base for exploring the sur-rounding area.

Condom is thirty kilometers northeast of Éauze, connected by a winding road that passes through acre after acre of colorful vineyards and gently rolling hills. Divided by the murky waters of the river Baise,

Condom is the home of several large armagnac shippers and also boasts a lofty sixteenth-century cathedral. Traveling south through the heart of the Ténarèze district will bring you to Auch, the largest city in Armagnac though today located outside the primary grape-growing areas. Among Auch's attractions are the Hôtel de France, presently the proud holder of two Michelin stars, and the Basilica Sainte-Marie. The highlight of the basilica, which is a mixture of Gothic and Renaissance styles, is the black-oak choir stalls, spectacularly carved with some fifteen hundred miniature sculptures.

The cuisine of Gascony is not often mentioned when gourmets discuss the great gastronomical regions of France, but the Armagnac area is fortunately blessed with several small, informal restaurants that offer good regional dishes at reasonable prices. Two worthy of particular mention are La Mosaïque, a very small restaurant some eight kilometers from Éauze in the village of Parleboscq, and La Bonne Auberge, in Manciet, between Éauze and Nogaro. One delight served at La Bonne Auberge is a delicious breast of specially fattened duck, *maigret de canard,* which is roasted and served with a rich brown armagnac sauce.

Each autumn, farms and vineyards are abandoned for a few days and the woods are filled with farmers bearing shotguns in search of *palombes,* the migrating wood pigeons that fly over the area on their way south for the winter. In season, these small birds are roasted in an armagnac sauce and constitute a local delicacy, with a flavor akin to duck or pheasant. Other specialties of the region include a hearty vegetable soup, *potage gascon; poulet aux cèpes,* chicken cooked with armagnac and the large, flavorful mushrooms found in the area; and, for dessert, *croustade,* a very flaky apple tart enhanced by a dash of the ubiquitous armagnac.

To help cut through the rich sauces and game that characterize much Gascon cooking, one traditionally pauses before the main course for a shot of white, unaged armagnac, served chilled. This is known as a *trou gascon,* similar to the better-known *trou normand* tradition in Calvados. This young armagnac is at its freshly distilled strength of up to 70% alcohol, but its fieriness in the mouth quickly gives way to a warm, almost flowery glow that refreshes both stomach and palate for the courses yet to come.

Administratively, Armagnac consists largely of the *département* of Gers, along with a bit of Lot-et-Garonne to the north and the forested

Landes in the west. More importantly, Armagnac is divided for purposes of brandy production into three subregions, arranged roughly like two crescent moons to the east of a central circular area. Farthest to the east is Haut-Armagnac, so named not because of its lofty elevation or the quality of its brandies, but because it is the most distant from the ocean of the subregions. Its chalky soil and the whiteness of its limestone outcroppings have given it an alternate title of Armagnac Blanc. Growers and shippers agree that the brandy from Haut-Armagnac is the lowest in quality of the three regions, and today only a small fraction of armagnac originates in this area. Many vines are still cultivated for table-wine production.

The central area of Armagnac is Ténarèze, whose principal city is Condom. The brandies of this subregion are forceful, fruity, and aromatic, and there are nearly as many vines planted here as in Bas-Armagnac. While seldom bottled on their own, the brandies of Ténarèze are considered by most producers as essential to a well-balanced armagnac blend.

In terms of production and over-all quality, the most important of the three subregions is Bas-Armagnac, the westernmost, circular area that includes the towns of La Bastide, Éauze, and Nogaro. Sometimes known as Armagnac Noir because of its dark oaks and pines, in the early 1970s it contained approximately twenty-five thousand acres of vineyards whose grapes were destined for distillation. The soil is a mixture of sand, slate, and clay called *boulbenes*. The commercial center of Bas-Armagnac is Éauze, which also houses the region's commercial and publicity organization, the Bureau National Interprofessionnel de l'Armagnac. The brandies of Bas-Armagnac are more elegant and refined than those of Ténarèze, and some merchants do bottle unblended Bas-Armagnac. Most, however, blend with brandy from the other regions and label the final product with the more general appellation of Armagnac.

Armagnac may well be the oldest of all French brandies. Written reference to its distillation can be found as early as 1411, some two hundred years before D'Artagnan set out for Paris and before cognac production had really begun, in the seventeenth century. The cultivation of the vine in the area dates from Roman times, while the technique of distillation was probably imported by the Moors who arrived from Spain in the Middle Ages.

Over the centuries, armagnac remained largely a spirit for local consumption, for its lack of easy access to the sea or to large rivers made commerce difficult. By the eighteenth century some brandy was being transported by ox-drawn carts to the town of Mont de Marsan, from where it could be transported by boat down the Midouze and Adour rivers to the port of Bayonne for shipment abroad. Cognac, on the other hand, had the early advantage of ready access to the Charente River and to the large port of La Rochelle for shipment to a well-developed network of overseas markets. By the mid-nineteenth century, canals and later the railroad opened up new markets, both in France and abroad, although even today the region has not fully overcome its early geographical disadvantages. While the houses of Cognac prospered from their rich trade in the nineteenth century and were rewarded with abundant capital reserves to finance further marketing, the production of armagnac remained essentially the province of the small farmer, who was subject to the vagaries of market conditions and easily hurt by such adversities as the widespread destruction of vineyards by Phylloxera in the late 1800s and the world-wide depression of the 1930s. Today, only one of every ten bottles of brandy consumed in France is armagnac, and of every one hundred exported only three are the fiery spirit of Gascony.

The climate of Armagnac is warm and well suited to the cultivation of the grape. In fact some authors, when describing the area, have gone so far as to talk of the sun-baked plains of Gascony, imparting visions of an arid region. The area is a well-watered one, however, and the green of the vineyards is matched by rolling hills covered with forests, orchards, and grasslands which impart a sense of richness to the land. Summer days can indeed be very warm, but spring and fall are usually quite pleasant, and the winters are mild.

Before the arrival of Phylloxera the vineyards of Armagnac covered some 250,000 acres (100,000 hectares). These were almost totally destroyed by the root louse, and it was not until after the First World War that replanting began in earnest, using grafted, resistant vines. Today the total acreage stands at about 100,000, but of this only about half is used for the production of armagnac.

The brandies of Armagnac are subject to the French *appellation contrôlée* laws, and only the following grapes may be used for the production of armagnac: Folle Blanche and Folle Jaune, Picquepoul, Saint-Émilion (Ugni Blanc), Colombard, Jurançon, Blanquette, Mozac,

Clairette, Meslier, Plant de Graisse, and Baco 22A. In terms of quantity the only ones that are important are the Folle Blanche, Saint-Émilion (Ugni Blanc), Colombard, and Baco 22A, as the remainder represent only very small plantings. The Baco 22A is a cross between the Folle Blanche and an American grape called the Noah. In the sandy soils of the southwestern part of the district it constitutes a large proportion of the vineyards and produces a wine similar to the Folle Blanche but less subject to molds and other plant diseases.

The white wine of the Armagnac region used in distillation averages about 9% alcohol, a bit higher than the average in Cognac, and is rather tart. Distillation takes place as soon as possible after fermentation and by law must be completed by the April 30 following the year of harvest. The wine must be left in contact with the yeast sediment known as lees, for this is thought to add extra flavor and aromatic components to the brandy. Much table wine is also made throughout the region for local use, although none is considered of sufficient quality to merit the coveted French status of *appellation contrôlée*. Both red and white grape vines dot the countryside, and in autumn their admixture produces a blazing sea of green, gold, and scarlet in some vineyards.

The traditional armagnac still was small and portable and consisted of little more than a heating chamber, or *chaudière*, and an adjacent condensing chamber. It was mounted on wheels and taken from farmyard to farmyard by itinerent distillers, the *bouilleurs de cru*. While such portable stills can still be occasionally found in Armagnac, to a large extent they have become relics of the past and have been replaced by larger, fixed stills owned by some of the more prosperous farmers or operated by co-operatives, merchants, or *bouilleurs de profession*.

The still for armagnac functions continuously (see diagram). Wine passes from a storage tank into the condenser, where it serves as a coolant for the alcoholic vapors in the serpentine. The wine in turn is heated and then passes into an adjacent unit consisting of two or three superimposed boilers or heating chambers mounted above a fire. The heat from below vaporizes the alcohol in the wine, which passes up through a short column containing several perforated plates and then over into the adjacent condenser. Some of the less volatile elements fall back onto the plates. The lowest *chaudière* is periodically drained of water and the nonvolatile residue of the wine.

Armagnac stills are relatively small compared to the continuous stills

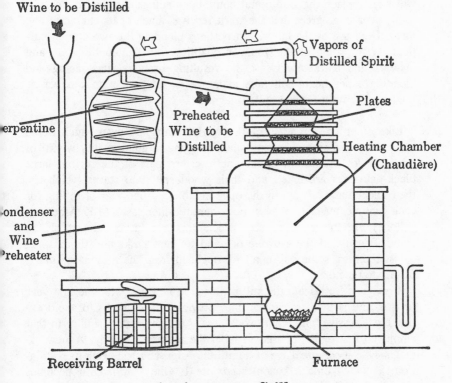

Wine to be Distilled

Vapors of
Distilled Spirit

Preheated
Wine to be
Distilled

Plates

erpentine

Heating Chamber
(Chaudière)

·ondenser
and
Wine
'reheater

Receiving Barrel

Furnace

An Armagnac Still

in operation elsewhere in the world; thus the distillate comes off at a lower alcoholic strength. In the past this averaged around 52–56% alcohol but regulations now permit the construction of slightly taller stills with more plates, capable of producing a distillate up to the new legal maximum of 72%. These limits are in the range where there is a rather high concentration of fusel alcohols and other congeners, higher than the pot distillates from Cognac, which undergo a double distillation.

A few producers have been experimenting with the use of a cognac-style pot still which has been permitted for the production of armagnac only since the 1972 harvest. The role this new distillation will play in the future remains to be seen, but at the moment it appears that armagnac produced in a pot still is a bit lighter and finer than the traditional product and will age more quickly. It is most unlikely that the pot still will ever replace the traditional continuous still of Armagnac, for virtually everyone agrees that the spirit receives much of its character and flavor from use of the latter. But perhaps blending the two spirits, particularly for some of the younger qualities, will lighten the style and increase the marketability of the resulting brandy. Since aging and blending experiments will take many years, no prediction can yet be made on the future of pot-still armagnacs.

Like other fine brandies of the world, armagnac owes much of its complexity and smoothness to years of aging in good-quality wood. In the forest of Monlezun, in the southwestern part of the region, large black-oak trees are felled and their wood split into staves which are then stacked and left out in the open air to dry—one year of drying for each centimenter of thickness. Four-hundred-liter casks (105 American gallons) are the standard size which are then fashioned out of the wood. Because of the growing demand for new casks and diminishing forest reserves, some oak is also brought in from the Limousin Forest, farther to the north.

Armagnac fresh from the still is placed in new casks for the first year or two, and is then transferred into previously used casks to avoid extracting excessive tannin and woodiness. An aging system similar to that employed in Cognac is used to label the maturing brandy. A new armagnac has a *compte d'âge* of 0 until the August 31 following its distillation, at which time it becomes *compte* 1. One year later it becomes *compte* 2, and so on. The legal minimum for marketing armagnac is *compte* 1, generally corresponding to a spirit of about eighteen months' age. The youngest brandies are usually labeled as 3-star, as in cognac. Armagnac labeled as V.O., V.S.O.P., Aide de Camp, or Réserve must be at least *compte* 4. The legal minimum for the designations Extra, Hors d'Âge, Napoléon, and Vieille Réserve is *compte* 5.

Armagnacs are generally bottled considerably above the legal minimums, particularly for the highest qualities. Three-star averages about three years, the V.S.O.P. class between five and ten, and the Hors d'Âge and Vieille Réserve fifteen to twenty-five. Some armagnacs are labeled as "10 years old," although in the past legal enforcement of this designation has been lax. Old barrels of vintaged armagnac are still kept by many firms, and when the records meet the satisfaction of the authorities these may be bottled with a vintage date. While only good brandies are usually aged in this manner, the vintage is more likely to be a guar-

1. A typical Charente farmhouse, surrounded by cognac vineyards
(photo by Briteau; courtesy of the Bureau National du Cognac)

2. Harvest in Armagnac

3. Fashioning a Limousin oak barrel in Cognac: the combination of fire and water renders the wood more supple, so that the ends may be drawn together to form the barrel (photo by J.Y. Boyer; courtesy of the Bureau National du Cognac)

4. A nineteenth-century cognac still room, showing the *chaudière, chauffe-vin,* and condenser; note the bed, essential to maintaining a round-the-clock watch on the distillation (photo by J.Y. Boyer; courtesy of the Bureau National du Cognac)

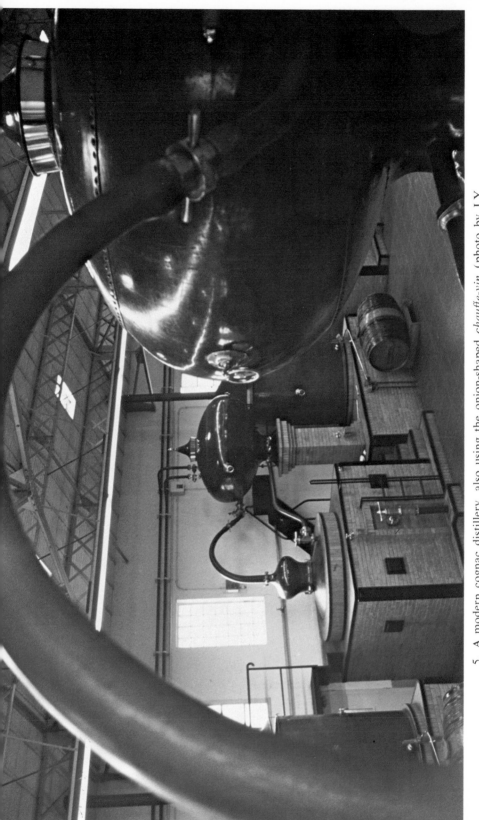

5. A modern cognac distillery, also using the onion-shaped *chauffe-vin* (photo by J.Y. Boyer; courtesy of the Bureau National du Cognac)

antee of age rather than a designation of particularly high quality as would be the case with champagne and port.

There are two traditional bottles used for armagnac, although other types may also occasionally be found. The most popular style is an oval bottle with flat sides and a long neck called the *basquaise*. It is similar to the *Bocksbeutel* used in Germany's Franconia district and is said to have derived its design from the goatskin wine bags of the old shepherds and smugglers of the Pyrenees. The other bottle, round and squat, is called a *pot gascon* and is often used for quantities of several liters.

Armagnac is certainly one of the world's most enjoyable spirits. In its youth it is a coarse and pungent spirit, less refined and elegant than cognac, but often with more intense flavors. With adequate aging a fine armagnac can acquire the complexity and balance to rival its famous neighbor to the north, and the differences are in style rather than quality. Armagnac has a characteristically grapy character in the aroma, one that may resemble, with a little imagination, prunes, nuts, or violets. Armagnac is fuller-bodied than cognac or California brandies, with higher levels of fusel alcohols. Its fieriness when young may not make it everyone's favorite spirit, but to those who have acquired a taste for it the brandy of the Gascons is a mouth-filling and warming drink of deep flavors and character.

Armagnac is excellent as an after-dinner *digestif,* for its robust flavors help cut through the satiating effect of a large, rich meal. Its liveliness even has restorative powers in midafternoon after a large luncheon, at a time when the lighter, more refined flavors of cognac seem more likely to promote comfort and sleep.

The production of armagnac has traditionally been the province of the small grape grower, and to some extent this is still true today. The largest producer of armagnac is a co-operative that numbers among its members seventy-two hundred of the eighteen thousand growers of the region, and many small farmers still offer their own labels. The first co-operatives were formed during the hard times of the 1930s, and today there are fourteen, all but one of which belong to a group called the UNION DES COOPÉRATIVES VITICOLES DE L'ARMAGNAC (U.C.V.A.), which is headquartered at Éauze and controls approximately 45 per cent of the armagnac currently being produced. Their marketing arm is the Société d'Intérêt Collectif Agricole Armagnacaise (S.I.C.A.), which controls the distribution of the co-operative's principal label,

Marquis de Caussade, as well as its other brands, which include *Oblin, Haut Baron,* and *Duc de St. Bar.* The co-operative also distills brandy for other merchants, who then age and bottle it under their own labels. The armagnacs from the co-operative are all of very fine quality. They include a *3-star* which is about two years old and is a typically pungent, grapy armagnac, a *V.S.O.P.* aged seven to ten years, and an *Hors d' Âge* fifteen to twenty years old, both of which have considerable complexity and refinement. At the aging cellars and tasting room in Éauze rare bottles of old vintage armagnac are occasionally offered for sale. We returned from a recent trip with a bottle of 1934, which we rationed and nursed through many a night in order to savor its wonderful old richness as long as possible. At the same time, a bottle of 1900 could have been purchased for about sixty dollars.

In Condom, the house of JANNEAU was founded in 1851 and is today run by members of the fifth and sixth generations of the family. The firm, largest of the independent houses, is experimenting with Charentais pot stills and has recently built a modern distillery on the outskirts of Condom. Janneau produces a good, typical *3-star* armagnac, labeled *Tradition,* which is young and grapy in nose and flavors and is aged in wood about three years. The *V.S.O.P.,* six to ten years old, has some wood in the aroma and is smoother and more complex in flavors than the *3-star.* The oldest blend is *Réserve du Fondateur,* which is about twenty years old and has aged vanilla flavors with a light, elegant finish that lingers very nicely on the palate.

The house of H. A. SEMPÉ, located at Aignan, in the Ténarèze, produce about 2 million bottles per year and is another large independent shipper, particularly to Germany and the United States. Many different labels are offered, and the age of the brandy depends on its ultimate market. The *3-star* is generally two years old, except in Britain, where it is three years of age. The *V.S.O.P.* sold in the United States and Britain approaches ten years of age, while the one sold in Germany as *Nicolas Napoléon V.S.O.P.* is just five years old. Sempé's domestic *3-star* and *V.S.O.P.* are typical armagnacs of good quality, and one labeled *10 Ans d'Âge* (10 years old) is especially flavorful. *Noces d'Argent* is a special bottling selected for its woody character and flavor, which Europeans traditionally associate with armagnac. Besides *Sempé,* other labels offered by this firm include *Cavalier, Château Perres, Giscard, La Vie,* and *Armagnac de Castillac.*

Several leading armagnac brands are now controlled by companies important in other aspects of the spirit's trade. Pernod, a leading anise-based French apéritif, owns the MARQUIS DE MONTESQUIOU label and offers a well-balanced armagnac with good spice and oak in the flavors. The Basque liqueur Izarra is based on armagnac, and it is not surprising that this company would also have its own armagnac house. Their brand is CLÉ DES DUCS, whose *V.S.O.P.* we found to have typical armagnac pungency and fruit in the aroma and good body, smoothness, and oak in the flavor.

Several cognac firms have also demonstrated an interest in the potential of armagnac. The MALLIAC firm is now owned by Courvoisier, and Camus has purchased a company in La Bastide d'Armagnac that bottles under the PRINCE DE CHABOT label. Their *Blason d'Or* (*3-star*) has little wood and fairly smooth, prune-like flavors; the *Napoléon* is not overly complex but does show some age; and the *X.O.* has a nice nutty-briar character and pleasant aftertaste. All have good fruit, though they are perhaps lighter than the average armagnac.

A list of the leading exporters of armagnac to the United Kingdom, Ireland, Canada, and the United States follows:

Company and Location	*Principal Brands*
S.I.C.A. Armagnacaise Éauze	Marquis de Caussade, Oblin, Haut Baron, Duc de Saint Bar
H. A. Sempé Aignan	Sempé, Cavalier, Château Perres, La Vie, Armagnac de Castillac, Giscard
Janneau Fils Condom	Janneau
Société des Produits d'Armagnac Condom	Marquis de Montesquiou
Établissements Papelorey Condom	Larressingle
Société J. Ryst Condom	Ryst
Compagnie Viticole des Grands Armagnacs La Bastide d'Armagnac	Prince de Chabot

Company and Location	Principal Brands
Léon Lafitte La Bastide d'Armagnac	Domaine Boingnères
Distillerie Côte Basque Bayonne	Clé des Ducs
Kressman & Cie. Bordeaux	Kressman
Établissements Besse & Paret Paris	Saint Vivant
Société Malliac Vic Fézensac	Malliac
Maison Nismes Delclou Lavardac	Nismes Delclou
Société des Vieilles Eaux-de-Vie Nogaro	Samalens
S. A. Pallas Nérac	San Gil
Cavé Frères Lannepax	Trianon

There are also a host of small farmers, producers, and *négociants* scattered throughout the countryside. Even those listed below as exporters will be hard to find, but as we have often been delighted by an armagnac from a small, relatively unknown property, we would encourage you to try a bottle should you happen upon one.

Henri Faget, propriétaire Château de Cassaigne
Condom

Laudet-Bastie, propriétaire Château de Laballe
Parleboscq

Établissements Gélas
Vic Fézensac

Maison Mader
Vic Fézensac

Maison Marcel Trepout
Vic Fézensac

Maison Michel Faure
Nogaro

Dartigalongue
Nogaro

G. Laberdolive
La Bastide d'Armagnac

Domaine d'Ognoas
Villeneuve de Marsan

Cooperative d'Armagnac Gerland
Villeneuve de Marsan

Maison Lafontan
Castelnau d'Auzan

Maison Ducastaing
Charenton

Maison Goudoulin
Courrensan Gondrin

Fruit preserved in armagnac and several local liqueurs complete the line of Gascon spirit-based products. Among the preserves the most famous are probably the *pruneaux à l'armagnac,* made from the famous prunes of nearby Agen, although chestnuts in armagnac syrup are also delicious. Other fruits prepared this way include apricots, clémentine oranges, and cherries. The liqueurs are for the most part rather simply flavored and sweetened spirits based on armagnac, but they are nevertheless pleasant enough to sample when visiting the area. The U.C.V.A. produces a sweet and heavy orange liqueur called POUSSE-RAPIÈRE, which has acquired some popularity as an apéritif when mixed with a tart local sparkling wine known as *vin sauvage.* The co-operative also produces ARMABELLE, which is a more complex liqueur with flavors of almond, citrus, and apricot. SABAZIA, produced by Sempé and labeled "Grande Crème de la Maison Sempé" is quite sweet and similar in style to Armabelle.

The future of armagnac appears bright, as the unified efforts of the co-operative and several large companies that have recently acquired interests in the area should increase recognition throughout the world through increased marketing capabilities. In addition, the price of armagnac has remained quite attractive in comparison to that of its northern neighbor, cognac. Since 1966, sales have risen steadily but not so quickly as to erode the stocks of older brandies necessary to maintain the quality of the finest blends. Armagnac's principal foreign markets are presently West Germany and Scandinavia, where the vast majority of brandy exported is sold in cask. This is far from ideal, for the producers of armagnac have no control over when their product will be bottled, or for that matter what cheaper spirit might be added to it. However, these markets are too economically important at the current time for major changes to be introduced, and it is unlikely that the practice of exportation in bulk will cease in the near future.

Almost all exportation to Britain and the United States is in bottle, although sales are low enough in both countries for armagnac to still be called a relatively undiscovered brandy. Next time you want to try a different spirit, full-flavored and reasonably priced, try the one from Gascony.

THE BRANDIES OF CALIFORNIA

THE BRANDIES OF CALIFORNIA

Brandy country in California is the warm and fertile Central Valley, particularly that part which stretches some two hundred miles from Lodi, a small town an hour and a half's drive east of San Francisco, south to Kern County, just across the Tehachapi Mountains from Los Angeles. Here the summers are long, the soil rich, and thousands upon thousands of acres of prolific vines cover the countryside.

In a bountiful year California's vineyards yield an adequate supply of grapes for her brandy producers. But in recent years an unprecedented demand for wine, coupled with growing seasons in which the harvest was reduced due to unseasonal frost and rain, have sent some brandy distillers to Arizona and even Mexico in search of grapes. A few bottlers of brandy, particularly those with an eastern base of operations, blend some imported brandy with what they buy from California. But for practical purposes virtually all, and certainly the finest, American brandies are from grapes grown, distilled, and bottled in California. In large part due to the efforts of the California Brandy Advisory Board, a California appellation has recently been recognized which requires that all brandy labeled "California" be produced exclusively from grapes grown and distilled in California.

Brandy has been made in California for nearly two centuries. As the Spanish fathers traveled northward establishing their chain of missions in the late-eighteenth century, they planted vineyards along the way. Grapes from these vines went into the production of table and sacramental wine, and some brandy was also made. In the early-nineteenth century such notables as General Vallejo of Sonoma and John Sutter of gold-discovery fame owned small distilleries. The primary grape used was the ubiquitous Mission, originally brought into the state by the missionaries from Mexico, which produced an unexciting wine and probably a mediocre brandy.

In the second half of the nineteenth century California vineyardists turned their attention to the noble vines of Europe. Since at this time cognac was being produced primarily from Folle Blanche and Colombard, these varieties were also planted in California for the purpose of distillation into brandy. The result was an immediate increase in quality in both pot and continuous-still distillates. By the 1880s California was exporting large quantities of brandy to Europe to help make up for the shortage created by the decimation of French vineyards by the Phylloxera root louse.

But California's growing interest in and production of brandy was to be short-lived, for French vineyards were replanted with pest-resistant vines and in 1918 America's noble experiment, Prohibition, began. Stills lay idle for fifteen years except for the production of small amounts of high-proof spirits for fortifying sacramental wines and for "medicinal" purposes.

Following the repeal of Prohibition, in 1933, the production of California brandy picked up again, although quality was at first rather poor and distillation was often used as a means of attempting to salvage poor wine and excess grapes. Many brandies were harsh and unpleasant, and most were not adequately aged. Since the end of the Second World War, however, both the techniques of production and the quality of California brandy have greatly improved. Conscientious efforts have been made to reduce the amounts of aldehydes and particularly fusel alcohols in the distillate, and the result has been a lighter, fruitier, cleaner product. Brandy is steadily increasing in popularity in this country, both as a mixer and for straight sipping, and no longer is brandy-making considered only an outlet for surplus grapes and wine.

Today Thompson Seedless and Flame Tokay are the principal brandy grapes of California; together they are responsible for more than 90 per cent of brandy production. Both produce clean, neutral wines, devoid of particularly strong aromas that might pass over into the distillate, which are ideal for the light, grapy brandies that are the goal of the California brandy industry. There are no regulations limiting the grape varieties that may be used for brandy, and at one time or another wines from most white and probably a few red vines have been distilled. Less important varietals most consistently mentioned by brandy producers include Emperor, Malaga, Mission, Palomino, and Grenache. Although considerable plantings of Muscat exist in the Central Valley, only small amounts of this varietal are used. Wine made from Muscat grapes has a particularly pungent aroma that easily carries over when distilled, and most producers feel this pungency is undesirable in a brandy.

Thompson and Tokay not only produce suitable wines for distillation, but are economically very attractive as well. Both types, especially the Thompson, are readily available and considerably less expensive than more distinctive wine grapes. The Flame Tokay grows best in the Lodi area, where in the fall its six-foot-high vines produce a blazing sea of colors worthy of its name. The Thompson is widely grown in the southern part of the Central Valley, with total plantings exceeding two hundred thousand acres. Besides its use in brandy, it is important as a wine, raisin, and table grape. It may also be used in inexpensive sparkling wines, perhaps explaining why a few California brandy producers have chosen to advertise that their products are distilled from so-called "champagne grapes."

It takes just over one ton of grapes to produce a fifty-gallon barrel of California brandy, or about one third as many gallons as you might expect a ton of grapes to yield in table wine. Thompson Seedless has sold for as little as one third the cost of other Central Valley white grapes suitable for distilling, and the price spread is considerably more when compared to the high-acid varieties such as Colombard, Folle Blanche, and Ugni Blanc grown in the premium wine districts of California's northern and central coasts. Any significant change to other grapes would thus add considerably to the raw-material cost of California brandy, although new plantings of Colombard, Ugni Blanc, and possibly Chenin Blanc in the Central Valley may alter this pattern somewhat.

Before Prohibition a number of pot stills could be found in California, but in recent years, as the trend toward lighter brandies has developed, most of the pot stills have been dismantled in favor of the more efficient column stills. A few pot stills remain in use for the production of blending brandies. Today, though, virtually all California brandy is distilled in large continuous column stills.

Beverage brandy may be distilled to a maximum of 85% ethyl alcohol (170 American proof). It is then usually cut to about 55–60% alcohol and barreled in fifty-gallon American oak. All California brandy must legally be aged for at least two years, although the average brandy is not sold until it is about four years old. Some companies have important stocks of aged brandies used for blending, although since most California brandies are relatively light in congeners, prolonged aging is less necessary than it is for cognac and armagnac.

The American oak used in brandy aging is mainly from the hills of Arkansas and Tennessee, some in the form of new barrels coopered especially for brandy and others in the form of recured casks formerly used for aging bourbon whiskey. American oak lends its own particular aroma and flavor to brandy, distinct from that imparted by European oak. This is perhaps best described as a dry, green, spicy-woody character less sweet and complex than that of Limousin oak, but intriguing in its own right.

Most California brandies are blended products which contain certain sweetening and flavoring ingredients added to them just prior to bottling. The legal limit for these additives, or "rectifying agents," is 2.5 per cent by volume. These materials are used to add both softness and flavor to light, neutral brandies in a style that brandy makers feel appeal to the American public. Each brandy maker has his own special formula of additives, which he usually keeps as a closely guarded secret. But everyone is happy to speculate on what the fellow down the road does, and with a little research it is possible to surface with a list of those flavoring elements most commonly employed.

The most important and most widely used rectifying agent is sugar, usually in the form of liquid or invert sugar. Some producers use only small amounts of sugar, although glycerine is another popular way to add sweetness and smoothness. Prune and other fruit extracts, fortified wines such as white port and sherry, and St.-John's-bread are among the more flavorful ingredients used as rectifying agents. The latter is derived from the pod of the Mediterranean carob tree and possesses a cocoa-vanilla flavor that is sometimes noticeable in young California brandies.

Small, well-balanced blends of such materials, when added to good four-to-five-year-old brandy, can contribute soft additional flavors that will not necessarily mask the basically clean, fruity character of California brandy. Such a spirit can be sipped after dinner and also serves well in mixed drinks and in cooking.

Some brandy producers are rather heavy-handed, however, and excessively sweetened and flavored California brandy does exist. These are most often spirits aged little more than the legal minimum of two years, and the producer may attempt to soften the harshness of youth with as much sweetening material as the law permits. Although novice brandy drinkers may appreciate such a sweetened spirit, more-experienced brandy buffs are likely to find the excess sugar a poor cover-up for an otherwise uninteresting brandy. Even these relatively uncommon products may be quite palatable in punches or mixed drinks.

Blended brandies make up the majority of California's production, but a few distillers also offer a brandy to which no sweetening or flavoring material has been added. These are called "straight" brandies, and they may legally contain no additives other than caramel for coloring. Straight brandies may occasionally be "bottled in bond," which guarantees the age of the product. Bottled-in-bond brandies must be a minimum of 100 proof rather than the usual 80; they must be aged at least four years in barrel; and each batch must be distilled within a single six-month period. The date of distillation and the date of bottling appear on the green tax stamp on the top of the bottle.

Some Technical Thoughts

The traditional American still conjures up visions of a large copper kettle topped with yards of twisting pipe and heated by a small wood fire secluded somewhere in the Blue Ridge Mountains of North Carolina or Virginia. The continuous column still used in the production of California brandy is far less romantic, if not because of its bevy of efficient dials, gauges, and meters, then at least because it is too huge to be hidden from the "revenooers."

Continuous column stills, also known as Coffey, or patent, stills, have been around since the early-nineteenth century and today are in widespread use throughout the world for the production of spirits. The California variety rises well over fifty feet high and is capable of distilling about a thousand gallons of spirits per hour. It is composed of two separate columns which may be mounted either side by side or one on top of the other (see diagram).

The lower one is called a stripping, or beer, column (the latter term stems from the use of the column to distill fermented mash (beer) into whiskey). In brandy production preheated wine is introduced near the top of the stripping column. Heat in the form of steam comes up from the very bottom. The heat volatizes the wine, and the alcohol-rich vapors pass on to the second column, called the rectifying column, while the water and nonvolatile components fall toward the bottom to be removed as waste.

The rectifying column contains many perforated plates, through which the vapors rise and upon which the liquid collects as it con-

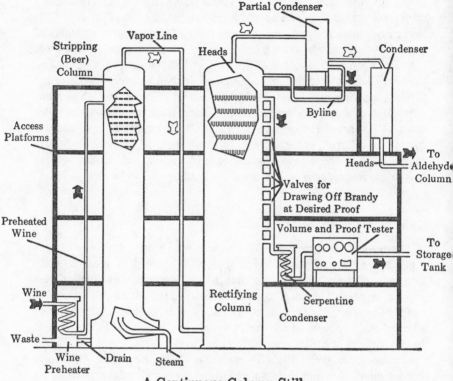

A Continuous Column Still

denses. The most volatile compounds rise farther up the column, while the least volatile collect on plates nearer the bottom of this second column. Beverage brandy may be taken off at a maximum of 85% ethyl alcohol (170 American proof). Fusel alcohols are present in greatest concentration about four plates below this, where the ethyl alcohol concentration is about 65%. Aldehydes and other highly volatile elements pass to the very top of the column, where they are taken off and passed through an aldehyde, or purifying, column.

The raw brandy is taken off the still at very close to its boiling temperature. On its way to storage tanks the spirit passes through a cooler and past gauges which measure alcoholic strength and flow rates.

The goal of most California brandy producers is to distill a product that is light and clean in both aroma and body—hence one that is relatively low in the higher alcohols called fusel alcohols. Brandy distilled from table wine and taken from the column at 85% alcohol will, under normal conditions, contain about 100–115 grams of fusels per hundred liters of spirits. This is somewhat higher than the level found in most commercial California brandy—indicating that additional steps must be taken somewhere along the line to achieve the lighter product geared to modern American tastes.

The first step in controlling the levels of fusel alcohols in brandy involves the raw product itself. Grapes vary considerably in their fusel oil formation; as a general rule white varieties yield lower levels than red grapes. Spoiled fruit increases fusels, while fermentation of clear rather than cloudy wines, removal of the skins prior to fermentation, and the avoidance of excessive oxidation all help keep levels down. Even the yeast strain used in the fermentation of the wine will have an effect on fusel concentrations.

Fortified wine will sometimes be used as part of the distilling material. Because about half the alcohol content of fortified wine is derived from neutral high-proof grape spirits, which are essentially devoid of fusels, the beverage brandy that results will be considerably lower in fusel oils than if a comparable amount of table wine were distilled.

Since fusels tend to concentrate at a certain level of the column, it seems logical that if this fraction were continuously drawn off the still, fewer of these pungent compounds would remain to pass over into the brandy. Such a practice is economically unfeasible, however, for up to one fifth of the total product would have to be sacrificed before there would be a sizable reduction of fusel content in the distilled spirit. Some producers claim they can reduce congener content by use of what is called a fusel oil decanter. Researchers at the University of California at Davis disagree, and state that in the production of beverage brandy it is not possible to concentrate fusel alcohols on any particular plate to a high enough degree to allow their separation.

At the top of the column, the vapors contain very high-proof (95%) ethyl alcohol and highly volatile compounds such as aldehydes. These may be removed and added to a purifying, or aldehyde, column. If steam is added, it is possible to separate the heads fraction of volatile compounds from the remaining ethyl alcohol, which is reduced to about 85% by the steam. This ethyl alcohol is virtually devoid of fusels, since it has passed through such a high-proof stage. When added back into the main stream of the brandy, it is still within the legal maximum of 170 proof, but it has the effect of reducing the over-all fusel alcohol level. This is probably one of the more common methods used by California distillers to keep their finished products low in fusel content.

The Wisconsin Mystery

Do you know which city in the world has the highest per capita consumption of brandy? Paris, London, New York, perhaps San Francisco? The answer may well be Milwaukee, Wisconsin. For reasons that are still not understood, despite intensive marketing-research studies undertaken by the California brandy industry, brandy rivals milk as the favorite drink of this northern dairy state. Until 1972, when it was surpassed by California, Wisconsin was the leading market for American brandy. The first two, and seven of the top ten, leading brands of all distilled spirits sold in Wisconsin are California brandy. One hundred and two domestic brandy labels are available in the state, far more than may be found in any other market.

Brandy in Wisconsin is drunk very much as bourbon and Scotch whiskies are in the rest of the country—in mixed drinks, with soda, over ice, or as a straight shot at the local tavern. But while very cold winters and the Scandinavian background of much of the state's populace are certainly conducive to the consumption of spirits, why brandy is preferred to other distilled spirits remains a mystery. One story we've heard is that the first enterprising liquor salesman to base his operations in Wisconsin after Prohibition sold brandy—and obviously was very successful. Perhaps the answer is as simple as that. Or perhaps the people of Wisconsin have just discovered a good thing a few years ahead of everyone else.

California Brandy: The Producers

The number of companies directly involved in the distillation of California brandy has steadily decreased as technical advances and economic factors have led to the concentration of production in fewer, more efficient plants. In 1971 the California Brandy Advisory Board was created to promote California brandy throughout the country, and today it is composed of fourteen members, who among them distill virtually all beverage brandy produced in the United States.

Even though the number of brandy producers has decreased over the years, several hundred different labels remain from which the consumer may choose. One reason for this diversity of labels is that a distiller may offer several different styles and qualities of brandy, each under its own brand. In other cases, a distiller may have chosen to retain a label purchased from another company during a consolidation of operations if the purchased brand had its own market identity. Some producers sell only young bulk brandy to others, who then age and blend according to their own specifications. And as with other distilled spirits, a considerable number of private labels may be provided by a producer who bottles brandy to meet the needs of a particular customer (winery, department store, liquor merchandiser, etc.) in a special market.

The Lodi area is the farthest north of the state's brandy-producing regions and is the home of two companies whose products are well known throughout the nation. Interestingly enough, both are grower-owned co-operatives.

The EAST-SIDE WINERY has been in business since 1934 and produces some six to seven hundred thousand gallons of brandy annually. All of it comes from two continuous stills, one built in 1933 and the other in 1934. The East-Side brandies are distilled as much as is possible from wine made from local Flame Tokay grapes, although some Thompson Seedless are brought in from other parts of the valley. Both blended and straight brandies are bottled.

The primary brand is *Royal Host,* which is offered as both a blended and a straight brandy. The blend is a pleasant brandy with light to medium sweetness, a fruity aroma, and slight wood character in the finish. It is aged an average of four and a half years in oak. A similar blended brandy is sold in New England under the *Pastene* label. Less expensive and younger blends aged for about two to three years are *Mission Host* and *Gold Bell.*

The *Royal Host* six-year-old straight brandy is light and dry, with a fruity aroma complemented by a fair amount of oakiness. It is an interesting, well-made brandy with good balance between oak and brandy flavors. The top-of-the-line product is a ten-year-old straight brandy labeled *Conti Royal.* This certainly is one of the most powerful of all California brandies, as it has lots of dry, green-spicy American-oak character in both aroma and taste. The color is quite deep and the aroma fairly clean and grapy. While such a forceful brandy will not be to everyone's taste, those who appreciate age and wood character should find this a pleasant sipping brandy. Both the Royal Host six-year-old and the Conti Royal are distilled entirely from Tokay grapes.

GUILD WINERIES AND DISTILLERIES is the largest grower-owned co-operative in the country, with a thousand members and seven wineries throughout the state of California. Guild began brandy operations in the late 1940s, in Lodi, and they now operate six distilleries in California. Their production was bolstered in 1971 with the acquisition of the Schenley distilling plant at the old Roma winery in Fresno. Guild is one of the most important California distillers, in terms of both quantity and quality. Column stills are used for the majority of distillation, although two pot stills at Fresno produce some brandy used for blending.

A number of different labels of blended brandy are offered for marketing in various parts of the United States. Those considered as the premium line are labeled *Winemasters' Guild, Guild Blue Ribbon,* and *Roma Director's Choice.* Other labels include *St. Mark* and *Citation.*

Guild is probably California's leading producer of aged straight brandies. Under the *Ceremony* label may be found both five- and eight-year-old straight brandies, both of which are dry, clean spirits with considerable wood flavors. The eight-year-old is particularly dominated by the spiciness of American oak, and, like the East-Side Conti Royal, will probably best be enjoyed by those who appreciate such a spicy, slightly astringent taste. Both *Ceremony* brandies are exceptionally good values. They contain brandy aged appreciably longer than the typical young blended brandy, yet are very nearly the same in price.

Guild's highest-quality brand is *Old San Francisco Brandy,* which is another straight brandy, eight to eleven years old. It is attractively packaged in a flat-sided flask bottle similar to the Armagnac *basquaise* or the *Bocksbeutel* of Germany, with a scene from early San Francisco pictured on the label. The color is fairly light, and the aroma is laden with an oak spiciness reminiscent of the eight-year-old *Ceremony.* In the mouth this is a dry, full-flavored brandy, with moderate body and considerable complexity. It is near the top of the price range of California brandies and should be considered one of the finest.

The FRANZIA BROTHERS WINERY is at Ripon, some thirty miles south of Lodi. Their production of brandy has increased considerably in the past few years. All distillation is done on a column still, and the base wine is about 90% Thompson Seedless with the remainder including Tokay from Lodi, Palamino, and small amounts of Muscat. Aging is done in both new and reused American-oak barrels.

All the brandies made here are blended products. The principal label is *Franzia,* which is a light, slightly sweet, and fairly simple brandy with some wood in the aroma. Its balance would be improved if there were more grapy-fruity character on the palate. Another label used in some markets is *Louis V.*

The giant of the California wine industry is the E. AND J. GALLO WINERY, headquartered in Modesto. For years Gallo has operated large column stills in the Modesto and Fresno areas, but for some time their use was limited to the production of high-proof grape spirits for their extensive line of fortified wines. A brandy bearing the Gallo label was marketed, but this was purchased from other distillers. Recently, however, the Gallo brothers decided to join the California Brandy Advisory Board and to begin production of their own brandy.

California's second-largest wine organization, UNITED VINTNERS, has long been active in the production of brandy. Only column stills are used, though in the days immediately following Prohibition some of the member wineries of what is now United Vintners were in the forefront of brandy production and depended heavily on pot distillates. Distillation today takes place at Lodi and Madera, in the Central Valley, while blending and bottling is at Asti, the northern-Sonoma County home of Italian Swiss Colony. Brandy is aged in barrel at all three locations.

The leading label for United Vintners is *Lejon,* which is available nationwide. This is a medium-bodied blended brandy, with some woody-spiciness in the aroma and light to medium sweetness underlying the grape flavors. The *Petri* label is similar in style but is available only in selected markets, most notably Wisconsin. A third brand is *Italian Swiss Colony,* which is somewhat lighter in color and body than Lejon and Petri, and also has light to medium sweetness.

Younger and less expensive blends include *Hartley,* which is available throughout the country, and *Jacques Bonet,* which is limited to special markets. These are light-bodied, simple, sweet brandies whose flavors are due primarily to rectifying agents. Nevertheless, they are smooth and mixable, and rather typify a certain style of California brandy. A bottled-in-bond Hartley brandy, which is a rather rough and fiery spirit, is also offered.

For years *Petri Grappa* was a familiar label on the California brandy scene. It was directed primarily at the Italian immigrants who enjoyed it in their homes and favorite bars of San Francisco's North Beach district. But as the older generation passed on, this became a diminishing market and several years ago United Vintners ceased producing America's only pomace brandy.

We remember several bottles in our own tasting experiences. The oldest Petri Grappa we tasted was made in the early 1940s under the Asti Colony label by Italian Swiss Colony. Its light-yellow color testified to a few years in wood, while the wild, tarlike fusel oils in the aroma were overwhelming. Bottles from the late 1960s were perfectly clear, for they saw no wood aging, and had a very fruity, grapy, almost sweet character in which the fusel alcohols seemed less prominent. Perhaps one day, as some of those who are now swelling the ranks of wine connoisseurs turn their attention to spirits, there will again be a market for this unique California product.

One out of every three bottles of California brandy sold in the United States comes from the Mount Tivy winery of THE CHRISTIAN BROTHERS, which is in Reedley, just a short drive from Fresno. The stock of aging brandy at The Christian Brothers is the largest in the Western Hemisphere, and the barrels, if laid end to end, would stretch from the winery to San Francisco.

Two continuous stills are used, each of which has a capacity of producing thirty-four hundred gallons of 169-proof spirit per hour. Two pot stills are also utilized to produce fuller-flavored brandies for blending purposes. Their capacity is four thousand gallons of wine apiece per fourteen-hour distilling run, larger than the six-hundred-gallon capacity of the traditional cognac pot still.

The Christian Brothers are proud of the fact that no brandy is brought from other producers, nor is any sold in bulk or under any different label. They distill all their brandy themselves, and each label can thus state, "Distilled, blended, and bottled exclusively by The Christian Brothers."

Brandy was first made at Mount Tivy in 1945, and The Christian Brothers were the leaders in the turn to a light, fruity, slightly sweet spirit that has now become established as the classic California brandy.

The regular *Christian Brothers* brandy is almost entirely a column distillate, although 7–10 per cent of pot-still brandy is added, and it is aged in oak for an average of four years. It possesses a sweet, nutty, sherry-like aroma mixed with grape fruitiness, and has a very smooth, slightly sweet finish. It is often the introduction to brandy for many Americans, and we remember a few camping trips on which a glass or two around the campfire did wonders to ward off the chill.

Although certainly pleasant enough, the regular *Christian Brothers* brandy is not what most brandy connoisseurs would consider a fine "sipping" spirit. The *Christian Brothers XO Rare Reserve* brandy may well be just that, however. This premium label was first released in 1972, and consists of a blend of 50 per cent pot-still brandy averaging eight years of age and 50 per cent five-to-eight-year-old continuous-still brandy. The result is a fairly full, well-balanced, complex brandy, which compares quite favorably with a number of more expensive *3-star* cognacs. Oak character is moderate, and a touch of sweetness (about 1 per cent) is added to ensure a smooth finish. Certainly it has been a welcome addition to the ranks of California brandy.

SCHENLEY DISTILLERS, producers of such well-known whiskies as I. W. Harper and Ancient Age as well as Schenley vodka and gin, are also important in the California brandy industry. For many years Schenley owned the Roma and Cresta Blanca labels, but then, in 1971, these, along with the Roma winery and distillery in Fresno, were sold to Guild. From their base in Fresno, Schenley remain very much involved in the marketing of California brandy.

Their most important brand is *Coronet VSQ*, which is one of the largest-selling brandies in the state of Wisconsin and also holds an important share of the market in other areas. Coronet, one of the lightest California brandies, is quite dry and clean in flavor with slight grapiness and essentially no wood in the aroma. Its lightness and lack of fusel alcohols make it a good spirit for mixing, although it lacks the complexity of a good sipping brandy.

Schenley also markets a number of other brandy labels, most of which are also quite light and somewhat sweeter than the *Coronet*. These brands include *J. Bavet, Certified, Jean Robert, Louis California, Park and Tilford,* and *Monastery*.

One of the fastest-growing names in California brandy is that marketed by the well-known PAUL MASSON winery of Saratoga. Masson is owned by the Seagram corporation, and their brandy is primarily supplied by another Seagram subsidiary, the Vie-Del Company of Fresno. Vie-Del produces beverage brandy for many people, but that destined for Paul Masson is to the specifications of Masson's own tasters and blenders, and final rectification and bottling are done at Saratoga.

The base brandy is mostly column-still, with small amounts of pot-still added, and is aged an average of four years in recoopered or previously used American oak. The regular *Paul Masson* is one of the most successful of California's medium-priced brandies. It is a pleasant and clean spirit with considerably more grapy flavor than many other brands, and a good balance of slight sweetness and wood flavors.

A special bottling is also available in a fancy apothecary jar; every few years, as a particular blend is sold out, a new-style jar is released. The *Masson Apothecary* is fuller and richer than the regular bottling, and enhanced by the addition of more pot distillate. The vanilla-oak aroma is pleasant, and the fruity flavor of the brandy is balanced by slight sweetness. Variations in the apothecary blend are occasionally noticeable, but the average quality remains fairly high.

The CALIFORNIA GROWERS WINERY is in the small town of Cutler, in the southern San Joaquin Valley. Their own label is *Growers Old Reserve,* but over the years they have been important as suppliers of base brandy to such well-known companies as *Gallo, Beringer Winery,* Consolidated Distilled Products (bottlers of *Bonadeaux, Henri C 10 Star, Pier 9,* and others), E. Martinoni (bottlers of *Mission Fathers*), and James Beam (bottlers of *Philip Boilieux, Chateaux, Holiday, St. Charles,* and others).

Robert Setrakian is the president of California Growers, and one of California's newest brandies bears his name. It is a straight brandy aged about six years and packaged in an attractive, narrow-necked, brown flask-shaped bottle. It is a medium-bodied brandy with excellent fruitiness and a bouquet that combines some wood with a delightful violet floweriness, which is especially noticeable when the brandy is cut with water for tasting purposes. *Setrakian* brandy is moderately priced and is a good example of a very fine column distillate.

Delano is the home of the large CALIFORNIA WINE ASSOCIATION, whose brands include some of the country's best-selling California brandies. The California Wine Association was founded in 1894 as a co-operative of some sixty-four wineries seeking to survive a period of wine depression. One of its early leaders was Almond R. Morrow, whose name now graces one of the company's most famous labels. The co-operative managed to survive Prohibition, but by the early 1950s numbered only eleven wineries among its members. In 1971 the family of Antonio Perelli-Minetti, owners of one of these wineries, purchased controlling interest, changed the co-operative into a corporation, and consolidated the headquarters in their Delano facility.

A number of different brands are offered by the California Wine Association, in many cases reflecting small specialty markets held by one of the early members of the co-operative. All the brandy is distilled in a continuous still, and the grapes are exclusively from California vineyards. Indeed, the CWA has been a leader in urging the adoption of a California appellation for brandy.

The two most important brands are *Aristocrat* and *A. R. Morrow,* and each is available in two styles. All are clean and light and are excellent examples of typical California brandies. The *Aristocrat* brand includes one blend with a small neck label containing six stars, and another with the signature A. R. Morrow on the neck band. The former seems a bit older and more complex, with some wood in the aroma, slight sweetness, and good grapy character in the flavors. The latter has similar flavors, if perhaps a bit less wood, and tastes slightly sweeter with a more intense peachlike quality to the aroma. The *A. R. Morrow Bottled-in-Bond* is usually aged about six years, contains a moderate amount of wood character that does not overpower the relatively light body, and is surprisingly smooth for its high alcohol content. The regular *A. R. Morrow* is similar to but younger than the *Aristocrat,* with grapy, slightly sweet flavors and less wood.

Other labels under which California Wine Association brandies are sold include *Eleven Cellars, F. I. Reserve, Guasti, L. & J., Old Constitution, Sun Maid, Wahtoke,* and *Victor Hugo.* In addition, many companies have chosen brandies from CWA for bottling under their own labels. Among these are *S. S. Pierce, Macy's Red Star,* and *A. & P.'s Coast to Coast* brandy.

There are four additional distillers who belong to the California Brandy Advisory Board: BEAR MOUNTAIN WINERY, SIERRA WINE CORPORATION, and GEORGE ZANINOVICH in the southern part of the San

Joaquin Valley, and WOODBRIDGE VINEYARDS ASSOCIATION of Lodi. To date these four have specialized in the production of bulk beverage brandy for sale to other companies rather than in the marketing of brandy under their own label.

Several California wineries offer brandies to round out their line of table, dessert, and sparkling wines. Some of these are sold primarily through the winery's tasting room or in very limited areas. Others are sold throughout the nation.

KORBEL is a very popular brand, light and clean in aroma, with pleasant flavors and a touch of sweetness. Formerly made by East-Side, it is now being being produced by California Growers to Korbel's specifications, and will be bottled at the Korbel winery in northern Sonoma County. The brandy from ALMADÉN, which is important in terms of sales and advertising, has a floral-vanilla bouquet, a touch of sweetness, and rather pleasant flavors with fairly nice grape character. BEAULIEU VINEYARD has also released a pleasant brandy that is slightly sweeter than the Almadén and has a flowery aroma and light, clean finish. Currently aging in a United Vintners warehouse (both Beaulieu and United Vintners are owned by Heublein) is a batch of brandy distilled from Colombard and Ugni Blanc grapes and placed in Limousin oak, in the cognac style—perhaps Beaulieu has interesting ideas for the future.

CRESTA BLANCA WINERY, now part of the Guild organization, has recently released California's first vintaged brandy, a 1966, selected from Guild's extensive aging stock. It is a well-balanced brandy entirely from Flame Tokay grapes, with considerable wood character in the aroma, nice flavors, and just a hint of sweetness.

Most large distilled spirits and cordials firms also include brandy in their line of products. Notable among these well-distributed products are *Arrow 5 Star, Leroux Deluxe,* and *Leroux 5 Star* (a blend of domestic and imported brandies), *Old Mr. Boston 5 Star,* and *Hiram Walker*. These are all lightly to moderately sweetened brandies with light body and little wood flavor—the type that lends itself best to mixing with soda or in cocktails. And of course the list of brandy labels goes on—far too long for the scope of any book—with many of those still unmentioned being private labels for stores or special blends for a limited market.

California brandy is available in many types and styles—from well-aged straight brandies to young, sweetend, blended products. The best are relatively light, fruity, yet flavorful spirits with some aged character that can be very nice for after-dinner sipping. The younger, less expensive California brandies mix well in apéritifs and cocktails in which their grapy character can be appreciated, and like other well-made brandies of the world, they add flair to many recipes. Even the finest California column-distillate brandies do not have the tremendous complexity of a well-aged pot-still cognac. But in fairness one should not compare the two, for each is a different product with its own style and uses. California brandy certainly represents an excellent value in the world of distilled spirits, and undoubtedly this is one of the reasons its popularity continues to grow. Its average quality is higher than Spanish and Italian products, and it compares well with many younger cognacs and armagnacs. As brandy producers look to the future with new ideas now only in their formative stages—distillates from high-acid grapes, experiments with new types of oak, greater emphasis on aging, and perhaps increased use of pot stills—the appeal and variety of California brandy are bound to expand. But the staple product will undoubtedly remain the same light, clean, grapy brandy that has already found a home in the American market.

OTHER BRANDIES OF THE WORLD

OTHER BRANDIES OF THE WORLD

Germany

Germany is in a unique position in the world of brandy. The German people certainly enjoy the spirit (28 per cent of the domestic liquor market is brandy), and a multitude of excellent vineyards are within the boundaries of the country, yet economic realities make domestic wines too expensive for distillation. Enterprising German distillers have thus turned to the warmer climates of Mediterranean countries for their source of base wine, where abundant supplies of less expensive wines may be found. Most of these are then imported into Germany in railway tank cars after having been fortified with grape spirits.

German law requires the aging of ordinary brandy for a minimum of only six months in containers of less than a thousand liters. Older brandies, often labeled *uralt,* must be aged a minimum of one year. As in other brandy-producing countries, caramel may be used to adjust color; sugar is permitted up to 2 per cent by volume; and an infusion of oak chips or essence may be added to increase wood flavors. Additional flavoring may come from up to 1 per cent by volume of fortified dessert wine and from extracts of plums, nuts, or almond shells. German brandies tend to be light in aroma and body, with considerably less of fusel alcohols than cognac or armagnac. They are usually relatively clean in style, often with slight sweetness but not highly flavored, and can be pleasant, easy-sipping spirits somewhat similar to the brandies of California.

Germany's largest distiller is ECKES, which was founded in 1857 and is today being run by members of the founding family's third generation. Until 1952 the company was a medium-sized brandy and liqueur producer, but in that year they introduced *Chantré,* a light blend which went on to become Germany's best-selling brandy. Another brandy, *Mariacron,* was introduced in 1961; it has surpassed *Chantré* in sales, and Eckes now produces the two most popular brandies in Germany.

Today, Eckes' plants at Nieder Olm and Oppenheim in the Rhineland distill more than sixty thousand gallons of wine a day, working around the clock. Dry white wines fortified with brandy before shipment are brought to the Eckes distilleries from France, Spain, Cyprus, and Italy and then distilled in large column stills with the brandy taken off at about 85% alcohol. The brandy is aged for six months to a year in 350-liter Limousin-oak casks and then is placed in large vats, also made of Limousin, for several months of final blending.

Chantré is a rather light brandy with a pleasant fruity aroma, simple flavors, and slight sweetness. Very much like California brandies in style, it is not at all unpleasant. Production and aging of the newer and now more popular *Mariacron* are similar to *Chantré*, with the primary differences being in the amount of sweetness and kind of flavoring materials used in the blend. The *Mariacron* is a bit fuller in style, sweeter, and with emphasis on a heavier, vanilla character.

Eckes has also introduced a white brandy, perhaps better called a grape *eau-de-vie,* which is sold in Germany under the label *Zinn 40.* It is distilled in a pot still topped by a rectifying column, and its water-whiteness is preserved by aging for a short time only in glass-lined tanks. Apart from a very slight fruity-mint character, it is not dissimilar to a rather ordinary vodka: the aroma and flavor are those of neutral alcohol, and there is little if any character of grapes or wine. The same product has been introduced in Britain under the *Mariacron* label.

Germany's most expensive brandy, and perhaps her best, is produced by ASBACH. The company operates two distilleries, one in Rudesheim in the Rheingau and the other in southwestern Germany at Baden-Baden. Ninety per cent of the wine is imported from France, from both Cognac and Armagnac, and the remainder comes from Italy. The company owns stills in all three areas to produce brandy to fortify the wines up to 23% prior to shipment to Germany. After arrival, the fortified wines undergo double distillation in 3000-liter pot stills, resulting in a final product of about 75% alcohol. A precondenser is used with some of the stills to reduce congeners, and an attempt is made to keep slightly more of the heads fraction than would be usual in Cognac, but considerably less of the tails than would find their way into the fuller, French product. The brandy is aged for about two years in 300-liter Limousin-oak casks, and then a further six months in large vats made of German oak. The final blend takes place in a huge, million-liter tank, known as the "swimming pool," with brandy drawn from the bottom to meet bottling requirements and refilled from the top to assure consistency of the blend. The only additive used by Asbach is caramel, to maintain the color.

The major brand is *Asbach-Uralt,* which accounts for some 95 per cent of the production, about 10 per cent of which is exported to the United Kingdom, Holland, and the United States. Small amounts of a slightly different blend are sold only in Germany as *Asbach Privat-Brand. Asbach-Uralt* is similar to a young cognac in style, though it is lighter-bodied and less woody in character. The flavors are not complex, but they are quite smooth and well balanced, making *Asbach* a very pleasant, drinkable brandy that could compete favorably with many 3-star cognacs.

Other smaller producers of German brandy include MELCHER BROTHERS (bottlers of *Dujardin*) and KAMMER, the latter being also known for their fruit *eau-de-vie.* Kammer uses wine from France, Italy, and Greece that has been fortified before leaving for Germany, and does all of its distillation in large column stills. Limousin-oak casks are used for aging, and judging from the taste of its brandy, some *boisé* may also be used to increase the wood character. The brandy is otherwise light and clean, with good flavors.

Italy

Brandy is distilled throughout Italy from a multitude of different grape varieties, while blending and bottling are often done at a central location by the more important producers. The largest of these is the DISTILLERIE STOCK, which was founded in 1884 in the city of Trieste (then part of the Austro-Hungarian Empire) by Lionello Stock. Brandy was Stock's first product, and it soon achieved considerable success throughout eastern Europe, probably due in no small part to the permission received from the authorities to label the product "medicinal." After World War I and the end of the Austro-Hungarian Empire, new plants were opened in Italy, Poland, Czechoslovakia, Yugoslavia, Hungary, and Austria, and the company continued to flourish. World War II intervened, but in the past thirty years Stock has managed to regroup and to re-establish its influence in the market. Today, from its headquarters in Trieste, brandy and liqueurs are shipped to over one hundred different countries, and new plants have been established in the United States, Australia, South Africa, and South America.

Stock is the largest-selling brandy in its native country, as indeed it is in many foreign markets. The company has eight distilling and aging plants throughout Italy, though wine for distillation comes primarily from the North. Both column and pot stills are used, and the latter are run in such a way that a single distillation produces a brandy of about 67% alcohol. Individual lots of brandy from different regions are aged separately in large, 20–40,000-liter Yugoslavian oak vats and also in small oak barrels. Final blending and bottling take place at a very modern facility in Portogruaro, near Trieste, and Stock's supply of aging brandy is equivalent to more than 70 million bottles.

By far the leading label is *Stock 84,* which is aged for a minimum of four years. This is a fairly pleasant brandy of light to moderate body and good grapy flavors with a touch of sweetness and slight wood tannin. Perhaps a bit fuller than the average California brandy, it is a good, consistent blend.

RoyalStock, sold only in Italy, is a sweeter brandy, deeper in color but less balanced than *Stock 84.* Stock *Original* brandy is a less important, younger blend, aged for one to three years, and based on Lionello Stock's medicinal brandy. The oldest and finest brandies are bottled as a reserve labeled *Bollino Oro,* which is intended primarily for the export market.

Another leading producer of Italian brandy is BUTON, located in Bologna, which also produces liqueurs and the popular Rosso Antico apéritif. Brandy is also made in Ozzano, Trieste, and Casapulla from a number of grape varieties, with an emphasis on Trebbiano (the Ugni Blanc or Saint-Émilion of France). Both column and pot stills are used, and, as at Stock, large and small oak containers are employed in aging. Buton bottles its brandy under the *Vecchia Romagna* label in three qualities: A *White Label* (*Etichetta Blanca*) is aged a minimum of two years, the most popular *Black Label* (*Etichetta Nera*) a minimum of three years, and the *Qualità Rara,* which is often sold in decanters, a minimum of fifteen years. There seems to be some difference between the Black Label sold in Italy and that available in the United States. The former is drier and somewhat harsh, with an odd, sage-like aroma, while the American version has a fruity cocoa-vanilla aroma, light-medium body, slight vanilla sweetness, and a touch of wood character. Perhaps the samples we tried were atypical, although it is certainly possible that the additives selected for a particular market may change the character of similar base brandies. In any event, the American blend is a not unpleasant brandy but one that lacks the complex fruit flavors and character of many French and California brandies.

DISTILLERIE RIUNITE, producer of Galliano, markets a brandy under the *Vittoria* label. This is produced from grapes grown primarily in the south of Italy and is aged for four years in both large and small oak. The result is a slightly sweet brandy with a vanilla-woody finish.

Scores of other Italian brandies are produced, but few are ever seen on the export market; most follow the general pattern of Stock and Vecchia Romagna—fairly light and slightly sweetened and flavored, falling between the heavier Spanish and somewhat grapier German brandies in style.

Spain

Brandy distillation in Spain used to be centered in the sherry-producing region, in southeastern Spain, using the local wine of Jerez. Today brandy is produced throughout Spain, although the well-known sherry houses remain the most important marketers of Spanish brandies. Such brands as Pedro Domecq, Duff Gordon, González Byass, Terry, and Sandeman are well distributed and exported. The brandies of these and other sherry producers tend to be quite sweet, with heavy doses of woodiness and rather pronounced sherry-like aromas and flavors, the latter often arising from the use of sherry as a flavor additive or from aging the brandy in barrels previously used for sherry. While Spanish brandies do have a large following among certain groups, the excessive use of flavoring and sweetening is unlikely to appeal to those who appreciate a cleaner, more classic style of brandy.

PEDRO DOMECQ is the most important exporter, and several different grades of brandy are offered. The least expensive is *Three Vines,* Domecq's equivalent of *3-star. Fundador* is probably the most popular quality and is slightly more expensive, although we found its heavy woodiness and rough character unpleasant. Still-higher grades include *Carlos III,* which is woodier and less sweet than the *Fundador,* though still not particularly complex, and *Carlos I,* highest-priced in the line.

TERRY offers a *Centenario,* which is quite dark in color, sweet, and has heavy vanilla flavors. More intriguing and complex is *Terry I,* which avoids some of the excessive woodiness and harshness that seems common, though it remains fairly heavy in style. The SANDEMAN *Capa*

Negra is less sweet than many other Spanish brandies and has relatively light, but straightforward, grape-brandy flavors.

Different in style and deserving to be better known on the export market are the brandies produced by the TORRES family at Vilafranca del Panadés, near Barcelona. These brandies are produced in pot stills, in contrast to those from other regions in Spain, where column stills are commonly used. Four grades of brandy are offered by Torres: *Imperial, Grande Rouge, Frontenac,* and *Hors d'Âge* (Grande Fine). The two youngest are bought from smaller producers in the region (who distill in pot stills) and then blended and aged in a three-tier solera system in barrels of American oak. The two more expensive qualities (*Frontenac* and *Hors d'Âge*) are distilled at the Torres winery in two 25-hectoliter pot stills, made in Cognac, from white press wine of Parellada, Macabei, and Xarello grapes. They are aged in new Limousin-oak barrels for six months, and then transferred to older barrels. As one can surmise from the label names, Torres considers its brandies to be in the French rather than the typical Spanish style, and tasting confirms this. The *Imperial,* with an average solera age of perhaps five years, is pleasant if fairly simple, with grapiness in the aroma and slight sweetness in the aftertaste. The dry *Grande Rouge* is about twice as old and has a clean, aged character and definite oakiness in aroma and flavor. The *Hors d'Âge,* which is sometimes labeled *Grande Fine,* has a nice nutty aroma, light-medium body, and fairly round, oaky flavors that evidence good complexity. It is perhaps closer in character to a good armagnac than to a cognac.

Portugal

Spain's neighbor on the Iberian Peninsula has been producing brandy at least as long as she has been making her celebrated dessert wines. Brandy production for the fortification of port is today controlled by the government, although a number of private companies produce brandy for general consumption. Brandy in Portuguese is *aquardiente,* and pomace brandy (*aquardiente bagaceira*) is also made. Portuguese brandies are similar to most Spanish brandies in their woody style, although most seem to be less sweetened. During World War II, when French brandies were unavailable, important quantities of brandy from Portugal were shipped to the United States and Britain, but after the war exports diminished considerably. Portuguese brandies are still sold in Canada, including much that is imported in cask and then bottled by the liquor-control boards of several Canadian provinces.

France

Brandy is made almost everywhere in France where wine is produced, although none of it rises to the heights of cognac or armagnac. There are eleven French regional brandies, or *eaux-de-vie de vin,* that are subject to the *appellation réglementée* laws, and others are sometimes exported and labeled simply "French brandy." While the latter are occasionally palatable, most are rather rough and uninteresting spirits that make liberal use of such labeling terms as "V.S.O.P." and "Napoléon." This is an obvious attempt to mislead some foreign consumer into thinking he is buying a bottle of celebrated brandy at a bargain price.

"Fine" is often used by the French to mean "brandy" and one of the regional brandies that has attained some reputation is *Fine de la Marne.* This is produced in the Champagne district and is named for the most important province of the region rather than being called "Fine de Champagne," which would cause confusion with the "champagne" *crus* of Cognac. Disgorged champagne (with yeast sediment from the champagne's secondary fermentation in the bottle) is the most common distilling material, for all the available wine is generally used in the production of champagne itself. JEAN GOYARD offers both a regular bottling labeled *Vieille Fine de la Marne* and an older *réserve.* Both are distilled by the same process as *marc de Champagne,* using the steam-extraction and rectification system of three vases or pots known as *distillation en calandre.* The younger *fine* is very fruity, light, and dry, with little wood flavor, and in many ways it is more appealing than an overly sweetened 3-star cognac. The older *réserve* has slightly more oak tannin, but at the same time is rougher; the brandy seems almost too delicate to carry the additional wood age.

Fine de Bourgogne is a wine brandy produced in Burgundy, although it is available only in small quantities. In character it resembles a light armagnac, with grapy flavors and light tannin.

Small amounts of *eau-de-vie de lie* (from the lees, a cloudy sediment left over after clear wine is racked off after fermentation or aging) are also produced in France, although the brandy is of mediocre quality.

Switzerland

Switzerland is not noted for its brandy, except of course for the clear fruit *eaux-de-vie* such as kirsch or poire Williams. Both *eau-de-vie de vin* and *eau-de-vie de lie* are distilled, and they are most often found at inexpensive prices in supermarkets or wine stores.

Eastern Mediterranean

The ancient Greeks, perhaps guided by Bacchus himself, were the first on the European continent to capture the nectar of the grape. A thousand years before the birth of Christ they spread knowledge of grape growing and wine making to what are now Italy, France, and Spain. Greek writings also contained abundant references to the art of distillation, although, curiously, it was left to other civilizations to combine the two sciences for the production of brandy. Today, vines cover more than half a million acres (220,000 hectares) of Greece, in areas spread throughout the mainland, the Peloponnese, and the islands, and brandy production is relatively important.

The largest-selling Greek brandy-based beverage is METAXA, which is exported to over one hundred countries around the world. The base spirit of Metaxa is grape brandy, although sufficient sweetening and flavoring elements are added so that it is marketed in the United States as a "Greek specialty liqueur," and we describe it elsewhere in this book. Three grades of Metaxa are produced: *5-star, 7-star,* and *Grande Fine,* as each contains progressively older blends of brandy. But even in the Grande Fine we found that the flavorings dominated any aged brandy character, so that the differences in quality among the three types may not be that noticeable.

Another leading Greek producer is CAMBAS, whose brandies are also widely exported. In addition to brandy, Cambas is a major producer of wines, a brandy-based specialty liqueur patterned after Metaxa called *Delicious,* a cordial named *Mastika,* and the anise-flavored Greek apéritif ouzo.

Neighboring Turkey has an extensive area of vines under cultivation, but because most of her population is Moslem, the consumption of wine and spirits is quite low. A brandy is made whose name, when translated into Latin script, curiously resembles the French word *cognac,* although the spirit itself bears considerably less resemblance to its namesake. Some wine is also distilled to be the base spirit of the anise-flavored raki. In nearby Lebanon, wine is also distilled for the same purpose, only here the anise-flavored spirit is called arack, a generic name which refers to different local spirits throughout the world.

Cyprus is the home of some fairly pleasant brandies, though, surprisingly, this stems not from her native Greek or Turkish populace, but, rather, from the influence of the spirit-loving British during the days of their colonial rule of the island.

Israel's wine industry is quite modern, and included in her produce is a well-made column-still brandy under the CARMEL label. This is a brandy with a touch of sweetness, cocoa-vanilla character in the aroma, and flavors that are light and clean, resembling many California brandies.

United States

Grapes are widely planted in certain areas of the eastern, midwestern, and southern Atlantic states of the United States for both table and wine use. We are sure that over the years people have tried to make brandy from these *Vitis labrusca* and *Vitis rotundifolia* vines, but we are unaware of any commercial brandy currently being produced from these eastern grapes.

By law, brandy is a term reserved for distilled spirits of not less than 80 American proof made only from fermented grapes. If any other material is used in distillation, a qualifying statement must appear on the label. In certain markets, most notably Wisconsin, a spirit has recently appeared that is prominently labeled as brandy but which, according to the small print on the label, is only about 30 per cent grape brandy and the remainder a distillate of citrus-fruit residue. To date, sales of such products have been minimal and it is unlikely they will ever make serious inroads on the sales of pure grape brandy.

Most major American liqueur manufacturers offer an assortment of fruit flavored brandies. As mentioned in the chapter on fruit liqueurs, these are not true fruit distillates but are sweetened spirits produced either by the maceration of fruit in grape brandy or by the addition of concentrated fruit flavors to brandy.

Mexico

Vines have been planted in Mexico since the sixteenth century, and from there were later transplanted to much of South America and California. The original vines were probably the Criolla, or as it is known in California, the Mission variety. Considerable acreage of this varietal remains, although recently there has been increased interest in the production of wine in Mexico and higher-quality grapes have been planted.

The climate in the Mexican vineyard areas is quite warm and, although improvements have been made, the quality of table wine does not approach that of California or Europe. More than half the wine produced in the country is distilled, and today there are some fifty wineries engaged in the production of brandy, although very few are imported into English-speaking countries. Most of the Mexican brandies we have sampled have been slightly sweetened, and some have had rather pronounced citrus or other flavorings added to them.

South America

Although 10 per cent of the world's supply of wine is produced in South America, this continent is responsible for none of the world's fine brandies. Most of the wine-growing countries on the continent produce brandy of one form or another, but virtually all is drunk locally. The one product that has achieved any international reputation is *pisco,* a pomace brandy first produced hundreds of years ago and introduced into the United States in the nineteenth century, when it was brought to California and sold to hordes of thirsty gold miners. In Peru, where it is perhaps most celebrated, pisco is distilled primarily from Muscat grapes grown in the Ica Valley. It may also be found in northern Chile, Bolivia, and Argentina. Pisco was traditionally stored in earthenware jugs and drunk when very young. Today, like many other pomace brandies, it is bottled without having seen wood and is therefore water-white in color. It has an intensely grapy, oily aroma, and when consumed straight, cuts a raw path across the palate in a way appreciated by few Americans. When mixed in a tangy cocktail called a "pisco sour," its wild flavors are reduced and are more likely to appeal to the non-aficionado of pisco.

The leading brand exported to the United States and Europe is INCA PISCO, which comes packaged in a series of ceramic figurines. However, we would not recommend buying a bottle unless you are attracted by the container, for the brandy inside is rather dismal stuff. A brand with cleaner and more attractive grapy flavors is SOLDEICA PISCO, produced by the Viña Vista Alegre. Unfortunately, all pisco sells at an elevated price, thanks to taxes and importers' markups, and we doubt that its quality can justify this. But should you have the fortune to make a trip to South America, don't hesitate to try pisco in its homeland, where it can be sampled for a fraction of the tariff demanded on the American market.

Australia

Australia's major brandy-producing areas include the irrigated vineyards of the Riverina district of New South Wales and the Upper Murray River and Barossa Valley districts of South Australia. The most common brandy-grape varieties include Doradillo, Sultana, Ugni Blanc (called White Hermitage), Grenache, and Malaga, which are distilled in both pot and continuous stills. The legal minimum for aging in cask is two years; brandy labeled "Old" must have been aged for at least five years in wood, while one labeled "Very Old" must not be less than ten years of age. The principal export market is the Commonwealth countries, particularly Canada and the United Kingdom, although some producers have begun limited shipments to the United States.

Australia's leading brand is CHATEAU TANUNDA, produced by B. Seppelt & Sons at Tanunda in the Barossa Valley. It is a blend of column and pot distillates which are both aged for slightly more than two years. In the same valley is the Barossa Co-operative Winery, which makes wines as well as brandy under the Kaiser Stuhl label. KAISER STUHL brandy is distilled in a pot still and aged or two years in new Limousin-oak casks before being transferred to older barrels for further aging. At the present time only small quantities are being produced for the Australian market.

The family-owned Angove's Pty. Ltd., in the Upper Murray River Valley, was founded in the late-nineteenth century by a physician from Cornwall. Three qualities of pot-still brandy are offered under the ST. AGNES label: the *3-Star* is primarily two-to-three-year-old brandy blended with small amounts of aged stock; the *Old Liqueur* is seven to ten years old; while the *Very Old* is aged more than fourteen years.

Several other companies also do some exporting, including the Emu Wine Company, producers of MARIE CLAIRE brandy, and the important Australian distilling concern, HAMILTON'S. Hamilton's exports a *3-Star* brandy that is a blend of both column and pot stills, and also produces a blend called *Hospital Brandy* for the domestic market.

South Africa

The first vines were planted in South Africa in 1655 by Jan van Riebeeck, commander of the first Dutch settlement at the Cape of Good Hope. Brandy production dates back almost as far, to the year 1672, and South Africans continue to be major consumers of brandy and other spirits. In some harvests, as much as half the total grape crush is distilled into brandy or high-proof neutral alcohol.

The southern and western areas of Cape Province are the major viticultural regions of the country. The Coastal Belt includes the districts of Stellenbosch and Paarl, and here the temperate influence of the nearby Atlantic favors the production of table wines and pale dry sherries. Across the mountains are Little Karoo and the Breede River Valley, warmer areas with less rainfall and deep, rich alluvial soils that yield large quantities of grapes per acre. This country is similar to the Central Valley of California, and it is here and in the outlying Olifants and Orange River valleys that brandy production is most common.

One of the first vines to be introduced into the country was a variety known as the Green Grape. Another early arrival was the Palomino, most famous today for its role in the great sherry vineyards of Spain, but for some reason known as the French grape in South Africa. These two, along with a Muscat locally called Hanepoot (Muscat of Alexandria), for years provided the bulk of all grapes destined for distillation. The former two varieties are still used, but the Muscat is considerably less popular today because of the strong aroma and flavor it imparts to its distilled spirit. The Cognac varieties of Saint-Émilion,

Colombard, and Folle Blanche are now being cultivated for brandy production, and in the prolific irrigated vineyards of the Little Karoo, wine from the black variety known as Hermitage (in France called Cinsault) is also distilled.

Both pot and column stills may be found in South Africa, and all brandy production is supervised by a government brandy board appointed by the Minister of Agriculture. All wines destined for pot distillation must first be approved by this board, and the spirits coming off a column still must also receive approval before they can be blended into commercial brandy.

Pot stills are operated in a manner similar to that practiced in the Charente, with two distillations producing a product that by law must not exceed 75% alcohol by volume. This is then aged in small oak barrels for a legal minimum of three years, at which time the producer becomes eligible for a rebate in excise duty. Because of this practice, such spirits are popularly known as "rebate brandy." To encourage additional aging, further tax credits are given for brandy aged four or five years.

Column distillates may not be taken off below 60% alcohol, but in practice "pure wine spirits" are usually removed at a strength of 96%. There is apparently no legal minimum for aging of this spirit, but it must be blended with a minimum of 25 per cent of three-year-old pot distillate before it can be offered as commercial brandy. As is common throughout the brandy-producing world, South Africa permits the addition of small amounts of sugar and flavoring elements prior to bottling, as well as the adjustment of color with caramel.

Most South African brandy is consumed domestically, although some is exported to the Commonwealth countries and a few other markets. The largest producer and exporter is the K.W.V., the CO-OPERATIVE WINEGROWERS ASSOCIATION OF SOUTH AFRICA LTD. For the South African market they offer a premium *V.S.O.P.* label which is pure pot-still brandy that has been aged a minimum of ten years in oak casks. In Canada, K.W.V.'s products constitute about one quarter of all brandy imports. The leading label is *Paarl Five Star,* which is a blend of equal amounts of pot-still brandy aged in Limousin oak for five years and two-to-three-year-old continuous-still wine spirits. The final blend is rounded out with the addition of a slight amount of sugarcane syrup and dessert wine. Several provincial liquor-control boards also import South African brandy in bulk for bottling in Canada.

Other South African companies which export brandy include: Bertrams Wines Ltd., Castle Wine & Brandy Co., and J. Sedgwick & Co., of Capetown; Gilbey-Santhagens Ltd. and Stellenbosch Farmers Winery, of Stellenbosch; and J. D. Bosman & Co. and Henry Taylor & Ries Ltd., of Johannesburg.

China

Although rice- and sorghum-based spirits are more widespread, grape wine and brandy are produced in China, primarily in the coastal province of Shantung. Brandy from the state-controlled distillery in Tsingtao is exported (since 1972) to the United States under the "Sunflower" label; fairly light-bodied and slightly sweet, with both wood and vanilla undertones, it resembles a slightly rough, young California brandy in style.

OF SKINS, STEMS, AND SEEDS

OF SKINS, STEMS, AND SEEDS

Brandy produced by distilling the grape skins, pulp, and seeds that remain after the wine has been pressed out is called pomace brandy. There is always a little alcohol that can be reclaimed this way, and through distillation this can be concentrated into a powerful spirit. Pomace brandies are made in many countries, but they are best known in Italy and France, where they are known respectively as *grappa* and *marc*.

A good pomace brandy is characterized by an intense grapy-pulpiness that can be refreshing after a rich meal or provide a powerful boost on a cold afternoon. Poor pomace brandies, however, can probably be drunk only when tossed into strong black coffee, if even then, and they rank among the least pleasant of alcoholic beverages. In between the extremes lie a host of full-bodied spirits with a rather coarse, oily, at times even varnish-like quality in flavor and aroma but which retain a certain distinctiveness. They never capture the elegance or complexity of a cognac or other fine wine brandy, because the strong, bitter character of the pomace is always present in the spirit. But while many people will never like even the best of pomace brandies, finding their typical high fusel-oil content objectionable, those who do take the time to acquire a taste for them may find an intriguing medley of strong flavors as well as some understanding of why millions of people consider *grappa, marc,* or *pisco* their national spirit.

Grappa

Italians are undoubtedly the largest consumers of pomace brandy. The homeland of the often raw and fiery *grappa* is in the Veneto region of northeastern Italy, especially around the small town of Bessano del Grappa, but it can be produced anywhere in Italy. It may also be labeled *Acquavite di Vinaccia* or *Acquavite di Graspe.* For centuries *grappa* was distilled in the hills as a clandestine spirit, much like American moonshine, and it is fair to assume that quality took second place to alcohol content. In the nineteenth century its production was legalized, and it gradually became accepted as a legitimate spirit. Today there are over thirty independent distillers, in addition to such large companies as Stock and Buton, active in the commercial production of *grappa*.

Both red and white grapes are used to provide distilling material for the large column stills in which *grappa* is made. The distillate is taken off at 75–80% alcohol and most often bottled directly, without aging, at strengths that vary from the standard 40° G.L. to as high as 58°. Some *grappa* is aged in large casks of Yugoslavian oak, though usually for not more than two years so as not to obscure the fresh pungency and character of the brandy. These older bottlings are labeled *vecchia* (old) or *stravecchia* (extra-old) and often are tinged with yellow in contrast to the waterlike clarity of a young *grappa*.

Because it is not usually aged in wood, *grappa* is among the most pungent and "oily" of the pomace brandies, and its appeal will certainly be limited. In recent years, however, there has been a change toward a somewhat lighter and cleaner spirit. This has been accomplished in part by the removal of the fusel-laden stems prior to distillation, as well as by more careful selection of the distilling material. The *grappas* of such large companies as Stock (GRAPPA JULIA), Distillerie Riunite (GRAPPA VITTORIA), and BUTON are a bit fruitier and fresher than the traditional style, although they certainly retain their distinctive fusel-alcohol character. Stronger, oilier spirits are still produced by the small distillers clustered around Bessano del Grappa.

Marc

Marc is produced throughout France, although Marc de Bourgogne (Burgundy) is one of the few to have attracted more than a purely local following. It used to be common practice for farmers throughout Burgundy to distill a little *marc* for their own use each year, but the French Government, as part of its battle against alcoholism, has ceased issuing new distilling permits, so that the home production of *marc* is slowly dying out. Many wine producers and shippers offer a *marc* they distill themselves or blend from purchases from smaller distillers. Two important names are MORIN and JULES BELIN; the former was probably the premier *marc* producer in the nineteenth century. Occasional bottlings of *marc* from celebrated individual vineyards may also be found, including Clos de Tart and the Domaine de la Romanée-Conti.

Charente-type pot stills are generally used for distillation in Burgundy, and both red and white grapes are employed. The trend today is to remove the stems in order to obtain a lighter spirit; such *marcs* are denoted as *égrappé*. As is common practice wherever pomace brandies are made, water is added prior to distillation to facilitate extraction of the alcohol and to prevent burning the fairly solid cake of skins and pulp. Preserving the freshness of the *marc* is also important in both France and Italy, for an improperly stored pomace may deteriorate and impart off flavors to the distillate. *Marc de Bourgogne* traditionally receives a few years of age in small oak barrels and acquires color, smoothness, and oak character that distinguish it from *grappa*. Like a wood-aged brandy, it can attain some complexity, as the oak tannins and flavors tend to mellow the strong fusel-oil character.

In Champagne, *marc* is still made in the traditional mobile stills called *alembics à vases*. This curious apparatus consists basically of three interconnected pots, each several hundred liters in size, and a small column mounted on a platform. Pomace (*marc*) is placed in each of the pots, and steam is introduced into the first one. The vapors pass successively through the three pots in perhaps thirty to forty minutes, picking up and concentrating alcohol and flavors on their way. Upon emerging from the third container the vapors contain about 20% alcohol; they then pass directly into a small rectifying column, where they are concentrated to 68–70%.

Marc de Champagne tends to be lighter and more perfumed than *marc de Bourgogne,* reflecting differences in climate, the resulting base wine, and distilling methods. The only commercial distillery in the region is that of JEAN GOYARD, in the small town of Ay-Champagne. *Marc* is received after the harvest and is distilled both at the distillery and by twelve mobile stills that make the rounds of the countryside up to one hundred kilometers away. The young brandy is cut to about 53° and then barreled in small oak from the nearby Champagne and Aube regions, as well as some from the Limousin Forest. *Marc* sold under the Goyard label is aged during the first year in attics or outside, where considerable evaporation occurs, and then is transferred to a cellar for several more years. Goyard also sells *marc* to champagne houses, some of whom do their own aging, for bottling under their own labels. Before bottling, the *marc* is cut to its final strength of 40–43°.

Alsace is the home of an interesting if fairly rare *marc* that must be produced entirely from the white Gewürztraminer grape, the one responsible for the spicy, perfumed Alsatian wine of that name. *Marc de Gewürztraminer d'Alsace* is always *égrappé* and must be twice distilled in a cognac-style pot still. It is aged in neutral containers so that it retains its clear color, like the Alsatian fruit *eaux-de-vie*. A few producers do use chestnut or other wood casks for a small amount of aging, but the resulting *marc* should remain virtually colorless. *Marc de Gewürztraminer* resembles other pomace brandies in its fairly high fusel-oil content, although it is lighter and fresher than most Italian *grappa*. A few of those we have tasted do capture some of the spice and character of the Gewürztraminer grape, and they are best served chilled.

Marc is also produced to some extent in Switzerland, although it is generally of fairly low quality and is quite inexpensive. In style it is close to a light *marc de Bourgogne* and usually receives some aging in wood. Little if any is exported.

Other pomace brandies

The Peruvian *pisco* has already been referred to in the chapter on Other Brandies of the World, for it is the best-known brandy from South America (at least in terms of exports). Almost colorless and quite strong, it resembles *grappa* in style.

The California firm of United Vintners used to produce a clear *grappa* under the PETRI label, but as demand for such an unusual product declined it was discontinued not too many years ago.

Wherever wine is made, some sort of pomace brandy is likely to be produced from the cake of seeds, stems, and pulp that remains after pressing. While a hundred kilograms of pomace may yield only a few liters of alcohol, the desire to capture as much alcohol as possible from the fermented grapes has encouraged the production of pomace brandies. The vast majority, however, are purely local products, perhaps part of a centuries-old tradition in the area but unlikely to make much of an impact in the larger world of spirits.

CALVADOS

CALVADOS

While no one has yet claimed that the Garden of Eden was in Normandy, it would certainly have been possible for Eve to choose her apple from the orchards that have covered the fertile soil of Normandy and Brittany for millennia. The Roman legions remarked on the number of apple trees during their conquest of the Gauls, and the production of both apples and cider was regulated as early as the ninth century, under the reign of Charlemagne.

It is certain that the Norman and Breton peasants began distilling their cider soon after the technique was introduced into Europe, during the Middle Ages, but the first written mention of an *eau-de-vie* of *"sydre"* is not to be found until 1553, in the journal of a Norman farmer. A pear *eau-de-vie* (*"poiré"*) was also produced in much smaller quantities and continues to be made today, almost entirely for home consumption. Both these spirits were first produced in pot stills made of glass, which were surrounded by stones and heated by a wood fire. As in Cognac, these were later replaced by copper stills, whose descendants are still utilized for the production of the finest fruit *eaux-de-vie*.

"Calvados" is actually a French corruption of the name of a ship of the Spanish Armada, *El Cavador,* which foundered on the Norman coast in 1588. During the reclassification of administrative boundaries that followed the French Revolution, Calvados became the designation for the *département* nearest the site of the sixteenth-century shipwreck, and by the nineteenth century the name Calvados had become synonymous with the cider *eau-de-vie* produced in both Normandy and Brittany.

Today three categories of "cider brandy" are recognized and regulated by the French Institut National des Appellations d'Origine. The only region granted the prestigious *appellation contrôlée,* which is reserved for those spirits (or wines) of particularly distinctive character, is the "Calvados du Pays d'Auge," a relatively small area in the heart of

Normandy bisected by the route from the casinos of Deauville and Trouville, through Pont-l'Évêque, Lisieux, and Livarot. Surrounding the Pays d'Auge are ten other regions of *appellation réglementée* Calvados, which, though they may be sold under their individual appellations, are generally blended and bottled simply as "Calvados." Finally, the large and more general appellation (also *réglementée*) of *"eau-de-vie de cidre"* of Normandie, Maine, and Bretagne embraces the majority of the traditional cider-producing region of western France.

While the *eau-de-vie de cidre* and many "Calvados" are young, rough, and better drunk in coffee or as a quick restorative after a cross-Channel swim, that of the Pays d'Auge may, at its best, attain a subtlety and a complexity that rival many of the more celebrated brandies. Indeed, it is with grape brandies that Calvados du Pays d'Auge should be compared, as the manner of its production is much closer to that of cognac than to the clear fruit *eaux-de-vie* of Alsace or Switzerland. Calvados du Pays d'Auge must be distilled in pot stills of the cognac type from Pays d'Auge cider that has fermented naturally for at least one month. Like cognac, it is distilled twice, finishing at approximately 70° G.L., before being aged in oak casks for a minimum period of one year. It is felt that even the result of the first distillation, the *"petits eaux,"* should be aged for some time in oak before it is redistilled, although this practice is in general restricted to the smaller producers. Most aging is done in large casks holding from a thousand to ten thousand liters, and the optimum maximum age for an old calvados is perhaps twenty-five to thirty years, though aging up to seventy years is practiced. Much of the oak now used is in fact from the Limousin Forest, though, previously, local oak from the Orne valley was employed. Between periods of aging calvados, the casks may be freshened by a few months of cider, both to render the wood more supple and to add to the aroma of the next calvados. While a *boisé* of oak chips may be employed and a limited amount of sugar may legally be added at the time of bottling, these techniques are only rarely employed, and most calvados is left naturally dry. Traditionally, calvados has been bottled at 45° G.L. (90 American proof), though today 43° and even 40° are common. Some producers maintain that the lower proof brings out more of the fruit in calvados; it is also less expensive to produce.

Calvados without the *appellation contrôlée* of "Pays d'Auge" is distilled in relatively small continuous column stills of the armagnac type, though it must be possible to separate the heads and tails from the *coeur,* or heart, of the spirit. Most of this *appellation réglementée* calvados is bottled when two to three years old, though older stocks are kept for blending. The best of these younger calvados have a delightful, fresh, apple aroma, though the flavors are direct and forceful rather than complex. The simple *eau-de-vie de cidre* is rarely seen outside France, and its absence is not often noticed.

Precise indications of age do not often appear on calvados labels, though general designations are controlled by the Bureau National Interprofessionnel des Calvados et Eaux-de-Vie de Cidre et de Poiré (B.N.I.C.E.). Thus, a designation of three stars (apples, fleurs-de-lis, etc.) may be used only for a calvados at least two years old; "Vieux" or "Réserve" indicates a minimum age of three years; "V.O." or "Vieille Réserve," a minimum of four years; "V.S.O.P." or "Grande Réserve," at least five years old; and only those calvados beyond *"compte 5"* (five and a half years or older) are entitled to the designation "Extra," "Hors d'Âge," or "Âge Inconnu." These regulations apply to the youngest calvados in the blend, not merely to the average age. In practice, a vieux calvados probably has an average age of four to five years, "Vieille Réserve" of ten to fifteen, and "Hors d'Âge" or "Âge Inconnu" of twenty years or more.

Until recently, the production of calvados has always been secondary to the less time-consuming but more profitable production of cider. Even in the early 1970s, only 20 per cent of the cider produced within the delimited region of Calvados was distilled, resulting in the production of approximately 1.2 million U.S. gallons of pure alcohol in the 1972–73 season, of which only 150,000 originated in the Pays d'Auge. This latter figure, which equals about 170,000 cases of calvados bottled at 40° G.L., is less than 4 per cent of the amount produced from the first three Cognac growths (Grande Champagne, Petite Champagne, and Borderies) in the same year, and is certainly far inferior to the production of any one of the largest Cognac houses. As apples become more expensive, however, the retail price of cider is becoming less competitive with such drinks as beer and wine, so that many producers in Calvados expect the ratio of *eau-de-vie* to cider to reverse itself, perhaps in as little as five years. One of the functions of the B.N.I.C.E. (created only in 1966) will be to ensure that this increased production does not in any way lower the quality of calvados; indeed, one of the Bureau's most important objectives at the moment is to increase existing stocks of old calvados and to emphasize the quality of aged calvados rather than mere quantity.

Commercial calvados producers range from the small grower-distiller,

who may sell fewer than a thousand cases annually, to the larger
négociants in the area, whose sales are more likely to be in the fifty-to-
one-hundred-thousand-case range. Even this latter amount is hardly
sufficient to make calvados a household word. Yet, of more significance
is the fact that sales of one large *négociant,* Busnel, have doubled since
1971, when they were bought by the giant Ricard company; that
another large producer, Debrise Dulac & Co. ("Père Magloire" brand),
is now linked to the Champagne firm of Veuve-Clicquot; and that the
Cidrerie de Montgomery, which produced about fifteen hundred liters
of pure alcohol in 1972–73, is in the process of building a new distillery, with new eight-hundred-gallon Charente stills and several continuous stills. While it will take some time to build up sufficient stocks,
which are currently hovering around 2.5 million gallons, it is clear that
we should be hearing much more from Calvados in the future.

When describing calvados, one must really speak of two different
drinks: the very fruity but fiery young calvados, and the more mature,
subtle calvados du Pays d'Auge. While the explosive perfume of the
former is certainly welcome at times, on the British and American
markets you will generally get more for your money if you seek out the
"Pays d'Auge" appellation and, if it is available, a *vieux* rather than a
younger blend. A good vieux calvados should retain much of the fresh
apple scent with which it is born, tempered by an oak spiciness that
does not overwhelm it. A twenty-to-thirty-year-old calvados actually
resembles some older brandies, as the years of slow aging and the
acquisition of wood character lessen the difference between grape and
apple. Among the larger producers, BUSNEL, BOULARD ("Arc de Triomphe" brand in the United States) and MORICE are generally consistent in quality.

Warmed in the palm of the hand like any good brandy, calvados can
provide a pleasant alternative to the usual cognac or armagnac—particularly at the end of a creamy Poulet Vallée d'Auge or a well-ripened
wedge of Pont-l'Éveque! In Normandy people love to eat well, and a
glass of young calvados is also traditionally taken as a *"trou normand,"*
a break at the midpoint of a large meal. The fiery young spirit cleans
the palate and refreshes it for what lies ahead.

In the United States, apple or cider brandy is known as APPLEJACK.
A popular spirit during colonial and revolutionary times, it was distilled
in fairly important quantities when it was found that grains and other

traditional sources of alcohol did not fare well in the cold eastern climate.

Applejack has greatly declined in importance, and today only two labels are widely distributed: LAIRD'S, whose distilleries are in New Jersey, New York, and Virginia; and SPEA'S, now also headquartered on the East Coast, whose original home was in the beautiful apple-growing country around Sebastapol, in northern California. Most applejack now on the market is a blend of straight cider brandy that has been aged several years in wood and grain neutral spirits, usually 35 per cent of the former and 65 per cent of the latter. The resulting product is quite light, reflecting the currently popular taste, and lacks the intensity and complexity of apple flavors found in a pure apple brandy such as calvados.

FRUIT EAUX-DE-VIE

FRUIT EAUX-DE-VIE

The highly perfumed, delicate, yet fiery fruit *eaux-de-vie* are sometimes referred to as white spirits because of their crystal-clear color.[1] Most are relatively unknown outside their region of production, although kirsch and perhaps poire and framboise are familiar names. Others, from wild berries, flowers, and buds of the mountains and forests of the Vosges, are esoteric products whose scarcity, high prices, and fanciful names have earned them a unique place in the world of spirits.

Distillation of fruit into *eau-de-vie* became common much later than did the production of brandy, and even in the early-eighteenth century, fruit *eaux-de-vie* were still little known. Of course, alchemists had distilled fruits and plants into secret elixirs for centuries, and fruit spirits were used medicinally even into the seventeenth century. An epidemic of cholera in Alsace in 1634 was fought by the mass consumption of locally produced kirsch.

During the eighteenth century, distillation of fruit spirits gradually became centered in northeastern France, the Black Forest (Schwarzwald) of Germany, and Switzerland. The restriction of fruit *eau-de-vie* production to this region is perhaps due to two reasons. First, and most importantly, there was an abundance of both cultivated and wild fruit in the surrounding hills and valleys. Secondly, the production of white fruit alcohols may have corresponded to regional or ethnic preferences in taste, following the northern European penchant for clear, strong spirits like schnapps and aquavit.

The *eau-de-vie* regions of the three countries share a common aspect of rolling forested hills, orchards, and rich vegetation, but each also presents its own particular geographical and cultural character. The Black Forest is the highest of the three regions, rising southeast of

---

[1] Distilled fruit spirits are known as fruit *eaux-de-vie* or true fruit brandies. Since we have generally used the term "brandy" in this book to refer only to grape brandy, we will use "fruit *eau-de-vie*" to mean the spirit that results from the distillation of all fruit other than grapes.

Freiburg to over three thousand feet. Modern roads crisscross much of the area, linking the small vacation resorts that dot the countryside, but the forest itself has remained unspoiled. Its green-covered hills and sudden valleys still conjure up images of Hänsel and Gretel, wolves at the door, and cuckoo-clock chalets. Most of the dozen or so commercial kirsch distilleries in the Schwarzwald are situated on the edges of the forest or in the Rhine Valley near the French-German border.

The Alsatian *eau-de-vie* country, which stretches between the Vosges Mountains and the Rhine River from Colmar to Strasbourg, begins just north of Alsace's major wine-producing area. Its wooded hillsides, more peaceful than the dark slopes of the Black Forest, are less dense but also richer in the wild berries that yield the region's more unusual *eaux-de-vie*. Most of the distilleries are quite small, self-styled as *artisanale,* and many are little more than a few pot stills and aging-tanks in what might otherwise pass for a garage. Nevertheless, these usually family-run operations are full-time commercial ventures, and most offer fifteen to twenty different types of fruit *eaux-de-vie*. In Alsace the gamut of varieties is so great that the goal often seems less to produce a pleasant-tasting spirit than to prove that an *eau-de-vie* can in fact be made from almost any fruit, bud, or flower at hand!

The clear, still lakes and towering mountains of Switzerland are without question the most impressive setting for the production of *eaux-de-vie*. There is no single region or canton that predominates, although the cherries of the Zug Valley, between Lucerne and Zurich, are justly famous. Like the Black Forest producers, the Swiss concentrate primarily on kirsch and the other three or four best-known fruit *eaux-de-vie,* leaving the more unusual spirits to the fertile hillsides and imaginations of Alsace.

Fermentation and distillation of the "stone fruits" (cherries, plums, sloeberries) and pears are similar to the double-distillation procedures utilized in the production of cognac. The fruits are first "crushed," although in many cases this may consist merely of breaking the skins. Care is taken *not* to crack or break the stones, for this would release unwanted bitter-almond flavors. Selected yeast strains may be added to initiate fermentation, but for most varieties this is not necessary, for there are sufficient wild yeasts.

Fermentation generally occurs in fiberglass, enamel, or stainless-steel vats rarely larger than five hundred liters. The process is much slower than that for grapes, and may last from two or three weeks up to three months. Because of the fairly low sugar content in the fruits, the resulting "wine" will have an alcohol content of only 3.5–4% (pears) up to a maximum of 7–8% (mirabelle plums). It is illegal to add sugar to the fruit in order to increase the alcoholic yield of fermentation.

As soon as fermentation is completed, the fruit and wine are distilled, most commonly in a Cognac-style copper pot still. Because of the delicacy of the fruit and the necessity for a relatively gentle heat, the still is generally placed in a *bain-marie* of water, a double-boiler arrangement which avoids direct contact of the heat source with the bottom of the heating chamber of the still. Should the fruit be in a relatively solid mass after fermentation, water may be added before distillation to prevent burning. The first distillation generally yields a spirit of 25–30% alcohol; this is then redistilled, either by itself or in the presence of additional fruit, to extract as much aromatic essence as possible. Only the heart of this final distillate is kept; the heads and tails are taken off to be redistilled. The average strength of an *eau-de-vie* as it comes from the still is 55–60°, although this can vary considerably depending on the type of fruit.

A variation of the traditional pot still has been adopted by most of the Swiss and German producers and by a few of the larger French firms. This consists of a pot still heated over a *bain-marie* and surmounted by a small column containing a series of condensing plates in a style similar to an armagnac still. The process is not continuous, however, for the *chaudière* must still be emptied and recharged once the distillation of a given batch is completed. Only the more volatile, alcohol-rich vapors are able to pass through all the plates, while the heavier ones condense on their way up and fall back toward the bubbling liquid to be redistilled. With this method, *eau-de-vie* can be taken off from the top of the still at 60–65° G.L., and there is thus no need for a second distillation. Of course, the distiller is more important than the method of distillation; we have tasted excellent results from both systems.

The above methods are standard for the stone fruits and pears, which have enough sugar to yield a "wine" sufficiently alcoholic to be distilled. All the alcohol in the *eau-de-vie* thus originates in the fruit itself. In Germany and Switzerland, such products are referred to as *"Wasser,"* as in Kirschwasser or Zwetschgenwasser. Soft fruits and all the wild berries, however, have so little sugar that it is impracticable to obtain enough alcohol to make an *eau-de-vie* solely from fermenting and distilling them on their own. Also, a "pure" raspberry *eau-de-vie* made in this way for example, is said to be thin and bitter, not reflecting the sweet perfume of the fresh fruit. To overcome this problem but still capture the essence of such soft fruits, they are first macerated in alcohol; the resulting infusion is then distilled to concentrate the flavors and character of the fruit.

In Germany and Switzerland, *eau-de-vie* prepared in this manner is known as *"Geist"*; Himbeergeist is thus "spirit of raspberry." Neutral, high-proof alcohol is used for the maceration. In France, the term *eau-de-vie* is maintained to describe the product, and the macerating alcohol must itself be a fruit *eau-de-vie* with a maximum strength of 70° G.L. The *eau-de-vie* most commonly used is a young grape brandy, and the better producers use only white (unaged) cognac, up to a maximum of the equivalent of twelve and a half liters of pure alcohol for each one hundred kilograms of fruit.

Since the resulting infusion is already quite alcoholic, only one distillation is necessary to concentrate the aroma and flavors of the fruit and also reach the desired strength of 55–60°. As with the second distillation of the stone fruits, the unwanted heads and tails are eliminated and redistilled with the next infusion. For distillation, either a traditional pot still or a pot surmounted by a column may be used.

No matter which system of distillation is employed, the low sugar content of the various fruits means that the yield in *eau-de-vie* is extremely small. *Mirabelle* (yellow plum) and *quetsch* (violet plum) are probably the most generous, yet only four to five liters of pure alcohol can be obtained from one hundred kilograms of fruit; this means that it takes approximately twenty-two pounds of mirabelle plums to produce a single liter bottle of *eau-de-vie de mirabelle* at 50° G.L. Williams (Bartlett) pears and strawberries are even more stingy, requiring over fifty pounds of fruit for a single liter!

When the *eau-de-vie* comes off the still it is crystal clear, as are all distilled spirits. Unlike many other spirits, however this clarity is considered an essential element in the character of a fruit *eau-de-vie,* and any tinge of yellow or amber is considered a major defect. Additionally, it is felt that such influences as cask aging will do nothing but detract from the perfumed essence of fruit that has been captured in the freshly distilled spirit. Traditionally, therefore, fruit *eaux-de-vie* are held in neutral containers until they are bottled; the most common vessels today are glass or enamel-lined, although stainless steel is also being increasingly used.

Even though the young *eaux-de-vie* are kept in neutral containers, most producers agree that the stone-fruit spirits do improve with aging. Kirsch benefits most from age, and almost all producers will keep it for at least a few months before bottling; in Germany and Switzerland, good-quality kirsch receives a minimum of two to three years' aging. This time is normally spent in relatively large vats (*cuves*), but some houses prefer three-to-five-gallon glass demijohns. These demijohns may have holes pricked in their caps and may also be uncorked and agitated several times a year to ensure that adequate oxidaton occurs. Some producers also consider that changes in temperature are important, and they thus prefer to age above ground rather than in the more constant temperatures of a cellar.

Aging is much less important for *Geist*, which is macerated before being distilled, although most distillers do hold *eaux-de-vie* like framboise (Himbeergeist) for a few weeks or months to round out the slightly sharp edge that may be present immediately after distillation. Others insist that if the distillation has been carefully controlled, the *eau-de-vie* can be bottled immediately.

The oldest operating commercial distillery in Alsace, that of MEYBLUM, in the Val de Villé, is unique in that all the processes involved in making their *eaux-de-vie* (except the actual distillation) occur in wood: both fermentation and maceration take place in old oak vats, while aging is only in large ash casks. The owners feel that wood aging permits better oxidation, but the *eaux-de-vie* are always removed and bottled before they acquire any perceptible color. KAMMER, one of the largest Black Forest distillers, also ages in large oval ash casks for a minimum of two years for kirsch, one year for Mirabellenwasser and Zwetschgenwasser.

Most fruit *eaux-de-vie* are aged at the strength at which they run off the still, around 60°. Although traditionally *eaux-de-vie* were sold at 50°, rising costs and customs duties have reduced that figure to 45°, and you can expect even that level to drop in the future. Today, metal screw tops are used by most producers rather than cork closures.

Those *eaux-de-vie* labeled with a specific geographic name (framboise d'Alsace, Schwarzwälder Kirschwasser) must be produced entirely from fruit grown within the designated region. The appellation of "old" (*vieux* or *vieille*) in Alsace has no legal significance, although most producers do offer a few *"réserve"* bottlings that are of higher quality and often older than the regular line. Many of the very large producers who market *eaux-de-vie* do not actually distill their own, but the wording on the label does not always make this clear.

Although an *eau-de-vie* is certainly meant to be drunk as soon as it is bottled, it would seem reasonable to expect that there might be some changes in its character due to aging in the bottle. While only a couple of producers seem aware of this possibility, a spirit that ages in large glass-lined vats should also age to some degree in a glass bottle. There is little danger of your bottle of framboise or quetsch deteriorating for a period of several years, although you should not leave a small amount of *eau-de-vie* in the bottom of the bottle for an extended period of time. And it just might be interesting to put a bottle of kirsch, for example, away for five years and see if a slightly rounder, smoother spirit emerges—if you can keep away from it that long!

Because of their delightful, perfumed fruitiness, the white fruit *eaux-de-vie* find their natural place at the table at the end of the meal, when they make a very refreshing *digestif,* or later in the evening either alone or in the company of coffee. But despite their floral-fruity scent, *eaux-de-vie* are *not* sweet, and their somewhat fiery alcohol, unmellowed by aging in wood, will prove too strong for some. Primarily for this reason, it is usually recommended that fruit *eaux-de-vie* be served ice-cold, in prechilled glasses. While the pungent aroma usually stands up well to such treatment, we must cast a dissenting vote and suggest that a well-made kirsch, mirabelle, or other fine *eau-de-vie* need not be frozen to be enjoyed. While it is true that they do not benefit from slight hand-warming, as is the case for cognac and other wood brandies, neither are they so potent that they must be tossed off in one cold gulp like high-proof vodka or raw schnapps. We would encourage you to try serving fruit *eaux-de-vie* chilled, but only to a cellar temperature of perhaps 55–60° Fahrenheit. This is cool enough to be refreshing, but not so cold as to obliterate the finer nuances of a well-made spirit.

Because of the overwhelming importance of the aroma in the appreciation of *eaux-de-vie,* they should not be served in the tall, narrow glasses often reserved for liqueurs. A moderate-sized balloon-style brandy glass is perfect for inhaling the bouquet of flowers or basket of fruits that rises to greet your nose, though it should have enough of a stem so that you need not hold the bowl in your warm hand.

There are almost as many *eaux-de-vie* as there are fruits, flowers, and berries in Alsace, but no more than five are of any real commercial importance: kirsch, Williams pear, raspberry, mirabelle, and quetsch.

KIRSCH, KIRSCHWASSER (cherry)

Produced from several types of cherries of the *Prunus avium* species, kirsch is without doubt the most important of the fruit *eaux-de-vie* and the one most familiar to consumers. In Switzerland, its production is regulated more closely than that of other *eaux-de-vie,* and no "kirsch-type" spirits are permitted other than true kirsch, distilled entirely from fermented cherries. The major kirsch-producing areas are the Zug Valley and the region around Basel, and cherries also come from Bern and the Fribourg-Vaud region. Each distiller must prove that he has purchased a sufficient quantity of cherries for the amount of kirsch he has produced, and only Swiss cherries may be employed; no additives are allowed.[2] While these regulations cannot guarantee that all Swiss kirsch is outstanding, well-known producers like DETTLING (who distill only kirsch) and FASSBIND can be relied on to produce *eaux-de-vie* of consistent quality. Dettling offers four qualities, the "Supérieur Vieux" (minimum of three years old), "Réserve" (six years old), "Réserve exceptionnelle" (twelve years old), and, unusually, a vintaged kirsch that has been aged for at least ten years. In general, the Swiss kirsches are of good average quality, with fairly fresh cherry character but slightly less roundness and body than the best German products.

The German Black Forest is kirsch country par excellence, and the finest German kirsches are almost invariably labeled "Schwarzwälder." They seem to be aged more than adequately, and most evidence a round, aged-spirit complexity, distinctively kirschlike rather than reflecting fresh cherry flavors. A mellow almond undertone is often present, but it should not be the primary sensation. Among the better producers of easily available kirsches are SCHLADERER, ADOLF HUBER, KAMMER, and 3-TANNEN, all of whom bottle Schwarzwälder Kirschwasser. There are only about a dozen important distillers in the Black Forest, but there are many more smaller producers.

The major French kirsch-producing region is centered around the small town of Fougerolles, situated west and a bit south of Alsace. The small Val de Villé, in Alsace, is also noted for its cherries. All French fruit *eaux-de-vie* tend to be slightly lighter and more delicate than their

---

[2] In contrast, Swiss regulations do permit the addition of "small quantities" of sugar and "inoffensive vegetable extracts" (*bonificateurs*) to improve the flavor of any *eaux-de-vie* except cherry, plum, or gentian.

German or Swiss counterparts, and kirsch is no exception. Among the large producers, DOLFI is the most consistent and well balanced, but it appears younger and lighter-bodied than the Schwarzwälder Kirschwassers.

Two somewhat misleading kirsch-type products are also permitted in France. KIRSCH DE COMMERCE is a blend of 20–25 per cent pure kirsch with 75–80 per cent neutral alcohol and is used primarily in pastry making. KIRSCH FANTAISIE, essentially a neutral alcohol flavored with bitter-almond extract and at most 5 per cent true kirsch, is also used in cooking.

Some kirsch is also produced by the large American cordial firms and is used both in cooking and for drinking.

POIRE WILLIAMS, WILLIAMS BIRNENBRAND (Williams, or Bartlett, pear)

A good pear *eau-de-vie* captures not only the aroma of fresh pears, but the flavors of pulp and even seeds as well—it is probably the most distinctive and easily identifiable of all the fruit *eaux-de-vie,* and it ranks with raspberry as the second-most-popular fruit spirit. The raw fruit must be very ripe (though not the slightest bit rotten), which makes transport somewhat difficult. Aging is not as essential as for kirsch, but some producers do keep their poire for one to two years before bottling. The pears distilled in Alsace originate primarily in the lush Rhône and Loire valleys of France, while German and Swiss producers depend on pears from Switzerland and the Italian Tyrol region. Pears are among the most difficult fruits to ferment; yeast is often added, and the alcoholic yield is very low.

The taste of many pear *eaux-de-vie* is somewhat disappointing compared to the often delightful aroma, and this is unfortunately the case with the major brands available in the United States. One of the best is perhaps the German KAMMER, which has well-balanced, smooth flavors that retain good pear character without any alcoholic harshness, and 3-TANNEN is also very good. Many of the smaller French distillers also offer excellent poire Williams, and the Alsatian producers as a whole seem to have better succeeded in capturing the essence of the pear than their cross-border competitors.

In Switzerland, pears provide much inexpensive, relatively neutral *eau-de-vie*, and may even be used in crude cider brandies. Poire Williams should be of higher quality and must come exclusively from the Williams pear, but the Swiss products seem to be less consistent than the French.

You can occasionally find unusual bottles of pear *eaux-de-vie* that contain a whole pear inside them. This is accomplished by tying the empty bottle on a tree branch, over a blossom or tiny developing fruit, which then matures inside the bottle. Although they are quite attractive conversation pieces, the *eau-de-vie* chosen for these bottlings is not generally of the highest quality; the best poire Williams needs no help from bottled fruit.

FRAMBOISE, HIMBEERGEIST (raspberry)

The queen of the soft-fruit *eaux-de-vie* is framboise, whose intense, ripe character of raspberry is finding increasing popularity, especially in America. It may be the largest-selling Alsatian *eau-de-vie* exported, and most Swiss and German distillers make "spirit of raspberry" as well.

The French framboise, it should be remembered, must be macerated in another *eau-de-vie* rather than neutral spirits, and this contributes to the character of the resulting distillate. One of the more delicate *eaux-de-vie,* framboise is rarely kept more than a few months before bottling and, unlike kirsch, does not benefit from additional aging. The aroma should be deep and pungent, sometimes acquiring a very ripe, almost "rotten" (but in a good sense) character. Many people are surprised at the dry, alcoholic finish of the *eau-de-vie* after the almost-sweet aroma, but a good framboise should be smooth and well balanced on the palate.

Alsace also offers FRAMBOISE SAUVAGE, from small wild raspberries gathered during July and August in the surrounding hills. Its character is very similar to the regular framboise, which is also made from small berries, but is perhaps just a bit more subtle.

The Swiss and German Himbeergeists (or framboise, in some areas of Switzerland) are made with high-proof neutral spirits rather than unaged, white brandies, and the resulting *eau-de-vie* is generally a bit lighter, "cleaner," and perhaps less complex than the Alsatian framboise.

MIRABELLE, MIRABELLENWASSER (yellow plum)

Mirabelle is primarily a French product, although it is also produced in both Germany and Switzerland. The plateaux and hillsides of Lorraine are well suited to the growth of the fairly small, sometimes red-blushed mirabelle, which is a variety of damson plum (*Prunus insititia*). MIRABELLE DE LORRAINE is the only French fruit *eau-de-vie* that benefits from an *appellation réglementée,* but little *eau-de-vie* is actually produced there. Rather, the mirabelles are sent to neighboring Alsace, where what many producers themselves consider to be the finest of all fruit *eaux-de-vie* is actually distilled.

While not as easily identifiable as raspberry or pear, the aroma of mirabelle is a perfumed, flowery delight that seems both rich and deli-cate at the same time. With proper aging (generally one to four years), it can attain the complexity of an old kirsch, yet retain its inherent fresh-ness. The flavors are round and very fruity, and should leave a pleasant, lingering aftertaste. Among the large distillers whose products are likely to be exported, both JACOBERT (now owned by Cointreau) and DOLFI (which belongs to the Martini group) offer good mirabelles, although the finest are to be found among such small producers as MEYBLUM and MICLO.

QUETSCH, ZWETSCHGENWASSER (violet plum)

Larger, blue-violet in color, and less well known than the yellow mirabelle, the quetsch is harvested in September and October in all the *eau-de-vie*-producing regions. A *Wasser* in German nomenclature, it is first fermented and then distilled like cherries, pears, and other plums.

Less subtle and complex than mirabelle, quetsch nevertheless has a distinctive spicy-plum character that is very pleasant and resembles the Satsuma plum grown in the western United States. The French, Ger-man, and Swiss quetsch *eaux-de-vie* are all similar in style, a bit fuller than the mirabelle, with good fruitiness.

SLIVOVITZ is a plum *eau-de-vie* produced primarily in Yugoslavia and eastern Europe, whose basic character is very similar to that of quetsch. Slivovitz, however, is traditionally aged in wood rather than neutral glass or stainless-steel vessels, and it should have a straw to medium-yellow color. When well balanced, the slight woody character softens rather than overwhelms the fruit, and slivovitz is definitely a fruit *eau-de-vie* rather than a wood-aged brandy. The most important Yugosla-vian distillers are SLOVIN, who offer an eight- and a twelve-year-old slivovitz, and NAVIP.

Some German producers also market a "slivovitz" or "slibovitz"; that of ADOLF HUBER is actually a quetsch, which is not aged in wood, while KAMMER does offer a slibovitz similar in color and style to the Yugoslavian product.

The above five varieties account for the vast majority of fruit *eaux-de-vie* produced in the world, but there remains a whole host of intriguing and unusual *eaux-de-vie* that you may find in your travels to France, though most will probably never be exported. These lesser-known spirits are distilled mainly in Alsace, so we have listed them alphabetically by their French names. Where there is a German or Swiss equivalent, the German appellation is also given.

ABRICOT, APRIKOSENGEIST (apricot)

Though relatively rare, a good apricot *eau-de-vie* can capture the rich, ripe apricot aroma that is sometimes difficult to find in the sweetened apricot-flavored brandies popular in the United States. There may be undertones of almond from the presence of the stones during distillation.

FLEURS D'ACACIA (acacia flowers)

Made by the small and relatively young firm of LEGOLL in Neubois, Alsace, this is a delicate, light-bodied *eau-de-vie* with a flowery, wet-woody aroma a bit like prunelle. The flowers are infused in an unaged white-wine brandy before distillation.

ALISIER (fruit of the service tree)

This is produced from the fruit of a wild variety of the Mediterranean service tree (probably *Sorbus torminalis*), a close relative of the better-known mountain ash (*Sorbus aucuparia*). Made by several distillers, the *eau-de-vie* has a fairly distinctive wet hay-almond-fruity aroma and flavor.

AIRELLE (whortleberry, bilberry)—see MYRTILLE.

AIRELLE ROUGE (red whortleberry, cowberry)

Also known as the mountain cranberry (*Vaccinium vitis-idaea*), this is a tart, red fruit closely related to the blueberry and cranberry. As produced by the small but modern distillery of NUSBAUMER, it yields a pleasant *eau-de-vie* of an almost-sweet, perfumed evergreen character.

CASSIS (black currant)

While most berries are macerated, cassis may be distilled directly— like the stone fruits. The *eau-de-vie* retains the fairly intense, spicy-minty-black currant aroma that one associates with the fruit, but the dry, slightly alcoholic taste is understandably quite a shock to those who might be used to the sweet, heavy creme de cassis from Dijon.

CERISE, KIRSCH (cherry)

Very rarely, one may find a French kirsch labeled "eau-de-vie de cerise," although there is no difference between this and the more normal "kirsch" appellation.

COING (quince)

Not one of the more popular fruits for either eating or distilling, quince becomes a relatively full-bodied *eau-de-vie* with a rather "wild," green woody-spicy character.

CYNORRHODEN (rose hip)—see ÉGLANTINE.

ÉGLANTINE (dog rose)

From wild shrubs that are members of the *Rosa* genus, although it is not exactly clear which of several shrubs are the source for this rather spicy, woody, slightly tealike *eau-de-vie*. No distinction is made in

France between Églantine and Cynorrhoden; both may also be labeled more colorfully as Gratte-Cul.

FRAISE (strawberry)

Because of the difficulty of capturing the subtle strawberry fragrance (and competition from the more easily identifiable framboise) fraise is not widely produced as an *eau-de-vie*. It is usually light in body, with pleasant if somewhat weak strawberry aromas and flavors.

GENTIANE, ENZIAN (gentian root)

This earthy, quinine-like *eau-de-vie* will probably not be everyone's favorite, although its herbal character might appeal to those who like digestive bitters or some of the bitter apéritifs like Campari or the French Suze. The roots are first dried and then reconstituted before being macerated in alcohol and distilled; Swiss regulations permit the addition of sugar prior to fermentation and subsequent distillation.

GRATTE-CUL—see ÉGLANTINE.

GROSEILLE (red or white currant)

Only rarely produced as an *eau-de-vie* (though it is popular in jam making), the red currant lacks the intense character of the more popular black currant.

HOUX (holly)

The most expensive and oft-discussed of the Alsatian *eaux-de-vie,* houx is produced from bright-red holly berries which are painfully hand-picked in November and December, often after the first snowfall. The cost of the berries may approach one dollar per pound, or up to fifteen to twenty dollars per liter for the raw materials alone! The flavors are complex, evoking the aroma of holly berries and leaves mingled with evergreens and wet, slightly rotten logs—a far cry from the

fruitiness that distinguishes most other Alsatian *eaux-de-vie*. Certainly
its character is distinctive, though whether it would be the ideal accompaniment to your Christmas pudding is a matter of highly individual
taste.

MÛRE (mulberry or blackberry)

Only rarely distilled, mûre has a vaguely woody-fruity slightly berry-
like character that lacks the distinction of its well-known cousin the
raspberry.

MÛRE SAUVAGE, MÛRON (blackberry)—see MÛRE

MYRTILLE (whortleberry, bilberry)

Also known as airelle, the myrtille is a member of the large *Vaccinium* genus, which includes several species of the American blueberry
among its approximately 130 members. Wild bilberry shrubs are found
throughout Europe, Asia, and Great Britain, and their dark-blue berries
are used in jams, preserves, and even one of the more popular varieties
of yogurt. The character of eau-de-vie de myrtille varies somewhat from
producer to producer but is usually fairly fresh, delicate, and slightly
perfumed, with some woody undertones. One tasting conjured up visions of branches overhanging a clear mountain stream, an example of
the powerful effects of too many *eaux-de-vie* in one afternoon!

PÊCHE (peach)

Quite rare, and treated in the same fashion as apricot.

POMME (apple)

Apple is the most common fruit used to produce alcohol in the *eau-
de-vie* regions, and Swiss supermarkets are full of liter bottles of inexpensive, essentially neutral apple spirits. No apple *eaux-de-vie* of any

6. An armagnac still, with its short rectifying column atop the *chaudière*

7. A modern continuous, or column, still as used in California

8. A dramatic view from the bottom of the fifty-foot rectifying column of a large continuous still (photo by Tom Vano; courtesy of The Christian Brothers of California)

9. The control panel of a modern California distillery (photo by Tom Vano; courtesy of The Christian Brothers of California)

10. The *paradis* of a cognac firm, where the finest and most ancient cognacs continue their slow aging (photo by J.Y. Boyer; courtesy of the Bureau National du Cognac)

11. A modern *chai,* or aging facility (photo courtesy of Stock, Italy)

12. Some popular brandies and liqueurs. Left to right: Cognac Otard, Schenley Import Co.; Amaretto di Saronno, Foreign Imports, Inc.; Liquore Galliano, McKesson Liquor Co.; Creme de Noyaux, Bols; Creme de Menthe, Hiram Walker

interest are produced, except of course the distinctive calvados from Normandy, which is discussed in the preceding chapter.

PRUNE SAUVAGE (wild plum)

Produced by NUSBAUMER as a light, flowery but fairly simple *eau-de-vie;* probably the same fruit as prunelle.

PRUNELLE (sloeberry, blackthorn)

From the same small, wild plum that gives us the American sloe gin and various prunelle liqueurs, prunelle is a delightfully fruity *eau-de-vie* that deserves to be better known. It is normally characterized by an intensely perfumed honeydew-melon aroma, often with undertones of almond, and very fruity and slightly "wild" flavors.

REINE-CLAUDE (greengage plum)

A fairly large, greenish-yellow fruit belonging to a different species (*Prunus domestica*) from the mirabelle and distilled by only a few producers.

BOURGEONS DE SAPIN (pine buds)

Yes, even fir or pine buds are distilled in Alsace, although their appreciation will doubtless be limited to devotees of retsina and turpentine! The buds are picked in April, and the *eau-de-vie* has a strongly resinous, slightly nutty character that is distinctive, to say the least.

SORBIER (sorb apple)

This *eau-de-vie* is probably derived from the fruit of the *Sorbus domestica, pomifera* variety, of the sorb, or service tree. While it is closely related to alisier (*S. torminalis*), distillers usually do distinguish between the two species.

SUREAU (elderberry)

These dark-purple berries are gathered in the autumn and in some areas are used to make elderberry wine, though in Alsace *eau-de-vie* is the more common final product. With light-moderate body and fairly soft flavors, sureau has a pleasant deep berry-like aroma and more fruit than many of the wild-berry *eaux-de-vie*.

While a few of the less common *eaux-de-vie* are merely oddities, like bourgeons de sapin or houx, others are delightful spirits that are well worth trying if a bottle comes your way or, better yet, you find yourself in Alsace. Certainly the intensely perfumed prunelle or the delicate myrtille can rival some of the better-known *eaux-de-vie* in interest and complexity, even if the limited quantities of fruit available means that they will remain difficult to find outside the producing areas.

All fruit *eaux-de-vie* are expensive. While some kirsches may sell in the United States for only eight to ten dollars per bottle, prices of twenty to twenty-five dollars are not uncommon for the longer-aged or less common varieties. Among the factors contributing to these prices are the ever-present taxes on alcohol; the scarcity of the raw product; the difficulty in picking many of the wild fruits, which are still gathered primarily by children, housewives, and farmers on a part-time basis; and the inordinate amount of fruit required to produce a single bottle of *eau-de-vie*. Most commercial fruit-*eau-de-vie* distillers are still very small, and even the larger firms are far from attaining the efficient scale of such grape-brandy producers as Courvoisier, Stock, or Christian Brothers. It is not too surprising that the cost of even a relatively "ordinary" *eau-de-vie* is high.

But none of the fruit *eaux-de-vie* are really ordinary; each is an almost unique product in which all the skill and art of the distiller are on display. From kirsch and mirabelle to prunelle or houx, the goal is to capture the very essence of the fruit, an essence that will not later be altered by wood tannin or sugar or flavorings, but an essence that will be drunk as pure as the moment it ran off the still. In these days of giant corporations and blending for the mass market, the perfumed *eaux-de-vie* of Alsace, Switzerland, and the Black Forest remain unique spirits.

PART TWO

Liqueurs

THE ALCHEMISTS' LEGACY—
A HISTORY OF LIQUEURS

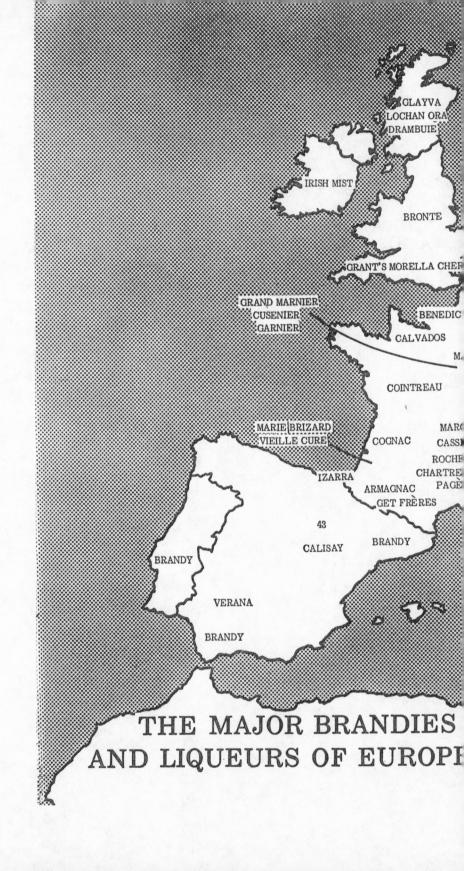

GLAYVA
LOCHAN ORA
DRAMBUIE

IRISH MIST

BRONTE

GRANT'S MORELLA CHEF

GRAND MARNIER
CUSENIER
GARNIER

BENEDIC

CALVADOS

M.

COINTREAU

MARIE BRIZARD
VIEILLE CURE

COGNAC

MARⒸ
CASSⒾ
ROCHⒽ
CHARTRE
PAGÈ

IZARRA

ARMAGNAC
GET FRÈRES

43

CALISAY

BRANDY

BRANDY

VERANA

BRANDY

**THE MAJOR BRANDIES
AND LIQUEURS OF EUROPE**

PETER HEERING
CHERRY KIJAFA

DERMINT
STONSDORFER
UYPER
GOLDWASSER

WISNIAK

ASBACH
ECKES
DOLFI
ESCORIAL GRUN
EAUX-DE-VIE

ERI-SUISSE
GRAPPA
OR d' ALPE
STOCK
AMARETTO
ALLIANO
LUXARDO
MARASCHINO
BUTON
TUACA
AURUM
SLIVOVITZ
MOLINARI SAMBUCA
STREGA

PASHA

METAXA
CAMBAS

THE ALCHEMISTS' LEGACY—A HISTORY OF LIQUEURS

Distillation was known and practiced for centuries prior to the Middle Ages—by the Egyptians, Chinese, Greeks, and Romans—but it was the inquisitiveness of the alchemists of this later time that eventually led to the creation of the flavored, sweetened spirits we today call liqueurs. The Catalan Arnold de Vila Nova, born about 1240, was one of the first to ascribe medicinal properties to flavored alcohol, though it remains unknown whether the first spices and fruits were added to alcohol for reasons of health or merely to render palatable what was probably a harsh, fiery, and often poorly distilled spirit. Many of the early experiments were more concerned with finding a universal solvent or transmuting base metals into gold than with creating an enjoyable alcoholic beverage.

From the fourteenth to the sixteenth or seventeenth centuries the production of "waters" and "elixirs" was generally confined to monasteries and the alchemists' laboratories. The experiments were slow and secret, as nearly every imaginable plant, fruit, and animal was investigated in the search for a life-restoring elixir. It was during this period that many of the monastic herbal elixirs were developed, their secrets to be later passed on from generation to generation before finally developing into such highly successful liqueurs as Chartreuse and Bénédictine.

At first the processes of distillation remained secret except to the initiated few. As distillation became better understood and as spices, herbs, and sugar from New World colonies arrived in Europe, the bitter medicines of the Middle Ages were transformed into intriguing new alcoholic drinks. No longer could the secrets of the alchemists remain hidden. The northern Europeans, perhaps inspired by the cold winters from which their Mediterranean neighbors were spared, seem to have been the first to realize the potential of what we now call "liqueurs" or "cordials."[1] Heronymous Braunschweig's treatise on distillation was published in the early-sixteenth century. In 1575 Lucas Bols founded in Amsterdam one of the world's first commercial liqueur houses, and the celebrated Danzig Goldwasser from Der Lachs appeared in 1598.

Liqueurs were first introduced to France by Catherine de Médicis during the Renaissance, but they did not become truly fashionable until the reign of the Sun King, Louis XIV. One favorite was *rossolis,* or *rissoly,* perhaps derived from the king's title of *Roi Soleil* or from the Italian liqueur *rosolio,* and the king's personal blend was said to have been based on a preparation of orange flowers, musk roses, lilies, jasmine, cinnamon, and cloves. The oldest distillery still operating in France, that of Rocher Frères at La Côte St. André, was founded near the end of the Sun King's reign, in 1705. As the court imitated the tastes of their king, the appreciation of liqueurs of various kinds spread throughout the French nobility. Liqueurs also were popular in Italy, and a form of *rosolio* is still produced in the North.

Although fruits were occasionally used, most of these early liqueurs remained based on flowers, plants, and herbs; not until the eighteenth and nineteenth centuries did fruit liqueurs and ratafias become popular, perhaps reflecting a gradual change in tastes in favor of lighter, fresher after-dinner drinks instead of the heavy, complex digestives of medicinal origin. While the average liqueur, or cordial, would have perhaps a dozen ingredients, macerated for a few days and then distilled, the most complex were likely to contain a myriad of rare and precious herbs and spices. The standard seventeenth-century English treatise on distillation, written by John French, gives the following recipe for the aptly named Aqua Celestis:

> "Take of Cinnamon
> Cloves
> Nutmegs
> Ginger
> Zedoary
> Galangall
> Long-Pepper
> Citron-pill

---

[1] The terms "cordial" and "liqueur" are today synonymous; the former is used primarily in America, while the British and Europeans use "liqueur." We will use the two interchangeably in this book.

Spicknard
Lignum-aloes
Cububs
Cardamums
Calamus aromaticus
Germander
Ground-pine
Mace
White Frankincense
Tormentill
Hermodactyle
the pitch of Dwarf Elder
Juniper berries
Bay-Berries
the seeds and flowers of Motherwort
the seeds of Smallage
        Fennell
        Anise
the leaves of Sorrell
        Sage
        Fel-wort
Rosemary
Marjoram
Mints
Penny-royall
Stechados
the flowers of Elder
        Roses red
            white
of the leaves of Scabious
Rue
the lesser Moonwort
Egrimonie
Centory
Fumitary
Pimpernell
Sow-thistle
Eye-bright
Mayden-hair
Endive
Red Saunders
Aloes, of each two ounces

Pure Amber
the best Rhubarb, of each two Drams

dryed Figges
Raisins of the Sun
Dates, stoned
Sweet-Almonds
Graines of the Pine, of each an ounce.

Of the best *Aqua vitae* to the quantity of
them all, of the best hard Sugar, a pound,
of white honey half a pound, then adde

the root of Gentiane
flowers of Rosemary
Pepperwort
the root of Briony
Sowbread
Wormwood, of each half an ounce.

Now before these are distilled, quench gold
being made red hot, oftentimes in the foresaid
water, put therein orientall Pearls beaten
small an ounce, and then distill it after
twenty foure houres infusion.
This is a very Cordiall water, good against
faintings and infection."

A "Cordiall water" indeed, even if one were to forgo the gold and the
crushed "orientall Pearls."

The practice of flavoring alcohol with medicinal herbs and plants
during the sixteenth and seventeenth centuries remained primarily the
province of the apothecary, descendant of the Middle Ages alchemists.
French's treatise begins by warning the reader that "There is a glut of
Chymical books, but a scarcity of Chymical truths . . ." and then
proceeds to offer alcoholic remedies for some 150 diseases and infirmi-
ties, including baldness, forgetfulness, madness, measles, pimples,
"Venereal distempers," and the classical promise of "Youth to renew."
The distillates recommended include not only plants and herbs, but also
animals. It is evident from such elixirs as essence of Mans-brains,
Viper-Wine, and water of Horse-dung that the primary purpose must
have been medicinal rather than gustatory!

Raw sugar and spices from every corner of the world began to arrive in important quantities to eighteenth-century Europe, and the production of liqueurs became more common. In France, the houses of Marie Brizard and Get Frères were founded, and the emphasis was increasingly placed on pleasant-tasting digestives rather than merely tolerable medicinal elixirs, although such traditional "medicinal" substances as anise, caraway, and angelica often continued to be used as essential ingredients. The producers in Germany and Holland continued to emphasize the restorative powers of liqueurs, however, preferring such elixirs as Dutch bitters and kümmel to the more delicate inventions of the French houses.

Many different liqueurs were grouped under the general rubric of "ratafia," the term allegedly being derived from the custom of drinking a toast upon the ratification of a treaty. The most common, or "red," ratafias were made by macerating soft fruits (cherries, gooseberries, strawberries, raspberries) in alcohol to which was also added a distillate of spices or herbs and sugar. Other ratafias were made by stopping the fermentation of various fruit juices by the addition of brandy, in much the same fashion that some apéritif and dessert wines are made today.

While John French's treatise dwelt almost entirely on the medicinal aspects of liqueurs, *The Complete Distiller,* published in 1757 by A. Cooper and subsequently plagiarized for over a century, offered much more pleasant concoctions to the reader, including a recipe for Ros Solis, or Sun-dew, cordial, possibly derived from the early French liqueur of a similar name. It consisted of various flowers, caraway seeds, raisins, and licorice root as well as the omnipresent cinnamon, cloves, and nutmeg. Cooper's four rules for making "compound Waters & Cordials" are still valid today and demonstrate that the basic processes of liqueur production have changed little in the ensuing two centuries:

1) use only neutral, "well-cleaned" spirits;
2) be sure to leave the fruits and plants to "digest" (macerate) for a sufficient length of time:
3) pay attention to the heat of the fire;
4) use only the "heart" of the distillate.

The third rule is directed not only at the quality of the distillate, which is impaired if distillation proceeds too quickly, but also to the protection of the distiller: we are warned that, even when distilling in the presence of water rather than alcohol, if the fire becomes too hot "the Plant will stop up the Pipe of the Still-head; and consequently, the rising Vapour finding no Passage, will blow off the Still-head, and throw the boiling Liquor about the Still-house, so as to do a great deal of Mischief, and even suffocate the Operator, without a proper Caution." Distillation in the eighteenth century was clearly not a profession for the careless!

The Napoleonic Wars, in the early-nineteenth century, slowed the growth of most liqueurs, particularly French, but the prosperity that accompanied the industrial age in the second half of the century encouraged a tremendous increase in production and the number of European liqueur firms. Many companies were oriented as much toward exportation as to their own domestic markets.

Of great importance was the development, in the early-nineteenth century, of the continuous rectification column. This allowed the distillation of an almost totally neutral spirit, which is today the base of the great majority of modern liqueurs and cordials. Among the well-known firms founded in this period were Bénédictine, Cointreau, Cusenier, and Marnier-Lapostelle in France; Buton and Stock in Italy, Luxardo in Yugoslavia; and, just after the turn of the twentieth century, Drambuie in Scotland.

By now totally freed from the constraints imposed by the apothecaries (although many liqueurs were still offered as digestives) and encouraged by the frivolous character of the Belle Époque, most houses offered a wide range of flavors and styles whose titles, at least, implied a fervent imagination. The Dutch proposed such libations as Rose without Thorns, Illicit Love, The Longer the Better, and Parfait Amour; the French countered with Old Woman's Milk, Liqueur des Belles, and Maiden's Cream, and America had its violet Creme Yvette. Most of these concoctions were sweet and flowery, designed to attract the ladies, who were increasingly forming an important part of the liqueur market. At the same time, many of today's "standard" liqueurs had already become quite well known. These include anisette, popularized by Marie Brizard; cherry "brandy" (Rocher and Heering); the orange curaçaos of Cointreau, Cusenier, and Grand Marnier; creme de cassis from Dijon; creme de cacao; and creme de menthe. Some of the more traditionally styled herbal liqueurs also became established; both Bénédictine and Izarra were founded in the second half of the nineteenth century, and Chartreuse was first brought to Paris in 1846. It was also during this period that many American cordial producers began, with the majority coming from European backgrounds.

Most of the well-known names from the nineteenth century are still with us today, though of course a few have fallen by the wayside and others have been absorbed into larger groups. Since the end of World War II, many new liqueurs have appeared on the international market, but most tend to be specialty products rather than new lines of liqueurs from a single company. Some, like Irish Mist, have been based on traditional recipes, while the majority have been created specifically to capture whatever may be the current taste fashion. Modern techniques of publicity and marketing have created a highly competitive situation, in which the system of sales and distribution will sometimes be more complex than the production of the liqueur itself. Most European liqueurs are now sold primarily for export; Galliano, for example, was a stunning marketing success in the United States in the 1960s and encouraged the rise of several imitators, but it remains little known in its native Italy.

While the need for the marketing techniques of big business has naturally resulted in the concentration of production in fewer hands (Cointreau alone claims a 25 per cent share of the world liqueur market), in fact the average consumer probably has a wider choice of liqueurs from which to choose today than ever before. In addition to such well-developed liqueur-producing nations as France, the Netherlands, Germany, and Italy, popular liqueurs can now be readily found from Scotland (Drambuie), Ireland (Irish Mist), Jamaica (Tia Maria), Mexico (Kahlúa), and Israel (Sabra), to name only some of the better known.

Of the multitude of colorful and light-hearted cordials of the eighteenth and nineteenth centuries only Parfait Amour now remains, though most modern liqueur houses continue to offer at least a score of different products, and often many more. A typical selection might include creme de cacao, creme de menthe, orange curaçao and/or triple sec (each often available in two or more colors), three or four fruit-brandy liqueurs (blackberry, apricot, cherry, raspberry, peach), anisette, creme de banane, mandarin (tangerine), coffee, kümmel, parfait amour, some kind of herbal liqueur, and perhaps two or three "house specialties."

While many people think of liqueurs as rather steady, if unexciting, products in terms of sales and profits, the opposite is actually the case. International sales of liqueurs have been rising an average of 5–10 per cent annually in recent years, and many companies have seen sales double or triple in the space of a few years. The volume of exports of French liqueurs, for example, rose by nearly 100 per cent between 1966 and 1972, while Cointreau's operations increased by a remarkable 466 per cent during the same period. In 1973, the French bought 32 million bottles of liqueurs, which far outdistanced sales of Scotch whisky (22 million bottles) and cognac (15 million bottles). Yet, imported products still constitute less than 15 per cent of the cordials and liqueurs consumed in the United States.

"Liqueur" is derived from the Latin *liquefacere,* meaning to melt or dissolve. In a sense, this does tell us of the basic quality of a liqueur or cordial, for these are spirits which derive their primary character not from their alcohol or *eau-de-vie* base, but, rather, from substances dissolved in it. Bruno Rocher, of Rocher Frères, compares liqueurs to the playing of a piano; the *eau-de-vie* is merely the left-hand accompaniment to the brilliant melody of aromatic plants or fruits.

Less poetically, a working definition of "liqueur" is simply a sweetened spirit flavored by vegetable substances. In France, the minimum alcohol content is 15%, with a minimum sugar content of two hundred grams per liter (20 per cent). Those liqueurs designated *"crème"* must contain at least four hundred grams of sugar per liter. The flavoring substances used in the production of most liqueurs, and certainly in all the best ones, are the skins, seeds, roots, flowers, leaves, and pulp of various fruits and vegetables. Natural extracts or concentrates are also used (many originate in the French perfume center of Grasse), particularly for such relatively unusual tastes as banana and grapefruit. Many of the larger liqueur houses (including most American firms) also buy concentrates of some products from specialized producers, and the production of such flavor concentrates is an industry in itself. Chemical extracts or essences are not necessarily illegal, but they are very rarely used except in the lowest-quality products. Where they are used, the liqueur must be designated as "imitation" or "artificial" (America) or "fantaisie" (in France) on the label. The brilliant colors of most liqueurs do not arise naturally during production but are, again, based on vegetable substances (such as saffron) or other natural food colorings.

There are two basic means by which the flavor and aroma of the raw products—plants, herbs, fruits—are transformed into the liquid base of a liqueur: *maceration* and *distillation*. The first is the simplest, consisting merely of soaking substances in the base alcohol (either neutral grain alcohol or an *eau-de-vie* like cognac or armagnac) for a sufficient period of time for the alcohol to become impregnated with the character of the substance being macerated. The principle is exactly the same as that involved in making tea. In practice, it is generally the soft fruits (strawberries, black currants, raspberries, etc.) that undergo this treatment, but stone fruits (cherries, apricots), coffee beans, vanilla pods, and orange peels may also be macerated. A related technique, also used for vanilla or cocoa beans, is *percolation*. As in the household coffee percolator, this consists simply of passing water or alcohol through a layer of beans or pods, extracting the flavor and color as the liquid drips through.

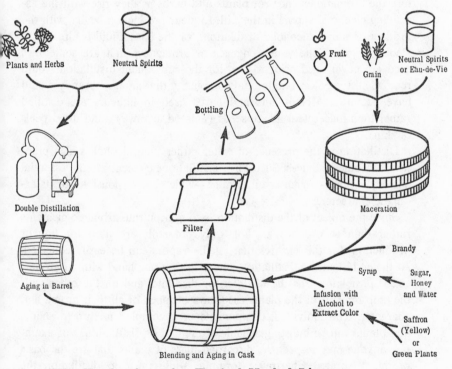

The Production of a Typical Herbal Liqueur

Maceration may last from only a few days up to several months and can take place in anything from a glass demijohn to gigantic vats of stainless steel, enamel, or wood. Where wood vessels are still used, they are generally very old and do not impart any character of their own, unlike the new oak casks used for brandy or whiskey. Of primary importance is the quality of the fruit utilized, which must be perfectly ripe and without any sign of rot. Neutral, high-proof (95–97%) alcohol is used for the great majority of liqueurs, and variations in flavor and quality depend essentially on the condition of the fruit and the length of maceration. Cognac, armagnac, and other brandies may also be used, and in this case the quality of such *eau-de-vie* will also have a major effect on the character of the resulting liqueur.

The process of distillation is discussed in some depth in the first chapter. In the fabrication of liqueurs, the object of distillation is not to concentrate the liquid into a highly alcoholic spirit but, rather, to capture the aromatic essences of plants and herbs as they rise with the ascending alcoholic vapors in the still. Liqueur production begins with the product of simple alcoholic distillation, for the base liquid is already an alcoholic spirit. The young cognacs or armagnacs that are sometimes used are never aged prior to use, for the subsequent distillation would remove all the color, tannin, and complexity that an aged brandy would have acquired. Most plants and herbs used in liqueurs are distilled rather than macerated, as are seeds (aniseed, caraway) and dried peels or skins.

Distillation in the presence of water rather than alcohol is also practiced in some instances. Successive distillations concentrate the essential oils of the plant— such as oil of mint—which are responsible for its aromatic character.

Since the object of the distillation is to concentrate aromatic elements rather than to produce alcohol, only pot stills are used for liqueur production, for this ensures that all the vapors can be easily collected. At the end of such a distillation, one is left on one hand with an aromatized spirit known as the *alcoolat,* or distillate, and on the other with the limp remains of the plants used, now stripped of all their aroma and character. The individual components of a complex mixture of herbs and plants will be indistinguishable at the end of distillation. For example, anyone may inspect the discarded mass of plants that are the basis of the celebrated Chartreuse formula, while prior to distillation the kinds and proportions of plants used is, not surprisingly, guarded in utmost secrecy.

The production of many liqueurs involves various combinations of the above techniques, as several different distillates and infusions (the aromatized spirit that results from maceration) may be blended together to create the final product. Distillation may also be preceded by a period of maceration, or the distillate itself may be redistilled two or three times, perhaps with the addition of fresh aromatizing substances, to obtain a greater concentration of flavor and aroma.

After the preparation of the necessary distillates and/or infusions, the particular "house blend" of the liqueur is made. A liqueur is almost never the result of the simple distillation or maceration of a single plant or fruit, as the primary flavor must be balanced and enhanced through the use of small amounts of supporting ingredients. Thus, anisette or mandarin will probably also contain a proportion of lemon-and orange-peel distillates; blackberry liqueur may include infusions of black currants and raspberries. These blending operations are extremely delicate, and they often determine whether the resulting liqueur is clumsy or elegant, well balanced or awkward.

This blend is then adjusted by the addition of sugar (usually in the form of a simple syrup) or honey, water, and alcohol. Neutral spirits and water are added in proportions calculated to give the desired alcohol content, which is generally 25–40% (though some of the herbal liqueurs may go as high as 55%). An aged brandy may also be added to give more complexity to the liqueur. At this point, color is given to many liqueurs, for distillates are always colorless, and the color extracted during infusion may not be sufficiently strong. Color may be derived from certified food colors or from infusions of plants or fruits: yellow from saffron; green from various leaves; brown from tea, coffee, or cocoa; red from cherries; red-violet from black currants.

Some liqueurs (particularly anisette, kümmel, and orange curaçaos) are cold-stabilized before being finally filtered, so that certain oils may be removed which would otherwise give the liquid a cloudy appearance in cold temperatures. Liqueurs are now expected to withstand extreme variations in temperature and climate throughout the world, so this final operation of filtering is very important. Except for a few days or weeks of resting (or "marrying") the final blend, most liqueurs do not need further aging and may be bottled as soon as is convenient after being filtered.

Thus the creation of most liqueurs comprises several essential stages:
1) preparation of the aromatized bases for the liqueurs by either distillation, percolation, or maceration, or by some combination of these methods;
2) mixing of the final blend and, if necessary, aging;
3) the addition of sugar, water, and alcohol;
4) a generally short period to rest the final product;
5) coloring;
6) cold-stabilizing and filtering;
7) bottling.

Of course, not every liqueur will go through all of these stages, but the preparation of many famous brands is certainly more complicated than merely flavoring and sweetening an alcoholic spirit.

The drinking and appreciation of modern liqueurs have progressed far beyond the original after-dinner or before-bed draught of sweetened medicinal spirit—although late evening remains one of the most pleasant times to enjoy the somewhat sweet, soft complexity of a drink that demands slow and relaxed sipping. Most liqueur houses recommend that their products be drunk chilled, either by cooling in a refrigerator or by being served over cracked or shaved ice. Apart from simply reflecting the current (particularly American) preference for cold drinks of all sorts, the primary function of such chilling is to cut the impression of sweetness that is characteristic to some degree of all liqueurs. Unlike wines, most liqueurs should not suffer any perceptible loss of character or aroma from this practice; in fact, many people do prefer the less intense, sometimes more subtle, flavors that result from the dilution of the melting ice. We would not, however, recommend freezing (as opposed to chilling) liqueurs before serving, for while such extreme cold may "soften" an ordinary liqueur or mask its lack of character, it can only dull the finer, more complex ones.

Most liqueurs and cordials, particularly the more modern ones, are today included in mixed-drink concoctions of all kinds, invented by barmen and marketing men from all over the world. Without going into the merits or faults of any particular drink (several creations are given in a later chapter), we would only remark that many of the complex herbal liqueurs in particular need a fine touch to be well blended, and that the simpler recipes are generally the more successful. One exception is perhaps the pousse café, a great showpiece that consists of several liqueurs of different colors carefully floated one on top of another in a narrow glass.

It is in the kitchen that liqueurs have perhaps seen their greatest renaissance in recent times, as the efforts of such firms as Grand Marnier have resulted in an important increase in the use of liqueurs in cooking. While their sweetness renders most liqueurs particularly suitable for desserts, interesting results can also be achieved by using small quantities of liqueurs in entrees or main dishes.

It is not true that a liqueur's high alcohol content prevents *any* change in flavor once the bottle has been opened, but most companies estimate that there should be no perceptible difference in their products for at least several years. Even then, detectable deterioration is likely to occur only if small quantities of the liqueur remain in an otherwise empty bottle, so you need have no real concern over a bottle that serves for several months or more before being finished. Perhaps the only exception to this general rule are a few low-alcohol (under 20%) fresh-fruit liqueurs, such as creme de cassis. The latter does change fairly rapidly in both color and flavor, and should be consumed within a few months at most.

Like other spirits, liqueurs should be stored in an upright position, whether open or sealed, to avoid any possible deterioration of the cork due to prolonged contact with the alcohol in the liqueur.

Finally, a few words on serving. As one of the ingredients in a cocktail, liqueurs are likely to appear in a tall, ice-frosted tumbler or perhaps in stemmed cone-shaped or shallow-bowled sherbet glasses. The latter would also serve for a creme de menthe or anisette poured over shaved or cracked ice. When served alone, liqueurs or cordials are for some reason invariably offered in the smallest glass in the house, usually filled to overflowing. Not only does the first sip require a very steady hand, but such minuscule containers make it almost impossible to enjoy the subtle perfume that is the primary attraction of many liqueurs. We would urge that you use a glass that will hold a reasonable amount of liquid when half to two-thirds full, and that it be in some form of the tulip or chimney shape, which permits concentration rather than diffusion of the aroma. It should also have a stem, to avoid the drink's being warmed by your hand, and be clear to allow one to appreciate the brilliant palette of colors so carefully presented by the producer. Certainly the friendly, relaxed atmosphere of an after-dinner liqueur is the perfect setting to display your finest crystal, be it the thin elegance of Baccarat or the multifaceted harmony of Waterford.

HERBAL LIQUEURS

HERBAL LIQUEURS

Herbs, plants, and spices of known (or suspected) medicinal or digestive properties were the first ingredients added to alcoholic drinks to render them more palatable as well as to improve their restorative qualities. The ancient Greeks and Romans toasted their gods with hippocras, an early "cordial" of wine, honey, and spices, while the honey-based hydromel is still produced in small quantities by Breton farmers. Doubtlessly many glasses of English mead were also drunk after first being flavored with cinnamon, cloves, and nutmeg.

As discussed in the previous chapter, the early medicinal liqueurs were primarily the province of the alchemist. But even more than the alchemist, it was the patience, learning—and often wealth to purchase rare spices—of the monastic orders that were best suited for centuries of experimentation in the search for those medicinal elixirs which were the forerunners of modern herbal liqueurs. The scientifically minded brothers of the Carthusians, Benedictines, Cistercians, and many others dedicated their lives to the development of these liqueurs, many of which did have certain restorative or medical value in comparison with what passed for medicine in the Middle Ages. The fame of some of these elixirs gradually spread, and the secret formulas of their production became the object of widespread imitation, particularly as the consumption and production of liqueurs expanded in the nineteenth century.

Besides their essentially herbal or plant-derived (as opposed to fruit) base, the primary characteristic of what we have grouped together as "herbal" cordials is that their flavor and aroma are derived from a combination of ingredients in which no single impression dominates. The single-flavor plant liqueurs—like kümmel or anisette—are discussed in the next chapter, for they have much more in common with such other single-flavor liqueurs as coffee or mint than with the complex elixirs that originated in French monasteries.

The simplest herbal liqueurs probably have two dozen different ingredients, but this number may swell to over one hundred. While an exhaustive listing would be impossible, the following probably represent some of the most "common" ingredients of today's herbal liqueurs: angelica root and flowers, hyssop (related to lavender), mint, cloves, cinnamon, pine buds, myrrh, coriander, saffron, thyme, artemisia, rose hips, vanilla pods, tea, nutmeg seeds and pods, juniper berries, bitter almond, aloes, aniseed, lemon peel, orange peel, balsamite, several varieties of wildflowers, honey, gentian root, quinine, caraway, cumin, ginger root, sage, rosemary, licorice root, fennel.

The early herbal elixirs were based almost exclusively on local plants and flowers, so regional variations in both style and ingredients could be fairly pronounced. Today, however, one has come to expect perhaps two fairly distinct styles which encompass the great majority of modern herbal-monastic liqueurs: the fairly intense, spicy-peppery-slightly anise elixirs, generally available in both yellow and green varieties, as typified by Chartreuse; and the slightly more mellow, less spicy, floral-vanilla liqueurs, brown or amber in color, typified by Bénédictine. Slightly different are such yellow Italian liqueurs as Galliano or Fior d'Alpe, which tend to be a bit sweeter and softer, with more vanilla-anise character.

CHARTREUSE is without doubt the dean of herbal liqueurs, by reputation if not by sales. Even its competitors acknowledge its complexity and finesse, although this does not necessarily mean that you, the consumer, will like it better than other, similar products. The basic Chartreuse recipe dates from 1605, when the secret of an "Elixir de Longue Vie" was given to a Carthusian monastery near Paris by the Maréchal d'Estrées, a captain under Henri IV. It was only after a century and a half that the final blend, consisting of some 130 plants, was finished in 1764 at the Carthusians' original home in the Massif de la Chartreuse, in southeastern France. Both an Elixir de Santé and an Elixir de Table were produced; the latter is today's green Chartreuse, while the yellow version of Chartreuse was not created until 1838, subsequent to the monks' flight during the French Revolution and their return to the monastery in 1817. After a second forced flight, at the end of the nineteenth century, a distillery was established in Tarragona, Spain (in 1903), which has continued to operate even after the Carthusians again returned to France. After World War I, both the production and distribution of Chartreuse liqueur was sold to a private, secular corporation, although the formula itself and direction of production remain in the hands of three Carthusian brothers who work daily in the Voiron distillery.

The formulas for both green and yellow Chartreuse are similar, although the latter is somewhat sweeter and contains honey rather than just sugar for sweetening. Several different batches of plants are distilled separately in the presence of neutral, high-proof grape alcohol, and the final blend—after the addition of water, sugar and/or honey, and coloring—is made almost immediately. The liqueur is then aged for several years in ancient eastern-European-oak vats, and it is doubtless this unusual period of aging in combination with the complexity of the ingredients that gives Chartreuse its inimitable character. Small quantities of both green and yellow are aged for twelve years and then bottled and offered as Chartreuse V.E.P. (Vieillissement exceptionnellement prolongé).

As with all the herbal liqueurs, it is extremely difficult to describe the taste of Chartreuse to one who has never tried it. The green, bottled at 55° (the V.E.P. loses one degree, to 54°, during its long aging), has a fairly forceful spicy-peppery-herbal-minty taste and aroma and only light sweetness; the over-all impression is of an extremely complex yet well-balanced liqueur. The yellow is less strong (40°, or 42° for the V.E.P.), though just as complex; its medium sweetness and slight honey undertones leave it softer and rounder than the green, particularly in the V.E.P. (which in style almost reminds one of a creamy, well-aged Sauternes). The original medicinal elixir is also still produced; unsweetened and bottled at 71°, it is sold primarily in pharmacies—though we've been told that some Americans insist on drinking it as a liqueur! In 1972, an apéritif mixture of green Chartreuse and orange juice was introduced under the name of Chartreuse Orange. It is a pleasant enough drink, a bit like an uncarbonated bitter orange, but retains only a little of the true Chartreuse character.

The Chartreuse distillery and aging cellars in Voiron, near Grenoble, are open throughout the year for visits and tasting; in nearby La Correrie is a museum dedicated to the Carthusian order.

The recipe for BÉNÉDICTINE, the best-known French herbal liqueur, actually dates from a century before that of Chartreuse, as it is thought to have been compounded around 1510 by the Benedictine monk Dom Bernardo Vincelli at the Abbey of Fécamp. However, the recipe was lost in the destruction of the Fécamp Abbey during the Revolution and did not reappear until discovered in some manuscripts by a Fécamp merchant, Alexandre Le Grand, in 1863, wherein he found a direct descendant of the original formula. Production of Bénédictine has been completely secular and in the hands of the Le Grand family ever since, although the religious history of the liqueur continues to be emphasized.

Le Grand built an ornate, Renaissance-style palace in Fécamp in 1876 which houses the Bénédictine distillery and aging cellars, as well as a religious museum and an interesting collection of Bénédictine imitators and counterfeits. The actual recipe consists of twenty-seven different herbs and dried plants, including Sri Lanka (Ceylon) tea, juniper berries, and balm (myrrh), as well as the more common angelica, cinnamon, cloves, nutmeg, and vanilla. Weighing and sorting the ingredients into five separate preparations is done by hand; these are then either distilled or macerated (lemon peel, vanilla pods) in neutral, 96% alcohol bought from state distilleries. Still separate, the semifinished batches are aged in old oak casks for about six months before being blended together for another several months' aging in larger oak. Finally, water, alcohol (if necessary), sugar syrup, honey, caramel (for color), and saffron (to fix the color and the blend) are thoroughly mixed in before a double filtration and bottling at 43°.

Noting the trend toward drier liqueurs, a combination of Bénédictine and brandy was developed in 1938; B AND B now accounts for nearly half of the total production at Fécamp and approximately 75 per cent of Bénédictine's sales in the United States. Bénédictine now owns the small firm of Comandon in Jarnac, whence it brings young cognacs to Fécamp to complete their aging. The final B and B blend is about 40 per cent five- or six-year-old cognac and 60 per cent Bénédictine.

The dark-amber color of both Bénédictine and B and B contrasts with the traditional green or yellow herbal liqueurs, and this reflects a slightly different style as well. Bénédictine is rounder, softer, and less spicy than most of the Chartreuse-type liqueurs; its flavors tend toward the darker, richer shades of vanilla, honey, and bitter almond rather than the intense, almost peppery character of Chartreuse or Izarra. Bénédictine is medium sweet; B and B has similar flavors, but is drier and possesses definite cognac character.

The Bénédictine distillery-museum in Fécamp is also open to visitors, though a small charge is made for a tour and tasting. The building itself is fairly impressive (if a bit ostentatious), and the entry charge is much less than you would pay for a glass of Bénédictine in a cafe. Should you be arriving in France via one of the cross-Channel ferries, a visit to Fécamp is an interesting detour.

Most of the other French herbal liqueurs, whether or not they had or maintain any monastic connections, follow the style of Chartreuse rather than Bénédictine. One of the best (Hemingway's opinion notwithstanding) is the Basque liqueur IZARRA, which is produced in Bayonne, just north of the Spanish frontier. *Izarra* means "star" in Basque, hence the red star that adorns the Izarra label, while the motto *"edari maite parregabea"* modestly claims that there is none other as good to drink!

While the Izarra recipe dates from the end of the seventeenth century, it has been produced commercially only since the mid-nineteenth century, appearing about the same time as Bénédictine. The Bayonne distillery now produces approximately 1 million bottles per year, and other plants are situated in Spain, Mexico, Switzerland, and Venezuela. Both green and yellow Izarra are offered, at 51° (50° in the United States due to import duties) and 40° respectively. Both include local sureau (elder) flowers from the Pyrenees in their ingredients, which number forty-eight for the green and thirty-two for the yellow. Three afternoons a week the various ingredients are sorted and blended by hand, amounting to a total of nearly forty thousand separate weighing operations per year to combine the five kilograms of plants which are required to produce each four hundred liters of liqueur. Some ingredients are distilled in pure alcohol, while others are macerated for three to four months in a blend of pure alcohol and armagnac. The final blend in fact includes about 15 per cent armagnac, testimony to the traditional contacts between the Armagnac region and the Bayonne shippers. The resulting infusion and distillates are then aged together for six months in 40-hectoliter oak casks, at which time sugar, acacia honey, water, and coloring matter are added prior to a further six months of aging.

While Izarra may lack some of the complexity and finesse of Chartreuse, its fresh, spicy-minty character is more straightforward and needs less concentration to be appreciated—perhaps reflecting the difference between the contemplative religious origins of Chartreuse and the warmer, secular atmosphere of the Pays Basque. While not so sweet as to require chilling, the flavors do stand up well to the chilling or ice cubes recommended.

Izarra has also recently acquired the nearby production of LIQUEUR D'HENDAYE, whose similar recipe is actually a bit older than that of

Izarra. It will probably remain a strictly regional product, though you might find an on-the-spot comparison between the two interesting.

The Bordeaux suburb of Cenon is the home of VIEILLE CURE, another herbal liqueur available in both yellow and green. Originally known as La Chaleureuse, the name was changed around the turn of this century when a company was formed around the product. Production is now controlled by Intermarque, a subsidiary of Bols, which is also responsible for Cordial Médoc and the French production from imported essences of both Bols liqueurs and Tia Maria.

All the fifty-odd ingredients of Vieille Cure are macerated for twenty-four hours in a mixture of water and neutral alcohol before being distilled. The resulting distillate is then aged for up to three years in various sizes of oak before the final blend, with sugar syrup, honey, water, and alcohol, is made. Somewhat unusually, both yellow and green varieties are made from the same blend, but the green contains a higher proportion of the extract-distillate and is bottled at a higher proof. A blend of cognac and armagnac is included in a special bottling of Vieille Cure, but the standard product employs neutral alcohol exclusively. The facilities at Cenon produce perhaps 250,000 liters of Vieille Cure annually, and extract is also shipped abroad to be finished in foreign plants.

Vieille Cure is a good, average liqueur of its type, with an anise-vanilla-herbal character, though it is perhaps a bit less well balanced than Chartreuse or Izarra; the yellow is slightly lighter and sweeter than the green.

Pagès's VERVEINE DU VELAY was introduced in 1859 and is a fairly well-known herbal liqueur in France, though it is not prominent in either the United States or Great Britain. Emphasis is placed on the digestive qualities of the yellow or green Verveine, the primary ingredient of which is harvested from special plantations in Auvergne; Pagès also offers tea infusions of verveine and other calmative herbs, in addition to several other liqueurs.

Among the many other French herbal liqueurs of both monastic and secular origins, note should perhaps be made of AIGUEBELLE, CARMELINE, LA SÉNANCOLE, TRAPPASTINE, SAPINDOR, and RASPAIL, most of which were commercially introduced in the nineteenth century. The first four were originally monastic elixirs (primarily Cistercian), Sapindor is bottled in a distinctive tree-trunk bottle, and Raspail was invented in the mid-nineteenth century by a scientist of the same name.

Raspail and Trappastine are Bénédictine-like; the rest are in the style of Chartreuse and are produced in green and/or yellow varieties.

The fame of several Italian herbal liqueurs is second only to that of the French, and Galliano is probably as well known in the United States as Bénédictine. There are several differences between the Italian and French products, though most are a matter of degree rather than totally distinct characteristics. First, the Italian herbal liqueurs are generally found only in one variety—yellow. Secondly, just as yellow Chartreuse is a bit sweeter than green, so most similar Italian products are sweeter than the French. Finally, the style in Italy tends to be less complex, slightly heavier, and with a greater emphasis on an anise-vanilla character not noticeable in French herbal liqueurs.

The southern-Italian STREGA, produced in the small coastal town of Benevento, is one of the closest in style to the strong herbal character of the French monastic liqueurs. Its forceful, somewhat medicinal flavors seem just a bit rough, however, and the medium body and sweetness could stand more finesse and better balance.

Most of the Italian herbal liqueurs are from the North of Italy and are traditionally based on the wildflowers that grow in abundance in the Alpine meadows. The recipes are generally similar, and many, such as FIOR D'ALPE and MILLEFIORI CUCCHI, are bottled with small branches inside each bottle, around which sugar crystals form. This is a fairly delicate operation, for the liqueur must be bottled when warm so that the crystallization will occur upon cooling. As might be expected, these liqueurs are fairly sweet; Millefiori Cucchi has a sugar content of 40 per cent, although its relatively high alcohol content of 45° keeps it from being cloying. Its herbal-vanilla character is quite pleasant, perhaps a bit more subtle and certainly as good as its better-known cousin, Galliano. The Fior d'Alpe from Isolabella may now be found with an obscene plastic branch in the bottle; its minty-herbal character is a bit heavy, but pleasant.

While many Americans think of it as a recently introduced product, GALLIANO was actually created around the turn of this century by Arturo Vaccari of Livorno, in honor of an Italian hero of the Italo-Abyssinian war in Ethiopia, Major Giuseppe Galliano. The liqueur commemorates the major's defense of Fort Enda Jesus, which is still pictured on the label. After World War II, the production of Galliano was taken over by the Distillerie Riunite di Liquori, which now operates from a modern plant in Solaro, near Milano, where Liquore Galliano constitutes 90 per cent of the production.

Galliano is based on several separate distillations of various herbs and plants, which produce a highly concentrated "essence" of 90–95% alcohol. This essence is then held in stainless-steel tanks for about three months before it is blended with water, sugar, and coloring, and after several more weeks, bottled in its distinctive tall bottle. Its color is bright gold-yellow, and the anise-vanilla-herbal character has some complexity and a clean finish. With moderate body and sweetness, its final alcohol content of 40° G.L. is well balanced, though its fairly soft, round flavors may seem a bit timid to those who prefer the more intense French products.

Although it was first introduced to the United States in 1925, Galliano's popularity was restricted to the Italian-American community until the 1960s. Largely due to the efforts of its U.S. distributor, McKesson and Co., who conducted an intensive advertising campaign based on the "Harvey Wallbanger" cocktail, Galliano achieved a tremendous marketing success; in 1973 its sales in the United States were in the vicinity of 4 million bottles. Oddly enough, it has never been one of the best-selling liqueurs in Italy, though it is available on the domestic market. There are now several other Galliano-style liqueurs on the market, including LIQUORE GAETANO, VALENTINO, and Stock's LIQUORE ROIANO. An American product, NEAPOLITAN LIQUEUR, is also available, which has a distinctly anise character.

Other Italian herbal liqueurs include CENTHERB, also referred to as MENTUCCIA, and CERTOSA, though most are known only in Italy itself.

Somewhat similar in style to Galliano is the Spanish CUARENTA Y TRES (43), which is a pale-gold liqueur produced, not surprisingly, from a blend of forty-three different herbs and plants. It is a "fat," sweet concoction whose primary flavor is rather neutral vanilla, with anise-orange undertones.

There is no German family of liqueurs as similar in style to one another as many of the French and Italian herbal creations, unless one includes the ever-present bitters, which are consumed in vast quantities. The best-known Chartreuse-type German liqueur may be Munich's ESCORIAL GRÜN, a fairly spicy green liqueur packaged in a distinctive flat, painted-ceramic bottle. A curious if very pleasant blend of herbal-bitter character can be found in JAGERMEISTER; many would probably recognize its rather medicinal-appearing stag-and-cross label. It is medium brown-green in color, with a complex herbal nose that might remind one in turn of anise, mint, gentian, quinine, and honey. Sweetness is light-medium, and the flavors are an interesting combination of Bénédictine-Chartreuse-bitters.

Another unusual German herbal-based liqueur is STONSDORFER, a generic name that includes bilberry (whortleberry) juice-herbal liqueurs from the Stonsdorf district. The original, made by the Koerner distillery since 1810, is labeled ECHT STONSDORFER, and it includes forty-three herbs and plants blended with deep red-purple bilberry juice. Fairly light-bodied and not too sweet, it is a slightly bitter, very spicy (pepper-nutmeg-cinnamon-anise-sage), and quite distinctive combination, in which only a hint of the fruit-juice base is apparent.

Two Spanish liqueurs popular in Andalucía are ESTOMACAL-BONET and CALISAY. The former is not really a bitters but is, rather, a dark-green liqueur similar to a rather simple Izarra, with herbal-citrus character. Calisay, on the other hand, is a fairly sweet, soft digestive with strong quinine character.

Switzerland also offers an herbal liqueur, GRANDE GRUYÈRE, which, despite its name, is not made from Swiss cheese.

Finally, mention should be made of the only English herbal liqueur (apart from those which are scotch-based and discussed separately), BRONTE. Known as the Yorkshire liqueur, it is a fairly simple blend of apricot-orange-spicy flavors and very slight brandy character. Light-moderate in body with moderate sweetness, it has a light-to-medium amber color.

While the specialty or individual brands described above are generally the more complex and interesting examples of herbal liqueurs, many of the large houses that offer a wide range of products also include an herbal blend or two. The best of these is probably GARNIER'S LIQUEUR D'OR, which is similar in both style and complexity to yellow Chartreuse. It is perhaps a touch less sweet and less intense, and is bottled with small flakes of gold leaf in suspension, as in German Goldwasser. Among the other large producers you will find

ROCHER FRÈRES GENALPY, which has a leafy-plant character rather than spiciness; LEJAY-LAGOUTE LIQUEUR JAUNE; GET FRÈRES CROIX D'OC; CUSENIER MAZARINE, a fairly pleasant, spicy-yellow liqueur that dates from a 1637 recipe of the Abbaye de Montbenoit; DE KUYPER DELECTA; BOLS BERNADINE, a simple orange-anise-vanilla blend, amber in color, vaguely in the style of Bénédictine; and STOCK LIQUORE ROIANO, a slightly unbalanced herbal-vanilla-anise liqueur between Galliano and Strega. American-produced herbals, none of which are well known, include LEROUX CLARISTINE, based on a formula from the Clarisse Convent in Dinant, Belgium. The prize for worst of breed goes to ECKES (who produce two of Germany's best-selling brandies, Chantré and Mariacron) LAURENTINER KLOSTER LIKOR, a dull, sugary, unpleasant blend which proves that there is more to making a good liqueur than just throwing a few plants into a still.

SEED AND PLANT LIQUEURS

SEED AND PLANT LIQUEURS

Seed liqueurs share the medicinal-*digestif* heritage of the herbal blends discussed in the preceding chapter, as caraway, anise, cumin, mint, and coffee are all known for their restorative properties as well as for their refreshing tastes. But while these may be found among the scores of ingredients out of which herbal liqueurs are created, they and some others have distinguished themselves from the rest of the spices, seeds, and plants by the fact that they also provide the base for "pure" liqueurs, in which a single flavor predominates. The word "predominates" is used purposely, for it is in fact rare that only a single raw product is utilized; subtle, complementary aromatic essences are almost always added to give each product its own particular style.

ANISETTE is one of the oldest liqueurs known, as anise-based beverages have long been enjoyed both for their digestive qualities and for their powerful character. Hippocrates, for example, drank "anisum" on special occasions. Anisette and anise-based apéritifs are particularly popular in southern France and Spain, while red anisette is a traditional drink in Creole Louisiana.

The best-known producer of anisette is MARIE BRIZARD, which was founded in Bordeaux in 1755. Marie Brizard was perhaps the best known of the eighteenth-century French liqueur houses, a reputation that was aided by the position of Bordeaux as a major port both to receive foreign spices and to export Marie Brizard's finished liqueurs. Today the company offers some twenty-eight liqueurs, but anisette remains by far the most important. Four fifths of all anisette consumed in France is that of Marie Brizard, and a separate plant in Spain produces anisette for thirsty Spaniards. It is quite common to add several other ingredients to anisettes, and Marie Brizard includes distillates of sixteen other seeds, plants, and citrus skins, in addition to aniseed.[1]

---

[1] Although the tastes are similar, anisette does not contain any licorice flavoring; the latter is obtained from the leguminous plant *Glycyrrhiza glabra,* while aniseed is from the herbaceous *Pimpinella anisum.*

The latter is distilled in pure alcohol, and 20–40 per cent of the liquid may be removed in the form of heads and tails, in order to eliminate the unwanted oils that are one of the major problems in the production of anisette (and also kümmel and curaçao). The resulting concentrate, at 83–86% alcohol, is then blended with the other distillates and finally finished by the addition of sugar syrup, water, and alcohol. Anisette must then be cooled to promote the coagulation of oils, which would otherwise turn the liquid cloudy at low temperatures, before it is finally filtered and bottled. One American producer, ARROW, purposely retains some of these oils so that their anisette turns cloudy when mixed with ice or water.

Anisette is one of the sweetest liqueurs, with the sugar content generally around 40 per cent, and contains only 25–30% alcohol. The Marie Brizard has a relatively subtle anise aroma, and its flavors are soft and delicate rather than powerful. Despite its sweetness, the aftertaste is clean and not cloying. Most other French anisettes, including GARNIER, ROCHER, and to a lesser extent CUSENIER, follow this soft style, while the Italian and Dutch products tend to be heavier, stronger, and possibly sweeter. Anisette is often served over ice, as this dilutes the sweetness but does not impair the strong aroma.

Related to anisette is the Italian liqueur SAMBUCA, which is derived from the white-flowered elder bush, *Sambucus nigra,* found on many Italian hillsides. Since its fruit is very similar to aniseed and the liqueur is traditionally flavored with anise, Sambuca is virtually indisinguishable from some anisettes. It should have a slightly lighter, more flowery character than anisette, and is traditionally served with three roasted coffee beans floating on the top of the liqueur. MOLINARI is considered one of the most important producers, and the largest exporter of Sambuca is LUXARDO. Some coffee-flavored Sambuca is also produced.

Anise-flavored alcoholic beverages are most often used as apéritifs, many of which were themselves designed as substitutes for ABSINTHE. The latter, in which macerated wormwood was an essential ingredient, was very popular in the late-nineteenth and early-twentieth centuries, until it was banned in most countries because of its potency and allegedly undesirable side effects. One need only look at Degas' brilliant portrait of *L'Absinthe* to note the vacant stare and lifelessness that were considered to be common among absinthe drinkers of the time. Absinthe was traditionally served dripped slowly over a sugar cube held in a specially perforated spoon or with ice and water, which gave it a cloudy appearance. Today, absinthe has been replaced by French *pastis*-like PERNOD and RICARD, Italy's MISTRA, Greek OUZO, and the American HERBSAINT. Many "liqueurs" such as Greece's MASTIC or the Turkish State Monopoly's CLUB RAKI are strong, only slightly sweetened anise drinks whose fiery alcoholic character is much closer to the anise apéritifs than to the sweet, soft anisette liqueurs.

Caraway and cumin seeds (both belong to the Umbelliferae family), which today are the basis of KÜMMEL, have been used in the preparation of digestive beverages for at least two thousand years; the ancient Greeks knew of their properties, and cumin is mentioned in the Book of Isaiah. The Amsterdam firm of LUCAS BOLS was the first to produce a kümmel liqueur, at the end of the sixteenth century. The Bols operation left family hands after over two hundred years and today offers a complete range of approximately seventy-five cordials and spirits, which are exported to over 130 countries, the most important product probably being Genever (Dutch) gin. The new Bols plant at Nieuw-Vennep is very modern, and Bols also controls foreign plants elsewhere in Europe, in South Africa, in Argentina, and in the United States. These plants operate independently, but samples are periodically sent to the head office in the Netherlands for analysis. While the Nieuw-Vennep plant is not open to casual visitors, a tasting bar is maintained near the site of the original Lucas Bols distillery in Amsterdam.

Kümmel is essentially a distillate of caraway and/or cumin seeds in neutral alcohol, and may also be flavored with small amounts of aniseed and fennel oil; the cheapest producers may cut corners by simply adding cumin oil to the alcohol. While kümmel remained a Dutch specialty, it soon became very popular in Russia, Germany, and the Baltic countries. "ALLASCH" KÜMMEL, named for a town in Latvia, is a generally high-quality product made from a distillate of cumin, coriander, aniseed, and violet roots, in which the use of cumin oil is forbidden. EISKÜMMEL is produced by bottling a sweet kümmel while it is still warm, thus inducing the formation of sugar crystals in the bottle, which may have a cone-shaped punt around which the crystals collect.

Most kümmel is fairly dry, clear in color, with a pronounced, somewhat bitter caraway-seed aroma and flavor and often slight undertones of anise. The best is from Holland and Germany, although kümmel may be found in the lists of almost every major liqueur producer. GILKA, a well-known German kümmel produced since 1836, has a clean caraway aroma and fairly light sweetness that nicely balances the caraway flavors and slightly alcoholic aftertaste.

A cool, refreshing taste as well as its digestive properties have made CREME DE MENTHE one of the most popular of all liqueurs, particularly in the United States. Because of the immediate and universal appeal of mint, it is one of the few liqueurs generally produced without the addition of complementary flavors. Most cremes de menthe are, however, blends of carefully selected mint leaves, most commonly from southern France, England, or the northwestern United States. While creme de menthe is traditionally an after-dinner drink, often served over crushed or shaved ice, recent publicity has emphasized the thirst-quenching properties of mint liqueurs when mixed with cold water or soda as a cocktail or long drink. This approach has been particularly successful for GET FRÈRES PIPPERMINT, which now sells a million bottles annually in France.

"Pippermint," which was introduced by Get in 1859 and trade-marked in 1868, is produced from a blend of five different mints (from Russia, Bulgaria, and Morocco, as well as France and England), which is successively distilled in the presence of water until the desired concentration of the essential mint oils is obtained. This concentrate, one liter of which will suffice for one thousand liters of Pippermint, is then blended with water, neutral alcohol, sugar syrup, and coloring (for green only).

Those mint liqueurs labeled PIPPERMINT, FREEZOMINT (Cusenier), or PEPPERMINT (several) might be thought to be lighter and fresher than the traditional "creme de menthe," but this is not universally the case. Certainly the Get Pippermint is delightfully fresh, with a crisp, candy-cane peppermint aroma and taste and a clean finish despite its high (46–48 per cent) sugar content. Other French products, whether labeled creme de menthe or peppermint, tend to be fresher and lighter than the more complex and somewhat sweeter one made by BOLS, although REGNIER (Cointreau) is disappointingly dull. American products are generally between the French and Dutch in style, with pleasant, fresh flavors and moderate body. There are also differences which result from the choice of mints used, with the emphasis usually on either peppermint or spearmint.

Creme de menthe is normally available in clear and green varieties, and occasionally other colors as well. There is no difference in taste among the various colors, which are created through the use of tasteless vegetable coloring.

PEPPERMINT SCHNAPPS is offered by several American houses; it is clear in color and is slightly lighter and less sweet than the traditional creme de menthe.

Rivaling creme de menthe and anisette in popularity is the mild, rich CREME DE CACAO, which is produced by all the major liqueur houses. Today, creme de cacao is almost universally blended with a proportion of an infusion of vanilla pods, which are the unripe fruit of a climbing plant that grows around the cocoa trees in the plantations of West Africa and South America. The best vanilla is said to come from the island of Réunion, near Madagascar, where it was introduced by French colonial planters.

While many think of creme de cacao as a very simple liqueur, a well-balanced result can be obtained only with careful attention to the treatment of both cocoa beans and vanilla pods. The former are first shelled and roasted, before being distilled with neutral alcohol. The dried vanilla pods are generally macerated, again in neutral alcohol, before being blended with the cacao distillate. Other infusions or distillates may also be added, depending on the style of the producer, before the final adjustment with water, alcohol, and sugar. A deep brown, instead of the natural clear color, may be obtained through the addition of coloring matter or by some changes in the production process; Bols, for example, percolates part of their cocoa beans, thus extracting color and other non-volatile substances from the beans.

"Chouao" refers to cocoa from the Chouao region of Venezuela but does not necessarily indicate a creme de cacao of any noticeably different style.

Most cremes de cacao are full-bodied and sweet, though you will find differences in the depth of flavor and the balance between cocoa and vanilla character. There do not seem to be many detectable national variations in style, although American cremes de cacao tend to be slightly less sweet than the Europeans. Among the French houses, ROCHER and MARIE BRIZARD are quite well balanced and not sugary, while GARNIER is rather weak in flavor. In America, LEROUX has a fairly rich cocoa-bean-chocolate aroma. A Swiss liqueur, MARMOT CHOCO-LATE, has actual pieces of chocolate floating in it.

Creme de cacao is most often drunk in combination with other spirits or foods, as its smooth character and sweetness make it an excellent mixer. It is an integral part of the well-known grasshopper and (brandy) alexander cocktails, and is often enjoyed poured over vanilla ice cream as a simple dessert.

The "mixability" of cocoa-chocolate flavors has led to the creation of several liqueurs that have two primary flavors instead of just one. The traditional after-dinner mint is reflected in VANDERMINT, a sweet, heavy Dutch liqueur in which the mint character predominates, and in ROYAL MINT-CHOCOLATE LIQUEUR, made in France for the English firm of Hallgarten. The latter is quite pleasant, as the fresh mint flavor nicely balances the heavy body and sweetness; unusually, it is nearly clear in color. Both America's LEROUX and HIRAM WALKER offer a line of chocolate cordials that include mint, cherry, banana, and raspberry. Orange, perhaps the most popular of the fruit flavors, is combined with chocolate in SABRA, from Israel, which is fairly sweet, rich, and well balanced between the softness of chocolate and the slightly bitter taste of oranges. A bit more complex is VERAÑA, an interesting combination of chocolate-orange-vanilla-citrus-bitter almond flavors produced by the Marie Brizard establishment in Seville, Spain. CHERI-SUISSE was introduced in the late 1960s by Seagram and marketed in the United States as a companion to Vandermint, Pasha, and Sabra. Its chocolate-covered-cherry character is quite sweet and fairly simple, but it is nevertheless pleasant. Similar to this sweet, candied maraschino-cherry style is the LEROUX CHOCOLATE CHERRY.

Chocolate-coconut cordials have also acquired some popularity. Usually quite sweet, these include AFRI KOKO, from the West African country of Sierra Leone, CHOCOCO, produced in the Virgin Islands, and the American CHOCLAIR from Arrow.

A few producers offer a CREME DE VANILLE, though vanilla is most often found as a complementary rather than a primary flavor. Vanilla extract is also well known to cooks throughout the world, and the chemically produced imitation flavor of "vanillin" is permitted in American liqueurs, without the mention "artificial" on the label, up to a maximum of forty parts per million.

In recent years many people have switched their allegiance from the cocoa-chocolate liqueurs to those based on COFFEE, sometimes labeled CREME DE MOCHA (or MOKA), a slightly less sweet taste that also has wide appeal. It is the specialty products that have been the leaders in this group, as both the Jamaican TIA MARIA and the Mexican KAHLÚA enjoy world-wide recognition. Kahlúa has a dry, roasted coffee-bean aroma, although the taste is very sweet. Moderate to full-bodied, it has smooth flavors and is often drunk in a black russian cocktail (Kahlúa and vodka), which cuts its sweetness but also lessens its flavor. Tia Maria is lighter and drier, with a pleasant coffee-cocoa aroma. There seems to be a bit more complexity in the finish, and the taste is less sweet than most other coffee liqueurs.

Coffee liqueurs may be quite distinctive, as the coffee beans employed vary greatly in style and character. PASHA TURKISH COFFEE LIQUEUR, for example, does manage to capture much of the sweet, spicy richness that is typical of actual Turkish coffee, although it may be just a bit too sweet for some. STOCK COFFEE ESPRESSO is rather sugary and weak in flavor, but what character that is present does possess some of the bitterness of an Italian *espresso*. Less distinctive is GALLWEY'S IRISH COFFEE LIQUEUR, which is produced in Waterford from coffee distillate, Irish whiskey, honey, and herbs. The strong coffee-bean aroma is pleasant, but the flavors are simple and weak compared to the distinctive combination of coffee, Irish whiskey, cream, and sugar that has made Irish coffee such a popular drink in the United States. Hawaiian coffee or Kona coffee liqueurs often have strong coffee flavors and tend to be quite sweet.

Many of the large companies also produce coffee liqueurs, although none have achieved the recognition of the specialty products. MARIE BRIZARD CAFÉ is quite good, with strong coffee flavors to balance the heavy body and sweetness, while BOLS MOCCAFÉ and some of the American products tend to be rather less distinctive, relying on the simple, if not unpleasant, flavors that typify American and English coffee. Coffee liqueurs of all types are generally medium sweet or sweeter, but the slight natural bitterness of the coffee flavors often make them seem less sweet than creme de cacao or creme de menthe.

Many liqueurs of all types—herbal, seed, fruit, etc.—have a slight undertone of bitter almond as a useful supporting flavor, and a few employ this or other nutlike flavors as their primary ingredient. These are not generally produced from edible nuts as we know them, but from the stones or kernels of several fruits, including apricots, sloeberries, and cherries. The resulting liqueurs may be offered under several different names, such as CREME DE NOYAUX, CREME DE ALMOND, CREME DE NOISETTE, PRUNELLE, PERSICO, and AMARETTO.

Probably the best known of these "nut" liqueurs is AMARETTO DI

SARONNO, Saronno being a small town in the Northwest of Italy, near Milano. It takes its name from the local biscuits known as "amaretti," which are made with crushed almonds, and the addition of crushed almonds to a bottle of brandy or alcohol has been practiced for centuries. Amaretto itself, however, is produced not from almonds but from apricot pits, a related fruit with very strong bitter-almond character. According to legend, the distillation of apricot pits to produce amaretto was discovered four centuries ago by one Bernardino Luini; the first written reference to "Amaretto di Saronno" was in 1807. Today "amaretto" is a generic term used by several producers, while "Amaretto di Saronno" is the trade-marked name of the best-known producer, the Industria Lombarda Liquori Vini Affini (Illva). Illva is owned by the Reina family, who have a history of liqueur production dating from the eighteenth century; they make the herbal Millefiori Cucchi and several other liqueurs. Amaretto di Saronno is based on neutral alcohol, a distillate of apricot pits, and a few aromatic herbs; some of the pits are crushed to further aid in the release of certain essential oils. It is not aged, but does pass a few months of "marrying" time in stainless-steel tanks before being finally filtered and bottled. The liqueur itself has a rich, fruity-almond aroma and taste that remind one of liquid marzipan; despite its fairly low alcohol content (28%) and medium sugar content (30 per cent), it is well balanced and not sugary, though definitely sweet. The nearby producers of Galliano market an amaretto, under the VACCARI brand, which is a bit simpler and lighter-bodied but retains pleasant almond flavors. American almond liqueurs are generally based on extracts of almond oil and labeled CREME DE ALMOND, though American-produced amaretto liqueurs have recently begun to appear, such as De Kuyper's AMARETTO DI CUPERA.

PRUNELLE is made from a small, berry-like variety of wild plum (*Prunus spinosa*) known in America as the sloe and in Britain and Ireland as the blackthorn. However, two quite different liqueurs may appear under this name: one, produced from the kernel of the sloe, has a nutty-almond taste; the other, from the pulp rather than the kernel, is more properly classed as a fruit liqueur and may at most have a faint almond undertone if a few uncrushed kernels are included. In addition, because *Prunus spinosa* grows wild throughout much of Europe, there may also be regional variations in the character of the fruit. In any event, the nutty prunelles have a rather particular personality that will not appeal to all. CUSENIER PRUNELLIA, made with a certain percentage of cognac, is fairly light-bodied and not too sweet, with a simple, if pleasant, fruity-almond aroma. ROCHER PRUNELLE is fuller-bodied and much sweeter, and has a distinctive raw (unroasted)-nutty character. MARIE BRIZARD PRUNELLE also has a nutty character, while the prunelles of LEJAY-LAGOUTE, STOCK, and BOLS are all fruity, closer in style to American sloe gin.

CREME DE NOISETTE is based on hazelnuts; the German HASELNUSSLIKOER is often blended with lemon peel, mace, and allspice. Pale yellow or amber in color, noisette is generally fairly sweet and simple with some hazelnut character; depending on the blend, it may resemble a light creme de cacao. Another "edible nut" liqueur is the American MACADAMIA NUT LIQUEUR, from Hawaii, which sometimes seems to have slight coffee undertones.

CREME DE NOYAUX is a more general label, but will most often include macerations and/or distillations of apricot or peach pits, perhaps with other fruit kernels or nuts as well. The character is primarily almond, though not always as pronounced as in most amaretti. Two regional armagnac liqueurs, U.C.V.A.'s L'ARMABELLE and Sempé's LIQUEUR SABAZIA, are based on a blend of bitter-almond (*noyaux*) and orange flavors.

PERSICO was an almond liqueur well known in England in the early-eighteenth century. Traditionally based on peaches, it is today produced by BOLS from a distillate of cherries, cherry stones, almonds, and nuts.

While TEA is fairly common in many liqueur recipes, it is rarely used as the basis for its own "pure" liqueur. However, green-tea liqueurs are a traditional Japanese drink, and among these SUNTORY GREEN TEA LIQUEUR is probably the best known outside Japan. Suntory is Japan's largest whiskey producer, but they also make a line of liqueurs, including most of the standard varieties, under the HERMES label. Both Matcha powdered tea and Gyokuro rolled tea are macerated in a blend of brandy and neutral alcohol to produce their distinctive green-tea liqueur, which is quite heavy in body and very sweet (50 per cent sugar). It does retain the character of strong Oriental tea, including the slight bitterness of tea leaves, but its heavy character will probably not have universal appeal.

One of the more unusual liqueurs is produced in Jamaica from the dried bud of the pimento tree, a member of the myrtle family, which produces the clove-like allspice. PIMENT-O-DRAM is medium brown to amber in color and has a distinctively spicy allspice-cinnamon-pepper aroma and definite clove-like taste. Full-bodied and moderately sweet, it is a well-balanced liqueur that, once the initial surprise of its taste is overcome, has a pleasant and certainly distinctive character.

Difficult to classify are the few Chinese liqueurs that have been available in the United States in small quantities since trade with the People's Republic began, in the early 1970s. Those exported are primarily regional specialties; many are sorghum-based and are bottled at 80 to a fiery 108 proof. A GINSENG liqueur is made, along with more esoteric spirits such as CHU YEH CHING, a clear, slightly sweet, rather weedy liqueur with an alcoholic finish, and WU CHIA PI, a spicy, oily, tangerine-colored liqueur of peppery character. Their high alcohol, relatively light sweetness, and unusual (to American and European palates) flavors will not appeal to all, and sales at present are almost exclusively limited to Chinese and Chinese-American communities.

FRUIT LIQUEURS

FRUIT LIQUEURS

Capturing the true flavors of ripe cherries, oranges, and other fruits has long been the goal of chefs and bakers; it is not surprising that liqueur producers have also found "fruitful" inspiration in fresh and dried fruits all over the world. Unlike the herbal and many of the seed liqueurs, fruit cordials have almost always been prepared primarily for gustatory appreciation and enjoyment rather than for medicinal or digestive purposes. While a glass of triple sec or raspberry liqueur may indeed provide a satisfying end to a meal, the taste must be refreshing and should not possess the bitter or very spicy undertones often associated with those beverages whose primary purpose is to aid digestion rather than please the palate. In addition, most people are familiar with the raw products—oranges, cherries, plums, blackberries, etc.—that form the basis of fruit liqueurs, and they thus expect what they are drinking to taste like the fresh fruit they know. You expect an apricot or peach liqueur to be identifiable as such, unlike the traditional herbal liqueurs whose major ingredients may be outside most persons' range of experience and whose over-all impression is that of a complex blend rather than of one, well-known flavor.

Because of the many uses for fruit flavors and essences, a major industry has grown up around the extraction and concentration of these flavors. Several American companies specialize in the production of fruit extracts for use in all phases of the food industry, and in Europe many important companies are situated in Grasse, France, the perfume capital of the world. Whether or not a given liqueur producer uses fresh fruit or concentrated essences depends on both the quality of the production and the availability of fresh fruits in the area. Most European firms seem to employ fresh or dried fruits as much as possible, and many are found in areas noted for their orchards or for particular fruit products. Extracts or essences for particular hard-to-obtain flavors may be purchased either from concentrate specialists or from other liqueur houses which specialize in the desired product. In the United States, on the contrary, the use of fresh fruit seems to be the exception rather than the rule, and the large firms rely on concentrates or extracts that are prepared specifically for use in liqueurs and cordials. These natural fruit extracts should be distinguished from purely chemical products, which are permitted only if the words "artificial" or "imitation" or, in France, *"fantaisie,"* appear on the label.

Orange—Curaçao—Triple Sec

The orange originated in the Orient, gradually spreading westward through the centuries. By the ninth century the bitter orange was known in Spain, while the sweeter variety was not introduced until the fifteenth. Louis XIV brought the first orange tree to the orangerie at Versailles in 1663, and French and Spanish explorers soon transplanted the golden fruit to the New World, establishing important orange plantations in the West Indies. Today, the best of the world's bitter oranges come from the Antilles, Haiti, and Curaçao, while most of the sweet oranges come from the Mediterranean area, especially Spain, North Africa, and Israel, and from the southern and western United States.

All citrus-based liqueurs, including orange, are made not with the fruit itself, but, rather, with the peel, which imparts a more intense, slightly more bitter flavor. The Dutch were the first to distill orange peels, which were brought from the West Indian island of Curaçao by seventeenth-century traders. The Dutch firm of DE KUYPER was founded during this period, in 1695, and is still noted for its Orange Curaçao, which is packaged in a tall, distinctive earthenware crock.

Today, Curaçao and other bitter oranges are dried before shipment to liqueur houses throughout the world; they are then reconstituted with water and/or alcohol, and the very bitter white inner fiber that clings to the peel is removed. The peels may be macerated, but most are distilled in the presence of high-proof neutral alcohol, giving a highly scented essence that concentrates the essential aromatic oils of the orange. (It is these oils that produce sparks if you pinch the mist from an orange peel into a candle flame.)

A few companies offer an orange liqueur labeled simply ORANGE or FINE ORANGE; almost all include both CURAÇAO and TRIPLE SEC in their lines. The first varies considerably from firm to firm, but it most often will be orange-amber in color and may contain brandy in addition to neutral alcohol, which adds to the liqueur's complexity. Triple secs are almost always clear, contain both sweet and bitter oranges, and (despite the implications of the name) are not necessarily any drier than curaçaos. The curaçaos often are available in a variety of colors and should contain a higher proportion of bitter, curaçao oranges; however, they generally seem to have less finesse than the clear triple secs and are subject to fairly substantial variations. All three varieties, however, should possess a definite and easily identifiable orange-peel character, even though most will often contain a small proportion of complementary aromatics (lemon peel, mandarin, orange-blossom water, orris root, spices, etc.). Most orange liqueurs are light to moderate in sweetness.

Probably the best-known and best-selling orange liqueur is COINTREAU, whose amber rectangular bottle can be found in over two hundred different countries. Founded by Adolphe and Édouard Cointreau in 1849 in the Loire Valley town of Angers, France, the family-owned operation now controls thirteen distilleries throughout the world as well as a new plant outside Angers that consumes over forty thousand hectoliters of alcohol and six hundred tons of orange peels annually. Some of the foreign subsidiaries produce Cointreau from a concentrate supplied by Angers; two, in Spain and Argentina, have a totally independent production. Cointreau does produce several other liqueurs, since 1956 under the REGNIER label, but the original Cointreau triple sec constitutes 70 per cent of the company's production. (The United States Regnier subsidiary produces a different line of cordials, geared to American tastes.)

The peels of both bitter (from Haiti and the Antilles) and sweet (from Spain and North Africa) oranges are used in the production of Cointreau; the former are dried and then reconstituted in France, while the latter are shipped frozen from their native regions to be macerated in pure alcohol. The two varieties, along with a small proportion of supporting ingredients, are then twice-distilled in copper pot stills in the presence of neutral alcohol to yield a highly aromatic concentrate of about 80% alcohol. From here the computers take over, as the concentrate is automatically blended with the correct proportions of water and sugar (27.5 per cent) before being cold-stabilized and filtered. No aging is necessary, and the clear liqueur is bottled as soon as necessary.

Cointreau has maintained its reputation, acquired in the late-nineteenth century, as a light, refreshing beverage, distinguishing itself from the heavier, more complex herbal liqueurs and sweet cordials then in vogue. Its aroma and flavor are straightforward, with a fresh orange-peel character; the light to moderate body and sweetness are well balanced, leaving a clean aftertaste. While not as complex as some other well-known orange liqueurs, it is certainly one of the most pleasant.

Rivaling Cointreau for the title of leading French orange liqueur producer is the house of MARNIER-LAPOSTELLE, makers of GRAND MARNIER. Founded by Jean-Baptiste Lapostelle in 1827, the family-owned company offered a fairly complete line of liqueurs until the end of the nineteenth century, when Grand Marnier began to emerge as their specialty. Today, Grand Marnier "Cordon Rouge" constitutes about 80 per cent of Marnier-Lapostelle's production, and the company's continuing emphasis over the past few decades on the culinary possibilities of Grand Marnier has made it as famous in kitchens and *patisseries* as in bars or drawing rooms.

Though basically an orange liqueur, Grand Marnier is very different in style from Cointreau. Most importantly, the Cordon Rouge is based exclusively on cognac rather than on neutral alcohol; in addition, only bitter oranges from Haiti are used in the formula, without the sweeter, Mediterranean peels. After being reconstituted with water, the bitter peels are macerated in young white cognac (at its freshly distilled strength of 70% alcohol) for about two months in large oak casks. This infusion is then distilled at the Lapostelle family distillery at Neauphle-le-Château, near Paris. The resulting essence is blended with more cognac, this time a blend three to four years old, water, sugar, and a few secret herbs before receiving about one and a half years of aging, again in large oak casks. The cognac used in both stages comes primarily from Marnier-Lapostelle's own château in the charming town of Bourg-Charente, in Cognac. (A limited amount of this cognac is sold under the Marnier-Lapostelle label.) After filtering and the addition of a small amount of caramel for color, the Grand Marnier is bottled.

A slightly less expensive version is also produced. Known as "Cordon Jaune," it employs a less distinctive, non-cognac brandy as base. Because of the only slight difference in price that remains after shipping costs and customs duties, only the cognac-based Cordon Rouge is sold in the United States, Great Britain, and Ireland, while both varieties are available in European markets.

Grand Marnier Cordon Rouge is a fairly complex liqueur of light-medium amber color, moderate body, and light-moderate sweetness. Its cognac character is noticeable and distinctive, as the impression is that of a well-balanced orange cognac rather than a straight orange liqueur. The Cordon Jaune is lighter-bodied and much less complex than the

Cordon Rouge; it has good orange flavors, is slightly less fresh, and is a bit sweeter than Cointreau.

Two other French houses noted for their curaçao-type liqueurs are CUSENIER and DOLFI, though neither specializes to the extent of Cointreau or Marnier-Lapostelle. While Cusenier offers over eighty apéritifs, spirits, syrups, and liqueurs, produced in five different establishments, all the liqueurs are prepared in their main plant near Paris, which was built in the 1930s. CUSENIER ORANGE is probably the best known of the cordial line, and has had a fine reputation since the nineteenth century. It is armagnac-based, similar in style to Grand Marnier but with more orange and less brandy character. Its bitter-orange flavors are bigger and more forceful than either Grand Marnier or Cointreau, and it might be just a touch sweeter. The CUSENIER TRIPLE SEC is in the Cointreau style, as it is distilled only with high-proof neutral alcohol. DOLFI is based in Strasbourg, and their CURAÇAO ORANGE SEC is prepared from a distillate of both sweet and bitter orange peels. An infusion of orange peels is also added to give the liqueur its light-amber color. In flavor it probably falls between the freshness of Cointreau and the cognac complexity of Grand Marnier; its light to moderate body and sweetness are well balanced, and the orange flavors are pleasant. Unusually, the DOLFI TRIPLE SEC is actually a bit sweeter than the curaçao, and contains a hint of mandarin character.

Curaçao-orange-triple sec liqueurs are produced in almost every country in the world; after the celebrated French products, one of the most widely known and certainly distinctive types is German GOLDWASSER. Created at the end of the sixteenth century by the firm of DER LACHS in Danzig, the liqueur continues to be associated with that city, even though many brands now originate in Germany. Clear in color, Goldwasser is a distillate of orange (and also lemon) peel, additionally flavored with coriander (most importantly), cardamom, and mace. The name comes from the fact that each bottle contains small particles of gold leaf floating in it, a traditional practice stemming from the alchemists' belief in the healing powers of gold. The aroma of Der Lachs has a spicy-citrus character, and the light-moderate sugar and 40° alcohol leave a clean, crisp aftertaste in which the spiciness predominates over the slightly bitter orange flavors.

Another German orange liqueur is APFELSINENLIKOER, a sweeter, lower-proof, orange-colored cordial based on orange juice as well as peel, cinnamon, cloves, and other spices.

Other distinctive orange-based liqueurs include Italy's AURUM, a very popular, pale-gold cordial with a brandy base; MERSIN, a clear, sweet liqueur from the Mersin orange-growing region in southern Turkey; the Cypriot FILFAR, a fairly simple, pale-yellow liqueur from local sweet oranges; Israel's chocolate-flavored SABRA, created by Seagram—using Jaffa oranges—in the late 1960s; and the curious Dutch HALF-OM-HALF, a generic name for a blend of half orange curaçao and half bitters said to have been discovered by mistake some centuries ago.

Most American cordial houses do offer a curaçao or a triple sec, although they are relatively unimportant in terms of sales or popularity. The most common use is in mixed cocktails, especially the margarita and sidecar. That of DE KUYPER'S American subsidiary is based on extracts prepared at the home plant in the Netherlands.

Other Citrus-based Liqueurs

Only the orange has been truly successful among the citrus-fruit liqueurs; the next most important is probably MANDARINE (tangerine), though its production is relatively limited. Almost always sweet and colored a bright orange, it may be a useful addition to punches or some cocktails, but many people will find its intense, sweet flavors overwhelming. Most of those mandarines from large firms are probably produced from natural extracts or concentrates.

Among the specialty products worth mentioning is the generic VAN DER HUM (the name is loosely translated as "whatshisname," after its unknown Dutch creator), produced primarily in South Africa from the local Nartze tangerine and South African brandy. The best-known producer is BERTRAM'S, which has pleasant if fairly simple orange-tangerine-herbal flavors and medium sweetness. MANDARINE NAPOLÉON is made by Pagès in Le Puy, France, and marketed for export as a specialty item by a Belgian concern. With more subtle character than most other tangerine-based liqueurs, perhaps due to its relatively high (40%) alcohol content, it has light-medium body and moderate sweetness. Other mandarin liqueurs include MARNIQUE, from Australia, and the Danish SAN MICHELE.

LEMON liqueurs are rare, although one is produced under the VACCARI label by the makers of Galliano; called DOPIO CEDRO, it is a clear, rather sweet liqueur that tastes a bit like American Girl Scout-produced lemonade. A slightly drier CITRON is offered under Irish Mist's ROYAL IRISH label. Almost equally rare are GRAPEFRUIT liqueurs, which are normally labeled with the French name PAMPLEMOUSSE. Their flavor is likely to be vaguely citrus, and most are probably produced from concentrates rather than fresh or dried fruit.

The American FORBIDDEN FRUIT liqueur was originally produced from the shaddock, a fruit similar to the grapefruit, but today the more common citrus varieties are used. Generally brandy- or whiskey-based, it can be a fairly pleasant, light-to-medium-sweet drink; that produced by JACQUIN has pleasant undertones of cocoa and herbs. ROCK AND RYE is another American product; essentially a citrus-flavored whiskey, it is discussed later. In Germany, BERGAMOT liqueur is produced from an infusion of the small, yellowish-green citrus fruit of that name, generally with brandy added.

Citrus peels, particularly orange and lemon, are also used as supporting ingredients in many liqueurs, even though their presence may not be immediately discernible. Dominating ingredients with which citrus flavors are often blended include anise, vanilla (parfait amour), and herbal-based recipes.

Cherry Liqueurs

Cherries are perhaps the most widespread wild fruit in the world (after grapes), and as a result of this easy accessibility and the inherent attraction of their dark red color and sweet cherry flavors, a multitude of cherry liqueurs are produced which rival orange types in popularity. Many different species of cherries are employed, ranging from the small, dark Marasca cherry of Yugoslavia and northern Italy to the sweeter, larger, red eating cherries that are found throughout France (known as *griottes*) and in southern Denmark. Often cherry liqueurs will contain a blend of several varieties, some for sweetness and flavor, others for color.

A few words of explanation should be offered here regarding cherry (and other fruit) "brandies." Grape brandy is a distillate of fermented grapes or grape juice; properly speaking, cherry brandy should then be a distillate of cherries. This is the position taken by the American alcoholic beverage authorities, who hold that only the distilled spirit of a particular fruit can be labeled "brandy" (what we generally refer to in the present book as *"eau-de-vie"*). Swiss regulations insist that "cherry brandy" be based on kirsch, to which cherry syrup and, if desired, natural aromatic substances have been added; no artificial coloring is permitted. The English, however, complicate the picture by using "fruit brandy" to designate those liqueurs which are primarily a maceration of fruits in a combination of fruit juices with (grape) brandy, resulting in a sweeter, colored cordial far removed from true fruit *eaux-de-vie* such as kirsch, mirabelle, or slivovitz. In the United States, such brandy-based liqueurs must be labeled "fruit-flavored brandies." Thus, the same liqueur might be labeled simply "cherry liqueur" in France, "cherry brandy" in Great Britain, and "cherry-flavored brandy" in the United States. While there is a minimal percentage of fruit-distillate brandy that English fruit brandies must contain, this does not guarantee that all "cherry brandies" will have any discernible (grape) brandy character.

Another variable in cherry liqueurs, in addition to the composition of the alcoholic base, is the amount of almond character present. In theory, such undertones are derived from the cherry kernels, which may be distilled or macerated, with or without being crushed. In fact, it is likely that bitter-almond extracts of various sources are often added where more almond character is desired. As with most fruit liqueurs, cherry "brandies" often have subtle supporting flavors added as well.

The oldest distillery in France, that of Rocher Frères, at La Côte St. André, in the *département* of Isère, was founded in 1705, during the reign of Louis XIV. A century and a half later, at the 1855 Paris international exposition, it was declared that, "without contradiction," Rocher was the first firm to generalize the drinking of liqueurs in France. While at that time Rocher offered over one hundred different products, since the late-nineteenth century it has been known particularly for its CHERRY ROCHER. Today, 80 per cent of Rocher Frères's production involves cherries, which are brought not only from the nearby Rhône Valley, but from all over France.

The large red cherries are harvested in late June and early July. They are then brought to La Côte St. André, where, along with a small percentage of black cherries related to the Marasca, the fruit and pits are crushed and put into high-proof neutral alcohol to macerate for approximately two years. This maceration takes place in large vats of eastern-European oak, which is very old and close-grained, minimizing evaporation and imparting no discernible oak character to the cherry-alcohol mixture. Stainless-steel vats are gradually being introduced as the old oak becomes unusable, and at any time Rocher may have up to two hundred tons of fruit and twenty-five hundred hectoliters (seventy thousand U.S. gallons) of alcohol aging. When the aging is completed, the now aromatized and colored alcohol is filtered, and water and sugar are added for the final blend. A small amount of the production, primarily exported, is labeled ROCHER CHERRY BRANDY; it contains perhaps 15–20 per cent wine brandy added to the blend. This is said to have little real effect on the flavors, which are derived primarily from the kind of cherries utilized and the length of maceration. The resulting liqueur, bottled at 30° G.L., is medium red-amber in color, with a pleasant character of fresh, ripe cherries. Its light-moderate body and sweetness are well balanced, with very little almond undertones.

The other French cherry liqueurs are also on the light, fresh side. CHERRY MARNIER, which constitutes only 5 per cent of the production of Marnier-Lapostelle, is a holdover from the nineteenth-century days when the company offered a whole line of liqueurs. It has a more pronounced and complex brandy-almond character than the Rocher, but is not quite as fresh-tasting. CUSENIER'S is produced from separate infusions of red and black cherries blended together; it has a spicy raspberry-almond fruitiness and a fairly dry brandy aftertaste. Other French cherry liqueurs, including MARIE BRIZARD, REGNIER, and GARNIER, are generally light and fruity, with light to moderate sweetness and only light brandy-bitter almond character.

Certainly the most well-known cherry liqueur is Denmark's PETER HEERING LIQUEUR, formerly known in the United States as CHERRY HEERING. "Heering's Cherry Brandy," as it was then known, was developed in 1818 from an old recipe utilizing the celebrated red cherries of southern Denmark, and its fame was soon spread by the ships of the Heering trading company. Liqueur production gradually overtook trading, and today Heering's cherry liqueur can be found throughout the world. This fairly low-alcohol (24½°) cordial is very dark red in color, light-bodied, with lightly sweet, intense, ripe cherry character. The flavors are relatively simple, but quite pleasant.

The English are probably the main consumers of cherry "brandy" liqueurs, and the best known of several British producers is undoubtedly GRANT'S MORELLA CHERRY BRANDY. Developed by Thomas Grant in 1774, it is based on Morella cherries from Kent and French brandy; the taste is light, fruity, and fairly dry, and the color is a tawny amber rather than the deep red of Continental producers. Other British brands include ROSS and JAMES HAWKER.

In Italy, CHERISTOCK is produced primarily from Yugoslavian Marasca cherries; it has a deep wine-red color, medium body, and good fruity flavors. The CHERRY BRANDY from BUTON (who make Vecchia Romagna brandy) has an orange tinge to its dark red color and is stronger in both brandy and bitter-almond character than the Stock. With medium body and sweetness, it is definitely heavier than both English and French brands. Also heavy and sweet but lacking any real brandy character is VACCARI. The producers of the well-known Aurum orange liqueur also offer a cherry liqueur under the name of CERASELLA.

Cherry cordials are also very popular in the eastern European countries. The somewhat spicy Polish WISNIAK can be found in several American markets.

In quite a different style but perhaps even more intense in its cherry character is MARASCHINO, first developed commercially by LUXARDO in the early-nineteenth century from a traditional Dalmatian recipe for a non-alcoholic beverage known as "Rosolio Maraschino." The eastern seaboard of the Adriatic Sea, known as Dalmatia, home of the small, dark Marasca cherries (*Prunus cerasus marasca*), has had a checkered political history: formerly part of the Republic of Venice, it was under the Austro-Hungarian Empire from the fall of Napoleon until the defeat of Austria-Hungary in World War I, at which time it again passed into Italian hands. Since World War II, it has been part of Yugoslavia. Girolamo Luxardo, member of an old Genova trading family, first settled in Zara (Zadar) in the early-nineteenth century as vice-consul for the King of Sardinia. In 1829 he was granted a "privilege" by the Austrian emperor for the production of maraschino and cinnamon rosolio, and he and his descendants gradually developed a world-wide market for their maraschino. (It was during these early times that Luxardo's distinctive round, straw-covered bottle was developed, to protect the fragile cargo from rough, lengthy journeys.) The Zara establishment was destroyed by Allied bombing raids during World War II, and at the end of the war the Luxardo family was forced to flee by Yugoslav partisans. A new factory was established in 1947 in Torreglia, Italy (near Padova), and Marasca cherry trees were planted in the surrounding volcanic hills. Today, Luxardo controls nearly one hundred thousand trees in the Torreglia region and is by far the most important producer of maraschino in the world.

The Marasca cherries follow a more complicated procedure than the simple maceration which is sufficient to produce most cherry liqueurs. First, the stones are removed and distilled separately, without being crushed, to concentrate their bitter-almond character. Meanwhile, the rest of the cherry-juice, pulp, even stems—is left to ferment. Once the proper stage is reached, the fermentation is stopped by the addition of alcohol (which inhibits any further fermenting action by the yeast); the resulting fortified cherry wine is used in the production of cherry brandy but is no longer needed in the maraschino process. The cake of pulp and stems that remains after the wine is pressed is added to the stone or kernel distillate, to be aged in porous larch-wood casks for six months. This mixture is then distilled three times, each distillation further concentrating the flavors, before being put away for further aging of at least three years, this time in neutral hickory wood. At the end of this time the final blend with sugar and water is made, and the maraschino is ready for bottling after a few months' "marrying" time in ash vats. A complicated process, and one that requires ten to thirteen pounds of cherries for each liter of maraschino, or a yield of only five liters from an average tree!

Much of Luxardo's production is sold in bulk to be used by fine pastry shops and in chocolates and sweets, as well as to other liqueur producers in concentrated form. The clear maraschino sold in Italy under the Luxardo label has 32° alcohol and 36 per cent sugar; for export, the alcohol is 40° G.L. and the sugar content a slightly drier 28 per cent. The aroma is an intense cherry-almond, and the light moderate body and sweetness leave a very smooth, clean aftertaste. Though most frequently used in cooking (a bit of maraschino can be delightful over a fresh fruit salad) or cocktails, its strong cherry flavors can also be appreciated straight.

The only other significant specialty producer of maraschino is DRIOLI, which was also founded in Zara in the early-nineteenth century. Today a Yugoslavian maraschino is produced under the MARASCA label, as an obvious (even down to the carrier-pigeon trademark) imitation of Luxardo. The liqueur is very disappointing, as its heavy sugariness masks minimal cherry character; it seems to have been poorly distilled.

Most large liqueur houses produce their maraschino from concentrates or extracts, perhaps including oil of bitter almond. Others produce a maraschino that is simply sweetened kirsch; this may be pleasant, but usually has more kernel and less cherry character.

Finally, Suntory offers an unusual SAKURA CHERRY BLOSSOM LIQUEUR, produced from the maceration of Japanese cherry blossoms in neutral alcohol. Light pink in color, it is a light-bodied, fairly sweet cordial with smooth, if somewhat insubstantial, flavors.

Berry-flavored Liqueurs

The soft berry fruits—blackberries, raspberries, strawberries, blueberries, bilberries—are invariably macerated in either neutral alcohol or some form of brandy to extract their flavor essences and color. While they are distilled to obtain the clear Alsatian or Black Forest *eaux-de-vie,* this process is almost never used in the production of liqueurs and cordials. Thus the so-called English blackberry or raspberry "brandy" liqueurs will not necessarily have any discernible brandy character; rather, most reflect primarily the flavors of the fruit, and we will refer to such products as simply "liqueurs."

While they do reflect the character of the dominant fruit, the berry liqueurs in particular are never pure extractions of a single fruit variety. Several different types of the same fruit may be used, and essences of different fruits are also generally added to yield a better-balanced flavor and aroma.

BLACKBERRY (MÛRE SAUVAGE, KROATZBEER) is the most popular of the berry flavors; this is probably due as much to the abundance of wild blackberry bushes, particularly in the Northern Hemisphere, as to the inherent taste preferences of the liqueur consumer. Blackberry liqueurs are generally full-bodied and fairly sweet, with a deep red-purple color. Often blended with a bit of raspberry to increase fruitiness, they are perhaps best served chilled, over ice cream or fruit, or used sparingly in cocktails. Blackberry-flavored brandy is the most popular of the American flavored-brandy varieties.

RASPBERRY (FRAMBOISE, HIMBEER), despite its wide appeal, is much less common than blackberry due to its relative scarcity and high price. Less intense in both color and flavor than blackberry, raspberry seems a difficult flavor to capture satisfactorily; most raspberry liqueurs have a raspberry-jam character rather than reflecting the essence of the fresh berries. One of the most successful is DOLFI FRAMBERRY (from *framboise* and "raspberry"), from the Strasbourg firm that also makes fruit *eaux-de-vie.* Framberry includes both wild and cultivated raspberries, primarily from Alsace, and is a blend of an alcoholic maceration of fresh juice and a distillate prepared from raspberries and neutral alcohol (like the German *Himbeergeist,* which is distilled with a high-proof neutral spirit, rather than French *eau-de-vie de framboise,* which must be distilled in the presence of a wine *eau-de-vie* with a maximum alcoholic content of 70%). The resulting liqueur has light to moderate body and sweetness and, although it contains only neutral alcohol, has a slightly "brandy-like" finish. The aroma is very pleasant, more akin to an *eau-de-vie* than the jam-like character of many other raspberry liqueurs, and the taste is drier than most.

Although not, strictly speaking, a raspberry liqueur, the dark-amber CORDIAL MÉDOC is based on a blend of fruits and plants in which raspberries probably play the most important part. Produced near Bordeaux by the makers of Vieille Cure, Cordial Médoc includes fruit-juice infusions as well as distillates; the resulting essences are then blended and aged for six to eight months in large vats. The final product is unusual in that it contains neutral alcohol and both cognac and armagnac, which are included in an attempt to duplicate the flavor of the Médoc wine brandy that originally was used as the base of this regional product. Certainly Cordial Médoc is a liqueur that deserves to be better known: its taste and aroma are distinctive, combining both brandy and fairly complex fruit flavors. It has only light sweetness and a clean, well-balanced finish in which the drier, brandy character predominates, in the style of Tuaca, Irish Mist, or some of the scotch-based liqueurs.

STRAWBERRY (FRAISE, ERDBEER) cordials are also fairly rare, even among the lines of many of the large producers. Again, DOLFI offers one of the more interesting liqueurs of this type, their wild strawberry, FRAISE DES BOIS. No other kind of fruit is used in the blend, which consists of several different varieties of small wild strawberries gathered in the surrounding area which are then macerated for several weeks in neutral alcohol. Light-bodied (only 20° alcohol) and delicate, it has good strawberry flavors and a pleasant, strawberry-jam nose; although quite sweet, the aftertaste is fresh rather than cloying. The German and eastern-European *Erdbeer* liqueurs are generally heavier and sweeter.

Various kinds of BLUEBERRY, BILBERRY, WHORTLEBERRY (MYRTILLE, HEIDELBEER), and ROWANBERRY liqueurs are occasionally produced, primarily in Germany (known as EBERESCHREN), the Baltic countries, and eastern Europe (the Polish RABINOWKA). Bilberry juice forms the base for the herbal STONSDORFER liqueur. The rowanberry, a small red berry from the mountain ash, yields a red, acid, slightly bitter-tasting liqueur.

Three fairly heavy, sweet cordials in the eastern-European style are produced in Finland from local wild berries. The best known is MESIMARJA, a red liqueur from the arctic nectarberry (*Rubus arcticus*); the others are SUOMUURAJN (cloudberry) and KARP (cranberry).

At least one American producer, REGNIER, also offers a CRANBERRY cordial, based on fruits from Massachusetts, New Jersey, Wisconsin, and Oregon.

CASSIS (BLACK CURRANT, JOHANNISBEER) is widely produced in both

France and other countries, but due to its low alcohol content and use as an apéritif, it is not generally classed as a true liqueur or cordial. An exception is the German version, *Johannisbeer* liqueur, which often includes orange oils, cinnamon, cloves, and cardamom, which are macerated along with the black-currant berries; it must have a minimum alcohol content of 25°.

Other Fruits

APRICOT (ABRICOT, APRIKOSEN) is the most popular of the stone-fruit liqueurs after cherry and has great appeal in France and Hungary as well as in the United States and the United Kingdom. Production always begins with the maceration of the pulp of small, ripe apricots (*Prunus armeniaca*), which originated in Asia Minor and are now widely grown in southern Europe, in either pure alcohol or a wine brandy such as cognac; depending on the producer, the stones may or may not be used. Other fruits and often a distillate of herbs and spices are commonly added, so that most apricot liqueurs are fairly complex, containing many nuances of flavor rather than the pure essence of apricot.

Among the French houses, GARNIER is probably the best-known producer of an apricot cordial; their ABRICOTINE dates from the founding of the family-owned company, in 1859. In 1870 the factory was moved to Enghien-les-Bains, a lovely lakeside resort near Paris, which is in a cherry-producing area; during the nineteenth century, cherry liqueurs were Garnier's most important product, being exported principally to the United States and Russia. Today, Garnier continues to offer a wide range of cordials, although their production seems relatively small and old-fashioned compared to such modern giants as Cointreau. Most aging and blending are still done in wood (oak and chestnut), but stainless steel is gradually being introduced when necessary. While they do control distilleries in other countries, the Garnier cordials sold in the United States are prepared from French-made essences which are then "finished" in America by the addition of sugar and water. Garnier is also famous for their production of fancy glass and ceramic bottles, which are avidly collected by aficionados.

The apricots for Abricotine are gathered both locally and from France's warm Midi region to the south. The pulp and stones are macerated separately and then blended with other ingredients to give a medium-amber, fairly complex nutty-apricot liqueur of light-moderate body and sweetness. MARIE BRIZARD APRY includes infusions of apricots and other fruits, as well as an aromatic distillate and a small amount of cognac in the final blend. Similar to the Garnier in sweetness, it has a complex apricot-strawberry-cherry aroma and smooth aftertaste, though some may expect more apricot character than is present. ROCHER APRICOT BRANDY is strong in both apricot and brandy flavors, while REGNIER and CUSENIER are simpler and sweeter, with more pronounced bitter-almond character.

Non-French apricot cordials are often sweeter, and most have many other ingredients. German apricots may contain plum *eau-de-vie*, sloe-berries, and dessert wine, and are usually derived from dried rather than fresh apricots. BOLS APRICOT includes a distillate of apricot stones and herbs, and has a fairly sweet apricot-almond-cherry character with a hint of brandy. Among the American producers, both apricot liqueurs and apricot-flavored brandies are offered, though the latter are by far the more popular. Sometimes the same fruit base may be used for both, and the apricot character is rarely overwhelming.

PEACH, like the apricot, is related to the almond and also originated in Asia. Its flavors are more delicate than that of the apricot, and most peach liqueurs fail to capture the subtlety of the fruit, leaving one only with a vaguely sweet, fruity impression. It traditionally formed the base of the English PERSICO liqueur.

SLOE GIN is not a gin at all, but an American and English cordial made from the fruit of the sloeberry (blackthorn, *prunelle*). Not a true berry either, the sloe is actually a small, wild purple plum (*Prunus spinosa*) belonging to the same genus that includes all the stone fruits. The bright-red, intensely flavored sloe gin is generally produced by macerating the slightly crushed berries, with or without pits, in neutral alcohol, although gin was the original maceration medium in England. Cherries are also traditionally blended with the sloeberries, and a slight cherry-bitter almond character is noticeable in many American sloe gins, particularly that of LEROUX. Of moderate body and sweetness and fairly simple fruitiness, sloe gin is rarely drunk on its own, but is often used as a mixer in such drinks as a sloe-gin fizz, in which its color, sweetness, and tart flavors are a useful additive.

As mentioned in a previous chapter, liqueurs labeled PRUNELLE may reflect the nutty-almond character of the sloeberry kernel, or they may be fruity cordials in the style of American sloe gin. Often the color will give you a clue: green generally indicates an almond emphasis, while red or purple is more likely to be based on a fruit infusion. Even the latter often retains a bit of almond character.

BANANA (BANANE, BANANEN) is one of the easiest flavor essences to reproduce artificially, and many standard banana cordials may contain imitation banana flavoring (this must be stated on the label). Natural banana concentrates are also commonly used. If fresh fruit is employed, very ripe bananas are macerated in neutral alcohol; the skins and other ingredients may also be employed, and sometimes a supporting distillate is added. Banana liqueurs made by any of these procedures generally have an intense, sweet banana aroma (in most cases reminiscent of banana oil or Turkish taffy rather than fresh bananas), heavy body, and a yellow color. All are in the "creme" category, medium to very sweet.

MELON liqueurs are rare, though a few have been offered in recent years. BOLS MELON LIQUEUR is from the European *Cucumus melo;* the Japanese house of Suntory offers a muskmelon-flavored MIDORI MELON LIQUEUR.

Other unusual fruit cordials include Hawaiian PINEAPPLE and the Australian and Hawaiian PASSION FRUIT. The latter has a sweet, peach-like character, and its tropical fruitiness seems more easily captured than that of the pineapple.

PARFAIT AMOUR is a very sweet (often over 50 per cent sugar), violet liqueur that is a holdover from more poetic days when fantasy cordials were in fashion. Originally a Dutch recipe, it is commonly based on orange and lemon peel, with the addition of vanilla, roses, orange-flower water, almond, coriander, and other spices. Its character is primarily vanilla-bubble gum, and its appeal today is very limited.

Of course, liqueurs can be (and probably are) produced from almost every fruit in the world; merely soaking any fruit in brandy or alcohol for a period of several weeks or longer and adding sugar will yield a liqueur of sorts. Only a relatively restricted number of fruit flavors, however, have gained enough popular acceptance to be commercially interesting for most producers. Orange and cherry liqueurs probably account for more than half the quantity of all fruit liqueurs and cordials made today; adding apricot, blackberry, raspberry, and sloe gin would leave only a very small proportion for the more exotic specialties.

BRANDY- AND WHISKEY-BASED LIQUEURS

BRANDY- AND WHISKEY-BASED LIQUEURS

The vast majority of liqueurs and cordials employ neutral, high-proof alcohol as their alcoholic base in the preparation of both infusions and distillates. This alcohol is generally 95–97% pure and is produced in continuous column stills primarily from grains or sugar beets. Certainly the availability of a clean, neutral spirit, which was made possible by the development of the continuous still, in the nineteenth century, has been a major factor in contributing to the consistency of modern liqueurs.

A much smaller number of liqueurs, primarily French, use small amounts of grape brandies or fruit *eaux-de-vie* to add complexity to an otherwise neutral-spirit base. These brandies may be added to the final blend in the form of, for example, aged cognac or armagnac, or they may appear earlier in infusions or distillates. In the latter case, clear young brandies at about 70° are used. This group of liqueurs would include some of the fruit-cordial "brandies" and a few herbal liqueurs as well.

Finally, a few liqueurs employ a distinctive brandy or whiskey not merely as an added flavor ingredient, but as their primary or exclusive alcoholic base. It is the spirit which gives the liqueur much of its character, and it is such liqueurs that we will be describing in the present chapter.

(Grape) Brandy

Brandy is an essential ingredient in several liqueurs we have discussed in earlier chapters, dealing with them according to their primary flavor characteristics. B AND B (herbal) and GRAND MARNIER (orange) are both based on cognac; the former is a blend of neutral-spirit-based Bénédictine (60 per cent) and five-to-six-year-old cognac (40 per cent), while Grand Marnier uses cognac exclusively, both young cognac in the preparation of the orange distillate and older cognac in the final blend. CORDIAL MÉDOC (raspberry-fruit) uses a majority of high-proof neutral spirits but obtains much of its character from the important proportion of cognac, armagnac, and other wine brandy which is also included in its formula.

One of the few liqueur houses to rely exclusively on cognac is the very small firm of GEORGES COURANT, which was founded in Cognac after the First World War. The business also includes the wholesaling of wines, syrups, spirits, etc., and its first liqueur, SÈVE PATRICIA, was based on a traditional Charente recipe dating from the emergence of cognac, in the seventeenth century. A traditional blend of coffee and cognac, known historically as Gloria, is offered under the name of SA'ALA, and four other, less unique cordials are available, with orange, apricot, prunelle, and herbal bases.

TUACA is an Italian brandy-based liqueur from Livorno whose primary flavoring ingredient is probably vanilla, along with cocoa and a hint of citrus peel. Produced from three-to-seven-year-old brandies purchased in both Italy and France, one of the secrets of Tuaca is the small percentage of milk which is also included; the result is a fairly full-bodied flavored brandy or a very light liqueur that reminds one of milk punch or egg nog, though it is certainly lighter and less sweet than either of those two concoctions. The flavors are soft and not particularly complex, but well balanced, with a fairly dry brandy aftertaste.

METAXA is a Greek brandy-based liqueur that was first produced in 1888 and is now one of a line of products (including the anise-based Ouzo and Mastic) that together represent 85 per cent of the total exports of Greek alcoholic beverages. Three qualities of the brandy liqueur are offered, *5-star, 7-star,* and *Grande Fine.* Metaxa *5-star* is essentially a flavored brandy, with citrus-apricot-brandy nose, light body, and only minimal sweetness. The *7-star* and *Grande Fine* are based on older brandies.

American "fruit flavored brandies" must be based exclusively on grape brandy, with a minimum alcohol content of 70 American proof, or 35° G.L. Legally they need not contain any sugar, which is normally a requirement of any "liqueur" or "cordial," but in practice almost all contain at least a minimal amount. Some firms may produce a fruit cordial and the corresponding fruit flavored brandy from exactly the same blend, the difference being that one has a neutral-spirit and the other a brandy base. The flavored brandies are generally less sweet than their cordial counterparts, and the fruit flavors may also be less pronounced.

All the major American producers, including ARROW, LEROUX, HIRAM
WALKER, DU BOUCHET, MOHAWK, DE KUYPER, and OLD MR. BOSTON,
offer flavored brandies. The most popular are blackberry and apricot,
though cherry, peach, banana, apple, coffee, and ginger flavored brandies may be found as well.

Scotch Whisky

Still the most popular whiskey and, for many years, the most popular
alcoholic spirit in the world, Scotch whisky (traditionally spelled without the "e") has, not surprisingly, become the focal point of several
liqueurs. One of the oldest and certainly the best known is DRAMBUIE,
which stems from a recipe given to a Captain Mackinnon by Prince
Charles Edward Stuart (Bonnie Prince Charlie) in 1746, when the captain hid Prince Charles on the Isle of Skye following the prince's defeat
at the battle of Culloden. The liqueur was made by the Mackinnon family for personal use until 1906, when a descendant in the whisky trade
began to produce Drambuie commercially in Edinburgh. Drambuie,
which is a contraction of the Gaelic *an dram buidheach,* or "the drink
that satisfies," is based on predominately malt whiskies selected from
over sixty different distilleries and aged by Drambuie for eight to twenty
years. Some five-year-old grain whisky is also used. After the whisky is
properly aged, sugar syrup, water, and a secret essence prepared from
herbal oils are blended with the whisky; when mixing is completed, it is
ready for bottling. Only one gallon of essence is used to flavor five
thousand gallons of whisky, so it is evident what importance the original
whisky selection and aging have. Drambuie has medium body and
sweetness, and the flavors are a fairly complex, distinctive blend of
honey-spicy-herbal-scotch elements.

Similar in style is LOCHAN ORA, which was introduced fairly recently
by the makers of Chivas Regal, a well-known premium Scotch whisky
blend. It is relatively light-bodied and moderately sweet, with peaty
Scotch whisky character and honey-herbal undertones. Also produced
by a well-known whisky distiller is GLEN MIST, which is said to be
slightly drier in taste.

Another traditional herbal recipe is the basis for GLAYVA (from *gle-
meth,* "the best"), which has been produced commercially since the
1940s. It is based on straight grain whisky bought from a single distiller, which is blended with about ten other ingredients added in the

form of a liquid essence. The resulting liqueur is lighter and perhaps less sweet than Drambuie, with definite anise undertones in the whisky-herbal-honeylike flavors. Not overly complex but pleasant and fairly distinctive, its mixability is being stressed by the producers, who opened a new distillery in Edinburgh in late 1974.

Just over the Scottish border, in northeastern England, is the Holy Island of Lindisfarne, where St. Aidan founded the first Celtic Christian church and monastery, in 635. Today, LINDISFARNE LIQUEUR is produced on the island from the standard traditional blend of Scotch whisky, honey, and herbs.

A few non-Scottish liqueur firms do use Scotch whisky in special blends, but these are relatively rare, and none is particularly well known. Among these are America's SCOTCH COMFORT, BOLS SKY CREAM and BOLSHERWHISK (a cherry whisky) from Holland, and ROCHER CHERRY WHISKY from France. The combination of scotch maltiness and cherry fruitiness strikes us as a bit odd, but it may be attractive to some.

Irish Whiskey

Irish *usquebaugh,* or whiskey, is probably older than that of Scotland, but it has never caught the public's eye or palate after the fashion of its neighbor. Unfortunately, many people think of Irish whiskey as a sweetish blend only to be put into Irish coffee, ignoring the fine, smooth flavors that an old Bushmill's or Jameson's can offer. Nevertheless, some reputation has been attained by the leading Irish whiskey-based liqueur, IRISH MIST. Loosely based on the traditional "heather wine" referred to in early Irish manuscripts, the actual Irish Mist recipe was brought to Tullamore by an Austrian refugee in 1948. Possibly dating from the flight of the Irish earls in the seventeenth century, the blend is based on approximately seven-year-old Irish whiskey aged at the Irish Mist distillery (which was founded in 1829) in Tullamore. To this, honey, sugar syrup, herbal extracts, and water are added; after three months "rest" in large glass-lined vats, the final blend is filtered and bottled. Irish Mist has light-moderate body and only light sweetness, and its pleasant aroma has undertones of honey-orange-bitter almond to complement the basic Irish-whiskey character. Smooth, with some complexity, it is probably best appreciated straight or with a bit of ice.

GALLWEY'S IRISH COFFEE LIQUEUR, which is produced in Waterford, does have some Irish-whiskey character, but it is primarily a coffee liqueur.

American Whiskeys

ROCK AND RYE is a generic name for an original American cordial which consists essentially of rye whiskey sweetened with rock sugar and often flavored with fruits. Neutral grain spirits may also be included. Perhaps the leading producer is LEROUX; their regular "Rock and Rye" is based on six-year-old Maryland whiskey blended with oranges, lemons, and cherries, while the "Irish Moss" brand contains crystals of rock sugar and employs a kind of seaweed (known as Irish moss) for flavoring instead of fruits. ARROW offers a Rock and Rye with honey.

The best-known American whiskey liqueur, though many think of it merely as sweet bourbon, is SOUTHERN COMFORT, a specialty product produced in St. Louis, Missouri. The flavors are primarily citrus and peach, with the latter predominating. The light body, alcohol, and fairly low sweetness are well balanced, and while the flavors are not overly complex, the dry finish is clean. Southern Comfort is generally used in mixed drinks and cocktails as a substitute for bourbon or blended whiskey, though it is not unpleasant served on its own as a liqueur.

FORBIDDEN FRUIT is also whiskey-based, and has already been discussed under "other citrus-based liqueurs."

Canadian Whisky

The most important liqueur based on the smooth, blended whiskies distilled in Canada is GEORGE M. TIDDY'S CANADIAN LIQUEUR, a light-amber, medium-sweet cordial with a fairly distinctive orange-herbal-earthy character. Sweeter than other herbal-type liqueurs, it is fairly smooth and is made exclusively with Canadian whisky. Another Canadian liqueur, recently introduced, is YUKON JACK, bottled at 100 proof.

Rum

In the early days of the development of modern, commercial liqueurs, the then-French colonies in the West Indies were the source of several rum-based liqueurs flavored with local spices. The most famous producer was the Veuve Amphoux, of Martinique, who is referred to as one of the eighteenth-century "queens of liqueurs" (the other was Marie Brizard) in an early-twentieth-century French work on liqueurs and spirits.

Today, no rum-based cordial has achieved international recognition and, while rum is doubtlessly used as a flavoring ingredient and spirit base in several West Indian liqueurs, it is unlikely to provide the primary flavor. Among those which originate in rum-producing countries are the Jamaican PIMENT-O-DRAM; NASSAU ROYALE, from the Bahamas; BALSAM, a banana liqueur popular in Haiti; and the Cuban ALDABO (orange) and RON COCO (coconut).

ARRACK is a spirit distilled variously from rice, millet, or coconut, and its fruity, slightly sweet character is very similar to the light rums of Cuba or Puerto Rico. It is used as the basis of several Scandinavian punch liqueurs, of which CARLSHAMN'S PUNSCH, from Sweden, is perhaps the best-known. A light-bodied sweet liqueur, its fruity flavors— date-fig-lemon-sugar—resemble a rum-based grog or fruit punch.

Gin and Vodka

Several American producers offer flavored gins and vodkas, many of which were introduced in response to laws in New York and New Jersey which, until 1972, prohibited the sale of all distilled spirits, except cordials, in half-pint bottles. Thus spirits were introduced which contained just enough sugar (2.5 per cent) to qualify for the "liqueur" designation. Citrus flavorings, including lime, are the most popular, but grape, cherry, and mint-flavored vodkas (or gins) have also been made.

Perhaps the only legitimate vodka liqueur is TAVA, recently introduced by Smirnoff. Clear in color and very sweet, it is smooth but very light in flavor, with slight undertones of mint-citrus-anise.

Fruit Eaux-de-Vie

Primarily because of the high cost involved in the production of most fruit *eaux-de-vie,* no generally available liqueurs employ large proportions of framboise, poire Williams, mirabelle, etc. An exception might be made for a few maraschino types which are essentially sweetened kirsch (cherry *eau-de-vie*). Apart from that, some local Alsatian liqueurs, particularly POIRE (PEAR) WILLIAMS and FRAMBOISE (RASPBERRY), are produced from true *eaux-de-vie* to which fruit juices and sugar have been added. The poire can be quite good, capturing the essence of fresh pears in a smooth, if somewhat sweet, form, although the availability of such products is understandably very limited.

13. "The Alchemist in His Workroom," a seventeenth-century Dutch painting by David Teniers showing the raw materials and primitive stills that were the forerunners of modern liqueur production (photo Giraudon, Paris)

14. Marasca cherries, gathered in the hills of northeastern Italy (photo courtesy of Luxardo, Italy)

15. The *torta* of skins, pulp, and pits which is distilled to produce maraschino (photo courtesy of Luxardo, Italy)

16. Some of the 130 secret ingredients in Chartreuse being removed from the primitive copper stills after distillation has been completed (photo courtesy of Chartreuse, France)

The Chartreuse aging cellars in Voiron (photo courtesy of Chartreuse, France)

18. A few of the many plants and herbs used in the preparation of Bénédictine, including nutmeg, saffron, hyssop, cinnamon, dried orange peel,
and angelica root (photo courtesy of Bénédictine, France)

There is at least one calvados-based apple liqueur although, again, the production is strictly local; we would be surprised if there is even enough to make the trip from Normandy to Paris. This is REINETTE, produced by the Calvados house of Lecompte, in Lisieux. Light gold in color, it is a very simple liqueur of slight apple-citrus character, light-bodied and fairly dry.

SOME FRIENDS AND RELATIVES

SOME FRIENDS AND RELATIVES

Several after-dinner or apéritif drinks are normally classed with liqueurs, even though their low alcohol content or particular method of manufacture may be quite different from those drinks we normally call liqueurs or cordials. Some, like creme de cassis, are alcoholic fruit juices similar to fortified fruit wines; other concoctions such as advockaat simply defy description.

CASSIS, or black currants, have been cultivated for centuries, and medicinal properties have long been ascribed to these small, blue-black, intensely flavored berries. As early as 1712, the abbot Bailly de Montaran, who was also a doctor at the Sorbonne, said that cassis was helpful in preventing colds; in fact, black currants have more vitamin C than any other fruit. Of course, the good doctor also said that cassis would cure snake and dog bites, fevers, small pox, cuts, and even the plague. In addition, "experience has shown that it is as useful for animals as for humans, but the dosage must be increased proportionally"! Several forms of cassis-based beverages were produced during the eighteenth century, utilizing the leaves as well as the fruit itself.

It was not until the mid-nineteenth century, however, that the modern formula for CREME DE CASSIS was developed. Its creator was L. LAGOUTE, then the only liqueur producer in Dijon, which is situated in the heart of Burgundy's famous vineyards. Interest in this new development spread rapidly, and soon Dijon was the center of the new cassis industry. L'HÉRITIER GUYOT, an important exporter of creme de cassis, was founded in 1845. By 1873 over three hundred nectares of cultivated black currants could be found on the slopes behind the great vineyards of the Côte d'Or, and as the vine-attacking Phylloxera louse invaded Burgundy, the cultivation of cassis became both more popular and more profitable. Dijon was soon the most renowned cassis-producing district, although important orchards could also be found in Touraine and Anjou, in the Loire valley.

Today, little has changed in the production methods of Lejay-Lagoute creme de cassis (which is now marketed under the SISCA label). The black currants are harvested in late June and July, and upon arrival they are crushed, put into oak vats with neutral, high-proof alcohol, and left to macerate for a period of several months. Cassis and its juice are very delicate, so the final blend with sugar and water is not made until just before bottling. Unusually, plain sugar rather than syrup is added (45–50 per cent), and great mechanical mixers then go to work to ensure that it is dissolved completely. The minimum alcoholic content for a creme de cassis is 15°; normally, it is bottled at 16°, although it may go as high as 25°. Due to this low alcohol content and the inherent delicacy of the fruit, cassis is one liqueur that should be consumed fairly quickly. Old cremes de cassis lose some of their intense flavor, and the dark color fades and acquires a slightly brownish tint. Ideally, it should be drunk within a few months after bottling, and once a bottle is opened it is best to finish it in a few weeks.

Creme de cassis is always very sweet, but its intense, sometimes minty, black-currant flavors and full body should leave it well balanced and less sugary than many other creme cordials. Because of its intensity and sweetness, though, cassis is often served as an apéritif when mixed with a simple, local white wine (in Burgundy, usually aligoté) or vermouth. This blend was made famous after World War II by the former mayor of Dijon, Canon KIR, who gave his name to the traditional blend of one part creme de cassis and four parts well-chilled dry white wine. It is a delightful drink, as the sweet fruitiness of cassis adds to the refreshing, palate-stimulating austerity of the wine.

Other low-alcohol fruit "liqueurs," particularly cherry, are made by the maceration of fresh fruits in pure alcohol. In France, several firms market a GUIGNOLET, which is based on the large red cherries grown primarily in the valleys of the Loire and Rhône and in Alsace. The moderately sweet, light-bodied result has only 15–20° alcohol and is often drunk as an apéritif. Generally quite fresh-tasting, and really closer to a cherry wine than to a liqueur, most are best appreciated served chilled or over ice. Several producers, including DOLFI, ROCHER FRÈRES, LEJAY-LAGOUTE, and COINTREAU (under the ROYAL ANJOU label), also offer a GUIGNOLET AU KIRSCH that contains 5–10 per cent of the cherry *eau-de-vie*. These are often less fresh and fruity than the plain guignolets, but seem a bit less sweet and more complex.

Denmark is the most famous cherry-producing country, and products like the French *guignolet* are generally offered as "cherry wine"—although more properly they may, again, be infusions of fresh cherries in pure alcohol. A bit fuller-bodied than their French counterparts, they also retain the fresh, fairly sweet character of ripe cherries. Among the better-known Danish brands are CHERRY KIJAFA and CHERRY ELSINORE. In America, LEROUX CHERRY KARISE is one of several similar products, though it is a bit heavier and less fresh than its Danish counterparts.

The sweet, fruity grape juice pressed during the autumn vineyard harvests forms the basis of the only apéritif-liqueur in France that has been awarded an *appellation contrôlée,* PINEAU DES CHARENTES. Pineau is a traditional drink of the Cognac region, and it is made by adding relatively young cognac to the grape must immediately after pressing. This prevents fermentation and guards the fresh fruitiness and sweetness of the grape juice. Further aging is important, and the best Pineaux spend up to five to eight years in old barrels to enable the cognac (which is about 25 per cent of the Pineau blend) to mature and integrate itself completely with the grape juice. Young Pineau is generally two to three years old, and all must be passed by a tasting committee before they are granted the *appellation contrôlée.*

Both white and rosé Pineaux are made, the latter from the Bordeaux varieties of Cabernet Franc, Cabernet Sauvignon, Malbec, and Merlot, which are grown in Cognac for personal use. The whites should have a fresh, grapy, nutty aroma and flavor in which the cognac plays an important part; the cognac flavors and 16–22° alcohol should prevent the moderate sweetness from being cloying. The older Pineaux should be complex and fuller in flavors, while the rosés generally seem just a bit less sweet. Among the large Cognac houses, both DENIS-MOUNIÉ and POLIGNAC (under the REYNAC label) offer Pineau des Charentes; RENÉ GOMBERT is one of the best of the smaller producers.

Similar in the technique of its production is RATAFIA DE CHAMPAGNE, another fruity, fortified grape-juice apéritif that originates in the French Champagne region surrounding the towns of Reims and Épernay. Although neutral, high-proof alcohol rather than cognac is used to fortify the grape juice and prevent fermentation, the high price of grapes in the

Champagne region makes Ratafia quite expensive. It is generally aged for about one and a half years before bottling and is similar in style to Pineau, though it lacks the nutty cognac complexity of the latter. Both should be served chilled but undiluted by ice.

Stock, the Italian brandy and liqueur house, produces two vermouth-based fruit "liqueurs," both 20° alcohol: CHERRY JULEP and BLACK-BERRY JULEP. The latter is the more popular, and its fairly smooth, fruity blackberry flavors are well balanced by light moderate sweetness. The vermouth is barely discernible, and the impression is pleasant and simple.

ADVOCKAAT is a thick, sweet, egg-and-brandy-based emulsion that has been produced in commercial quantities only in this century. Traditionally, it was produced at home by Dutch farmers from their own brandy, fresh eggs, and sugar. As the amount of brandy could vary considerably, the unwary often had their tongues pleasantly loosened until they began to talk as much as a lawyer—which in Dutch is "advockaat"! Today the brandy, eggs, sugar, and often such other flavoring elements as fennel or maraschino are carefully heated in large stainless-steel *bains-marie* (double boilers) until the mixture begins to emulsify, the point where the ingredients are thoroughly mixed without dissolving. When this critical stage is reached, the advockaat is then quickly cooled and, after perhaps three weeks' settling, bottled. The thickness of the mixture will depend on the heating and also on the relation of egg whites to yolks; it is said that ten eggs are needed for each liter of advockaat.

The Dutch and German advockaats, of which perhaps BOLS and VERPOORTEN are the most famous, are very thick and often best "drunk" with a spoon. They are very sweet, almost meringue-like concoctions, about the consistency of a thick American milkshake. A thinner version is made for export; in Great Britain and Ireland this drinkable rather than spoonable advockaat may be mixed with sparkling lemonade to make the currently popular snowball cocktail. Both thick and thin varieties should be shaken well before serving, as the ingredients do tend to separate slightly.

In Italy, a similar egg-emulsion product, based on the sweet dessert wine of Marsala, is offered called vov. Subtitled *"Zabajone confort-ante,"* it is a very heavy, thick, very sweet drink that seems rather sugary and unbalanced despite the interesting complexity added to the sugar-egg taste by the marsala.

All the advockaat-type "liqueurs" have a sweet, thick, egg-nog character; while, out of interest, they are certainly worth a try, they are unlikely to be everyone's favorite spoonful.

BITTERS of varous sorts are in many cases the modern incarnation of the old, bitter herbal elixirs that were the forerunners of today's liqueurs and cordials. While a few of the apéritif bitters may be quite pleasing to some palates, most are designed to stimulate or aid digestion rather than to provide a satisfying gustatory finale to a fine repast. Certain bitters are used almost exclusively as flavorings in other drinks and are not intended to be drunk by themselves. These would include the celebrated rum-based ANGOSTURA bitters from Trinidad and several brands of orange, peach, and other fruit-flavored bitters.

BOONEKAMP is a generic term for digestive bitters of the Dutch type, whose ingredients normally include quinine bark, bitter-orange peel, aniseed, licorice, cloves, fennel, coriander, gentian, calamus roots, rhubarb, and other, similar herbs and plants. Such dark-brown, slightly sweet bitters are especially popular in Italy (perhaps it's all that pasta), though their heavy herbal-quinine character is unlikely to be attractive to the casual imbiber. The best known is undoubtedly FERNET BRANCA, which has recently introduced a mint-flavored version, FERNET MENTA. Buton's PETRUS BOONEKAMP is also fairly well known in Italy, while the Vaccari AMARO SALUS is one of the more palatable of the innumerable Italian bitters. Similar in style is the German UNDERBERG bitters; it is estimated that a million single-serving bottles of Underberg may be drunk every day throughout Europe. France does not produce many digestive bitters, nor are they popular (except as flavorings) in the United States or the United Kingdom.

Another strain of the bitters family includes those products which, while they may also be taken as after-dinner digestives, are generally served with soda water as apéritifs. Here their rather bitter yet often somewhat fruity flavors stimulate both saliva and gastric juices to prepare for a dinner ahead. Again, Italy probably leads the way with CAMPARI, a brilliant-red, fairly sweet, quinine-gentian apéritif bitter that is generally served with soda and a twist of lemon. CYNAR is also Italian, and is unusually based on a maceration of artichoke leaves (and other herbs). France's most celebrated bitter apéritif is AMER

PICON; the Pernod organization also makes the gentian-based SUZE apéritif.

AQUAVIT or AKVAVIT is the national spirit of the Scandinavian countries, and it is also exported throughout the world. Based on neutral spirits from grain or potatoes, it is flavored with caraway (primarily) and other herbs and spices, from which it obtains its distinctive character. Aquavit contains no sugar, however, and thus is not classified as a true liqueur; as a flavored neutral spirit, its closest cousin would be gin. Generally colorless, some aquavits become pale yellow after aging in oak. Aquavit is most often served straight and well chilled. The best-known producers are the Danish firm of AALBORG, GAMEL and LINIE from Norway, and O. P. ANDERSON from Sweden.

Like aquavit, GIN is an unsweetened, flavored neutral spirit that falls outside the category of either cordials or fruit brandies. Juniper berries are an important ingredient, although a wide range of other flavorings are also employed by the various firms to create their own particular style of product. There are two broad categories of gin produced today: the heavier, fuller-flavored DUTCH or GENEVER gin, produced from malted grains and often aged for some time in oak casks; and the lighter, more neutral ENGLISH gin, which is popular in cocktails and mixed drinks.

VODKA is normally a neutral, unflavored, unsweetened spirit outside the realm of liqueurs, although some Russian vodka is traditionally flavored with buffalo grass.

PART THREE

NOGS, GROGS, AND A PUNCH OR TWO

NOGS, GROGS, AND A PUNCH OR TWO

The number of intriguing, unique drinks that can be prepared from brandies and liqueurs is practically infinite; thousands have already been listed in the many cocktail-recipe books on the market, and hundreds more appear each week from the hands of creative bartenders throughout the world. Without searching too far for exotica, the following well-known favorites have been selected to acquaint you with some of the standard items in the brandy-cordial repertoire. All are easy to make and can be prepared from ingredients that should be handy in your kitchen or home bar.

In experimenting with your own concoctions, you might keep these hints in mind: Most liqueurs are quite sweet, and many recipes thus call for "cutting" their sweetness with a dry spirit like vodka or brandy; for the same reason, most liqueur-based cocktails are served chilled. Be sure the liqueurs you mix are complementary; chocolate-mint, anise-orange, cherry-peach, or cocoa-orange, for example, are generally well liked, while stranger mixtures like raspberry and kümmel will surely have a more limited appeal. The herbal liqueurs, such as Bénédictine and Chartreuse, are among the most difficult to use in mixed drinks because of their complex character. When different colors of creme de menthe or creme de cacao are called for, this is purely for aesthetic reasons; there is no difference in flavor.

Where a recipe calls for "brandy," almost any fairly young grape brandy can be used. California brandies are generally the best mixers, though cognac and armagnac may be used where the brandy itself is an important ingredient and the mixture is not too complex. The heavy, sweet Spanish brandies are more difficult to integrate with other flavors, as are the pomace brandies like *grappa* and *pisco*. In any event, a young, grapy brandy is preferable to an older, more complex, woody one for the purpose of most cocktails.

Glasses of almost any sort may be employed, depending on the way the drink is to be served: by itself, on the rocks, or over shaved ice as a frappé. A clear glass allows the colors in the drink to shine through, and a stem prevents the chilled cocktails from being heated by the hand.

The drinks have been presented in no particular order; we hope you'll browse through until you find something that sounds interesting! Each recipe makes one drink, except where indicated otherwise.

Brandy Alexander
(along with the stinger, a true classic)

⅓ brandy
⅓ creme de cacao brown or white
⅓ heavy cream

Shake vigorously with ice; strain and serve.

Stinger

⅔ brandy
⅓ creme de menthe white

Shake with cracked ice; strain and serve.

Grasshopper

⅓ creme de cacao white
⅓ creme de menthe green
⅓ heavy cream

Shake with crushed ice; strain and serve.

Angel's Tip

Fill small liqueur glass ⅔ full with creme de cacao brown; gently float heavy cream on top.

Snowball

2 oz. advockaat
dash of lime

Add sparkling lemonade to taste.

Pink Squirrel

⅓ creme de noyau or creme de almond
⅓ creme de cacao white
⅓ light cream

Shake well with ice; strain and serve.

Mint Frappé

Pour creme de menthe green over shaved ice heaped in a shallow cocktail glass. Serve with short straws.

Chocolate-Mint Frappé

½ creme de menthe green
½ creme de cacao white

Combine creme de menthe and creme de cacao. Pour over shaved ice heaped in a shallow cocktail glass. Serve with short straws.

Rusty Nail

⅔ Scotch whisky
⅓ Drambuie

Stir and serve on the rocks.

Margarita

⅗ tequila
⅕ triple sec
⅕ fresh lime juice

Rub the rim of a cocktail glass with the squeezed lime and dip in coarse salt to coat. Shake ingredients with ice; strain and serve in the crusted glass.

Sloe-Gin Fizz

2 oz. sloe gin
1 teaspoon powdered sugar
juice of ¼ lemon

Shake ingredients well with cracked ice strain into tall 8-oz. glass and fill with sparkling soda water.

Black Russian

½ Kahlúa or other coffee liqueur
½ vodka

Stir and serve on the rocks.

Sidecar

½ brandy
¼ triple sec
¼ lemon juice

Shake with ice; strain and serve.

Harvey Wallbanger
(popularized by Galliano)

$\frac{2}{7}$ vodka
$\frac{4}{7}$ orange juice
$\frac{1}{7}$ Galliano

Mix vodka and orange juice in a tall glass; carefully float Galliano on top.

Saronno

1 oz. Amaretto di Saronno
1 oz. brandy
1 oz. heavy cream

Shake well with cracked ice, strain, and serve in a cocktail glass.

Menthe Julep

1 oz. creme de menthe
1 oz. bourbon

Pour over crushed ice into a brandy glass and sip through a straw. Garnish with fresh mint leaves.

Cassis Vin Blanc (Kir)
(a refreshing wine-based apéritif)

½ oz. creme de cassis (vary to taste)
4 oz. chilled dry white wine; preferably a white burgundy
  such as Aligoté, Mâcon, or Pouilly-Fuissé

Pour creme de cassis into wine glass. Add chilled wine and stir.

Vermouth Cassis
(another great apéritif)

½ oz. creme de cassis
2 oz. dry vermouth or Lillet Blanc

Pour over ice into a large goblet or old-fashioned glass and
add sparkling water to taste.

Curaçao-Apricot Delight

1 oz. orange curaçao or Cointreau
1 oz. apricot liqueur

Shake with crushed ice and strain into a glass.

Café Mocha

1 oz. creme de cacao
1 oz. coffee-flavored brandy
¾ oz. heavy cream

Shake with cracked ice and strain into a shallow cocktail
glass.

Apricot Delight

¼ fresh orange juice
¼ fresh lemon juice
½ apricot-flavored brandy or apricot liqueur

Shake well with cracked ice, strain, and serve.

Singapore Sling

1 oz. gin
juice of ¼ lemon
½ oz. cherry-flavored brandy or cherry liqueur

Shake well with cracked ice; strain into a 6–8-oz. glass.
Fill with sparkling water and garnish with a maraschino
cherry.

Netherlands Cocktail

1 oz. cognac
1 oz. curaçao
dash of orange bitters

Stir with cracked ice, and strain into a glass.

Rock and Rye Toddy

1 whole clove
1 stick cinnamon
1 twist lemon peel
1½ oz. Rock and Rye
boiling water
1 pat butter (optional)

Put clove, cinnamon, lemon peel, and Rock and Rye in a
mug. Fill to top with boiling water and stir. Float butter on
top if desired.

Brandy Manhattan

⅔ brandy
⅓ sweet vermouth
dash of bitters

Stir well with cracked ice; strain and serve garnished with a
maraschino cherry.

Brandy Old-Fashioned
(traditionally made with whiskey,
but better this way!)

dash of Angostura bitters
dash of orange curaçao
sugar to taste
2 teaspoons water
2 oz. brandy (or Rock and Rye)

Dissolve bitters, curaçao, and sugar in water. Add brandy
and stir. Add ice cubes. Garnish with a maraschino cherry
and an orange slice.

Brandy Sour

2 oz. brandy
1 teaspoon powdered sugar
1 tablespoon lemon juice

Shake the above with cracked ice, strain, and serve deco-
rated with a maraschino cherry and an orange slice. Sparkling water may be added if desired.

Brandy Grog
(instant warmth for a winter's night)

1½ oz. brandy
2 teaspoons sugar
boiling water
juice of a lemon slice

In a grog glass mix brandy and sugar. Add boiling water
to fill the glass. Squeeze lemon juice into grog and stir.
Garnish with a piece of lemon rind.

California Sunset

6–8 oz. orange juice
1½ oz. brandy
grenadine syrup

Add brandy to orange juice and stir well. Carefully pour
grenadine syrup down the side of the glass; do not stir.

Brandy Fizz

1½ oz. brandy
1 tablespoon powdered sugar
1 egg white
1 tablespoon lemon juice

Shake well with crushed ice and strain into a 6-oz. glass.
Fill the glass with sparkling water.

Brandy Highball

Pour 2 oz. fruit-flavored brandy of your taste (apricot,
peach, blackberry, etc.) into a highball glass. Add ice and
sparkling water.

The Pit's Sangría
(for a large crowd you don't mind becoming a bit rowdy!)

5 gallons red wine (cheap)
1 quart brandy
½–1 pint apricot or other fruit liqueur
sugar to taste (3–5 lbs.)
6 oranges
6 lemons

Mix liquid ingredients, adding sugar gradually as it dis-
solves. Slice oranges and lemons (other compatible fruits
may also be used) and let soak for at least twelve hours before serving. Serve chilled.

Mulled Wine

1 bottle dry red wine
6 oz. cherry liqueur or cherry brandy (the former will make a sweeter
    drink)
1 tablespoon curaçao or Cointreau
dash of orange bitters
juice of ½ lemon
½ teaspoon cloves

Combine ingredients and heat in a pan. Serve in mugs with a cinnamon
stick. Makes 4–5 servings.

Mrs. Garrett's Egg Nog

1½ dozen eggs; separated
1 pound sugar
1 pint brandy
1 pint heavy cream
1 pint whole milk

Beat egg yolks thoroughly. Add sugar gradually until dissolved, then add brandy slowly, stirring constantly. Continue stirring slowly while adding milk, then whipped cream beaten stiff. Fold in the beaten egg whites. Garnish with freshly grated nutmeg. Serves 25.

Champagne and Brandy Punch

6 bottles extra-dry champagne
1 bottle brandy
½ bottle Cointreau or triple sec
3 quarts sparkling water
limes
strawberries

Combine very cold champagne and sparkling water with the brandy and triple sec in a punch bowl. Garnish with slices of lime and fresh or frozen whole strawberries. More or less sparkling water may be added according to your own preferences. Float a piece of dry ice into the punch for a dramatic bubbling effect. Makes about 70 punch-cup servings.

Pisco Sour

6 oz. pisco   2 egg whites
3 tablespoons sugar   12 ice cubes
2 oz. lemon juice

Dissolve sugar in pisco, then add lemon juice, egg whites, and ice. Stir vigorously in a shaker, or mix in a blender. Makes four 4-ounce servings.

Pousse Café

One of the most stunning of liqueur drinks is the Pousse Café, which consists of several liqueurs floated carefully one on top of the other. The liqueurs will remain layered, without mixing, because of their different specific gravities; the sweeter liqueurs are heavier, and will support drier liqueurs or brandy. Since the same liqueur type, from different firms, often differs in sweetness, however, some caution is necessary. As a guide, very sweet grenadine syrup can almost always serve as a bright red base for your Pousse Café while straight or flavored brandies are relatively light and dry and may often be used for the top layer. Different-colored liqueurs can be arranged to portray national flags or festive occasions, as well as to provide a delightful series of different taste sensations. For example, you might try these variations on the timely Spirit of '76, using products of two well-known firms:

⅓ grenadine liqueur or syrup   ⅓ Bols anisette (red)
⅓ Arrow creme de cacao (white)   ⅓ Bols creme de menthe (white)
⅓ Arrow curaçao (blue)   ⅓ Bols curaçao (blue)

Pour carefully over the back of a spoon, in the order given, into a tall, narrow liqueur glass.

Bols offers a guide to preparing Pousse Café that lists the "Bolsweight" of each of their liqueurs, thus allowing you to prepare your own special recipes. Although the products of other houses may be different, the following are the listings for Bols from the heaviest to the lightest. (To ensure that the liqueurs do not mix, allow at least one point between each.)

ANISETTE (red, white)	17.8
CREME de MENTHE (green, white, gold)	15.9
CREME de BANANA (yellow)	15.0
CREME de CACAO (brown, white)	15.0
MARASCHINO (white)	14.9
COFFEE (brown)	14.2
CHERRY LIQUEUR (red)	12.7
PARFAIT AMOUR (violet)	12.7
BLUE CURAÇAO	11.7
BLACKBERRY LIQUEUR (purple)	11.2
APRICOT LIQUEUR (orange-amber)	10.0
DRY ORANGE CURAÇAO	9.8
TRIPLE SEC (white)	9.8

PEACH-FLAVORED BRANDY (amber)	7.0
CHERRY-FLAVORED BRANDY (dark red)	6.8
BLACKBERRY-FLAVORED BRANDY (purple)	6.7
APRICOT-FLAVORED BRANDY (amber)	6.6
ROCK & RYE (red-amber)	6.5
PEPPERMINT SCHNAPPS (white)	5.2
KÜMMEL (white)	4.2
PEACH LIQUEUR (amber)	4.1
SLOE GIN (red)	4.0

To celebrate St. Patrick's Day, try the green, white, and orange of the tricolor:

⅓ creme de menthe (green)
⅓ creme de cacao (white)
⅓ peach liqueur

Coffee Drinks

Almost any brandy or liqueur can be added to a mug or glass of hot coffee for a delightful end to dinner. Many are prepared with a garnish of cream and may also have grated chocolate added as a final touch. Although made with whiskey, *Gaelic* or *Irish Coffee* is the classic. A flavorful alternative is *Venetian Coffee,* prepared as follows:

1 oz. brandy
3 teaspoons sugar
strong, hot coffee
2–3 oz. heavy cream

Put sugar and brandy into a preheated 6–8-oz. stemmed tempered glass. Fill to ¾ inch from top with coffee and stir well to dissolve sugar. Carefully float enough lightly whipped cream on top to fill the glass. Serve immediately.

Mexican Coffee

1 oz. Kahlúa
1 teaspoon sugar
dash of powdered cloves
1 cup strong black coffee
cinnamon stick

Add coffee to Kahlúa, sugar, and cloves in mug or heated glass. Stir with a cinnamon stick.

Café au Cognac Flambé

1 cup hot coffee
1 tablespoon cognac
1 lump sugar
cognac

Float 1 tablespoon cognac on coffee in a cup. Put sugar
lump in a metal tablespoon, fill it with cognac, and warm
it over a flame. Ignite the cognac in the metal spoon and
float on the cognac and coffee. Stir gently until flame is ex-
tinguished.

The possibilities are endless. Here are a few selections as served
at the famous Enrico's in San Francisco:

Caffè Anise (anisette liqueur, caffè espresso, topped with
whipped cream)

Caffè Cacao (caffè espresso, creme de cacao, whipped
cream)

Café Cointreau (caffè espresso, Cointreau, and citrus)

Cappuccino San Francisco (hot chocolate with brandy)

Cappuccino Venetia (caffè espresso, dark chocolate, milk,
and brandy)

Kona Grog (Hawaiian coffee with rum and herbsaint)

Enrico's Original Ambrosia (coffee, Galliano, and cognac)

Iced Café Kahlúa (Kahlúa, Kona coffee, Turkish ice cream
with whipped cream and cherry)

COOKING WITH
BRANDY AND LIQUEURS

COOKING WITH BRANDY AND LIQUEURS

by Marion A. Blumberg

Cognac, armagnac, and calvados are frequently called for in French recipes, especially in dishes originating in the areas where these spirits are distilled. The French housewife uses brandy in much the same way that she uses herbs and spices, judiciously in small amounts to add that extra touch to her meals. Americans are fortunate in having available California brandy, which can be used equally well in cooking.

Many new dishes can be created by the careful addition of brandy to a favorite old recipe. For example, brandy and applejack make excellent marinades for steaks. A half cup of brandy may be added to a hearty soup or stew fifteen minutes before serving to add a warming touch to supper on a cold, wintry night. Veal or chicken may be sautéed in butter and brandy, then covered with a sauce that incorporates the drippings in the pan, often thickened with cream. When the sauce calls for heavy cream, the cream should be brought to the boiling point and allowed to simmer for a few minutes before the brandy is added, to insure that the two ingredients will blend together smoothly.

One important technique to master in cooking with brandy is the art of flaming. The secret is to warm the brandy before holding a match to it. After meat has been sautéed for several minutes, brandy may be added to the skillet, allowed to heat up for a minute or two, lighted with a match, and the pan held up off the heat and gently shaken back and forth until the flame burns itself out. The pan is then returned to the heat and further ingredients added to complete the sauce. Be careful that there is not too much butter or oil in the pan when the brandy is ignited, or an excessive flame may result. Most of the butter used to sauté the meat should be poured off before the brandy is added; it may be reserved and returned to the pan for incorporation into the sauce after the flaming step is completed.

An alternate method of cooking meat in brandy is to allow the sautéed meat to simmer in the brandy until the liquid has cooked down and nearly evaporated. This technique imparts more of the brandy flavor to the meat than does the flaming method.

Brandy and fruit *eaux-de-vie* will also enhance certain desserts. One to two tablespoons of brandy may be used in place of vanilla or almond extract in many pound-cake recipes. Brandy is the traditional spirit used to age and cure fruitcake: after baking, the cake is wrapped in cheesecloth that has been soaked in brandy and set aside to age for several weeks. As the cloth dries, more brandy is poured over it.

The custard of an apple tart may be flavored with a quarter cup of calvados or applejack, while that of a berry tart may be enhanced by one to two tablespoons of kirsch or other fruit *eau-de-vie*. The individual pieces of fruit may be soaked in a little of the same spirit, or they may be coated with a glaze made by thinning a fruit jelly with the spirit. In either case, caution must be used, for a little goes a long way.

Liqueurs, being sweet, tend to find their way most frequently into dessert recipes. The number of recipes using liqueurs is surprisingly large, principally because the producers all have a host of recipes promoting their own product. On close inspection, most will be found to be virtually identical, with only the type of liqueur differing.

Liqueurs may be used to add new flavors to standard dishes. Orange-flavored liqueur may be employed as a marinade for fruit either to be served alone or to be incorporated into a tart, pie, or cobbler. Chocolate-, mint-, and coffee-flavored liqueurs are delicious over ice cream. Two tablespoons of liqueur may be added to a cake batter or frosting—for example, coffee liqueur in a mocha cake, orange liqueur in a sponge cake, and almond-flavored liqueur in a pound cake.

Two dishes in which liqueurs are the featured ingredient are crêpes suzette and soufflés. In preparing the crêpes, orange-flavored liqueur contributes the major flavor of the sauce, while brandy is ignited to provide the spectacular finale to the tableside preparation. Again, as always, the brandy must be heated before it will catch fire.

Dessert soufflés occur in two forms, hot and cold (actually frozen). The hot dessert soufflés are a variation of the entree soufflé, with stiffly beaten egg whites providing the lightness. They may be prepared in one of two ways: The liqueur may be added directly to the soufflé batter before baking, in which case the soufflé is served without an accompanying sauce. The alternative is to soak ladyfingers in a little liqueur and layer them in the middle of the soufflé batter. The finished soufflé is then served with a liqueur-flavored sauce. The cold soufflé is composed mainly of whipped cream that is flavored with the liqueur, poured into a mold lined with ladyfingers, and placed in a freezer for several hours before serving.

The recipes that follow have been carefully chosen to represent the various ways in which brandy, *eaux-de-vie,* and liqueurs are used in cooking. I hope they will add an interesting new dimension to your menus.

PÂTÉ WITH ARMAGNAC

1 pound thickly sliced bacon	2 egg yolks, beaten slightly
1 quart water	½ cup armagnac
½ cup chopped onions	½ tablespoon salt
2 tablespoons butter	⅛ teaspoon pepper
1 pound chicken liver, cut in	⅛ teaspoon allspice
¼-inch cubes	½ teaspoon dried thyme
¾ pound lean pork, ground	1 teaspoon chopped fresh parsley
¾ pound lean veal, ground	1 bay leaf, powdered
½ cup heavy cream	

Preheat oven to 350°. Simmer bacon strips in water for 10 minutes. Line bottom and sides of 8½ × 4½ × 2½-inch covered baking dish with the bacon strips, reserving some to cover top. Sauté onions in butter for 10 minutes, until translucent. Add liver and sauté 3 to 5 minutes. Cool and chop finely. In a large bowl combine chopped liver with ground pork and veal. Blend with cream, egg yolks, armagnac, salt, pepper, allspice, thyme, parsley, and bay. Put into lined baking dish, smooth the top, and cover with remaining bacon strips. Cover and set baking dish in pan of boiling water (water should reach halfway up side of baking dish), and bake for 1 to 1½ hours, until skewer inserted into middle comes out clean. Remove from water, uncover, place weight on top of pâté, and chill overnight.

Serves 12 as an appetizer.

ROQUEFORT-AND-COGNAC SPREAD

½ pound Roquefort cheese	½ cup cognac
½ pound cream cheese, softened	½ cup chopped pecans

Combine Roquefort, cream cheese, cognac, and nuts, and beat until smooth and fluffy. Serve with crackers or wedges of unpeeled apples and pears.

Makes about 3½ cups.

FRENCH ONION SOUP

4 medium onions, sliced thin
4 tablespoons butter
¼ teaspoon sugar
2 tablespoons flour
6 cups beef stock or beef bouillon
1 teaspoon salt

¼ teaspoon freshly ground black
  pepper
¼ cup brandy
6 slices French bread
2 cups grated Gruyère cheese

Preheat oven to 400°. Cook onions in butter in covered 4-quart saucepan for 15 minutes. Add sugar and cook uncovered for 45 minutes, stirring frequently, until onions are golden brown. Add flour and cook, stirring, for 3 minutes. Add beef stock, salt, and pepper, and simmer uncovered for 1 hour. Add brandy and simmer uncovered for 15 minutes. Pour into individual ovenproof bowls. Float slice of bread on each and sprinkle with grated cheese. Bake for 10 to 15 minutes until cheese melts and starts to brown.

Serves 6.

CHEESE FONDUE

1 clove garlic, peeled and halved
2 cups dry white wine
juice of ¼ lemon
10 oz. Emmentaler cheese cut in
  ¼-inch cubes
10 oz. Gruyère cheese cut in
  ¼-inch cubes

1 tablespoon potato flour
1 tablespoon kirsch
salt
freshly ground black pepper
½ teaspoon freshly ground nutmeg
1 loaf French bread cut in ½-inch
  cubes

Rub cut surfaces of garlic clove over inside surface of ceramic fondue pot. Put wine and lemon juice in pot, place on high heat, and bring to a boil. Add cut-up cheese. Stir continuously in a figure 8 until cheese is melted and is the consistency of chewing gum. Stir potato flour in kirsch to dissolve, then add to the melted-cheese mixture. Season with salt, pepper, and nutmeg. Remove pot to burner. Spear pieces of French bread on long-handled forks, dip bread in fondue to coat, and eat immediately.

Serves 4 as a main course or 8 as an appetizer.

CHICKEN WITH BRANDY AND RIESLING

3–4-pound frying chicken, cut
   into 8 pieces
salt
white pepper
½ cup (¼ pound) butter
8 slices bacon, cut into 2-inch
   pieces

2 medium onions, chopped
½ cup California brandy
1 tablespoon whole thyme
2 bay leaves
6–8 whole cloves
1 cup California or Alsatian
   riesling

Remove skin from chicken pieces, wash, and pat dry. Sprinkle with salt and pepper and sauté in butter in a large, heavy skillet until brown on both sides, about 15 minutes. Remove chicken from skillet. In skillet, sauté bacon pieces and onion for 5–10 minutes, until onion is translucent. Return chicken to skillet, pour brandy over the pieces, allow it to heat for 1–2 minutes, then ignite. When flame has gone out, add thyme, bay, cloves, and wine. Cover and simmer 45 minutes, until chicken is tender. Remove chicken to serving dish. Remove pieces of bacon and reserve. Pour sauce into gravy dish. Return bacon to skillet and cook until crisp. Serve sauce over steamed brown rice garnished with bacon bits.
Serves 4.

POULET VALLÉE D'AUGE (CHICKEN WITH CALVADOS)

2–2½-pound chicken
½ cup butter
salt

white pepper
¼ cup calvados
1 cup heavy cream

Brown whole chicken in butter in a heavy-bottomed casserole. Season with salt and white pepper, cover, and cook slowly on top of stove for 30 minutes. Pour in calvados, heat for 1 to 2 minutes, and ignite. When flame dies, remove chicken to a serving platter and keep warm. Pour cream into casserole and bring to a slight boil, scraping bottom of casserole and stirring to mix scrapings into cream. Pour sauce over chicken and serve with fresh garden vegetables.
Serves 4.

LOBSTER WITH CALVADOS

4 lobster tails
salt
white pepper
⅛ teaspoon cayenne pepper
½ cup butter
2 shallots, chopped

⅓ cup calvados
4 tablespoons flour
1 cup heavy cream
juice of 1 lemon
freshly snipped parsley

Season lobster tails with salt, white pepper, and cayenne pepper, and sauté in butter until uniformly red. Remove and keep warm. Add shallots and calvados to pan, warm for 1 to 2 minutes, and ignite. When flame goes out, scrape bottom of pan to dislodge juices. Add flour and stir to blend, then add cream. Bring to a slight boil, stirring to blend with the butter. Remove from heat and add lemon juice. Pour over lobster tails and garnish with parsley.

Serves 4.

SHRIMP FRA DIAVOLO

2 pounds raw medium-sized
   shrimp
2 cloves garlic, peeled and crushed
6 tablespoons olive oil
¼ cup cognac
6 tomatoes, peeled, seeded, and
   chopped

1 teaspoon salt
½ teaspoon orégano
⅛ teaspoon cayenne pepper
¼ teaspoon fresh parsley, snipped

Shell and devein shrimp and rinse in cold water. Sauté the shrimp in garlic and olive oil until they turn pink. Add cognac and steam, covered, for 2 minutes. Add tomatoes, salt, orégano, and cayenne and cook for 15 minutes, stirring occasionally. Serve over steamed brown rice, garnished with parsley.

Serves 4.

BRANDIED BEEF STEW

2 pounds chuck roast cut in 2-inch
   cubes
salt
freshly ground pepper
4 tablespoons butter
2 tablespoons flour
½ cup brandy
1½ cups dry red wine
1 pound fresh tomatoes, skinned
   and quartered

1 bay leaf
½ teaspoon thyme
1 medium onion, chopped
2 cloves garlic, crushed
freshly snipped parsley
4 carrots, sliced
4 stalks celery, diced

Preheat oven to 300°. Season meat with salt and pepper, and brown in butter in Dutch oven. Add flour and sauté 5 minutes. Add brandy, wine, tomatoes, bay, thyme, onion, garlic, parsley, carrots, and celery. Cover and bake for 2 hours.

Serves 4.

COGNAC SAUCE FOR BEEF

¼ cup butter
1 cup light-brown sugar, firmly
   packed

½ teaspoon salt
½ cup heavy cream
6 tablespoons cognac

Melt butter in saucepan. Add sugar and stir until dissolved. Add salt. Stir in cream and bring to a full boil, stirring constantly. Remove from heat and whisk in cognac. Serve as a sauce for beef fondue or over a broiled steak.

Makes 1½ cups.

PORK CHOPS WITH APPLES AND BRANDY

6 center-cut pork chops
4 tablespoons butter
salt
white pepper
½ cup calvados or applejack
2 tablespoons butter

½ cup chopped onions
½ cup chopped celery
2 medium tart apples, peeled,
   cored, and chopped
1 teaspoon thyme

Brown pork chops in butter, seasoning with salt and pepper. Add brandy and cook over low flame for 15 minutes. In a small saucepan melt butter, add onions, celery, apples, and thyme, and sauté, stirring occasionally, until apples are lightly brown. Spoon over pork chops and simmer for 10 minutes.

Serves 4–6.

VEAL CHARENTE (VEAL WITH COGNAC AND MUSHROOMS)

1½ pounds veal for scaloppine
salt
white pepper
½ cup (¼ pound) butter
1 pound fresh mushrooms, washed
and quartered

1 teaspoon salt
¼ teaspoon white pepper
½ cup cognac
2 cups heavy cream
2 tablespoons flour
2 tablespoons Dijon-style mustard

Sprinkle pieces of veal with salt and pepper and sauté in butter until brown, about 3 minutes on each side. Remove to serving platter and keep warm. Sauté mushrooms in butter for 5 minutes. Add salt, pepper, and cognac, and sauté for 2 minutes. Blend cream with flour and mustard, and add to mushrooms. Bring to a boil and simmer for 5 minutes. Pour over veal and serve immediately.

Serves 4.

ALMOND POUND CAKE

½ pound butter, softened
2 cups confectioners' sugar
5 medium eggs, separated
2 cups sifted flour

1 tablespoon Amaretto di
Saronno
½ tablespoon vanilla extract

Preheat oven to 300°. Butter a 9×5-inch loaf pan. Cream butter and gradually cream in sugar. Add beaten egg yolks. Beat egg whites to a stiff peak. Alternate adding flour and egg whites, beating well after each addition. Add liqueur and vanilla. Pour into prepared pan and bake for 1 hour or until tester comes out clean. Cool ½ hour in pan, then remove, and cool completely. Dust top with powdered sugar before serving.

Serves 12.

APPLE TART

1½ cups sifted flour
3 tablespoons sugar
¼ teaspoon salt
¼ cup butter
2 tablespoons shortening
1 teaspoon grated lemon peel
1 egg, lightly beaten
1 teaspoon cold water
3 egg yolks
¼ cup sugar
¼ cup sifted flour
1 cup hot milk

1 tablespoon butter
½ tablespoon vanilla
1½ tablespoons calvados or
   applejack
½ cup whipping cream
4 Golden Delicious apples
½ cup sugar
½ cup apricot jam
1 cup water
2 tablespoons lemon juice
2 tablespoons calvados or applejack

Combine flour, sugar, and salt. Cut in butter and shortening. Add lemon peel, egg, and water, and mix to a stiff dough. Chill for 2 hours. Preheat oven to 400°. Roll dough out on lightly floured board to a diameter of 12 inches. Fit into a 10-inch flan pan. Prick pastry and bake for 15 to 20 minutes, until lightly browned. Cool thoroughly.

In top of double boiler beat egg yolks until thick. Gradually beat in sugar and continue beating for 2 to 3 minutes, until mixture is lemon-yellow in color and forms a ribbon when whisk is lifted up out of mixture. Gradually beat in flour. Beat in milk a few drops at a time. Heat over boiling water, stirring constantly, until custard thickens. Remove from heat and beat in butter. Beat mixture as it cools, then stir in vanilla and brandy. Whip cream to stiff peaks and fold into custard. Turn mixture into cooled pastry shell and chill 2 hours.

Pare, core, and cut apples into eighths. Combine sugar, jam, water, and lemon juice, and heat to boiling. Strain, pressing jam through a sieve. Return to saucepan, add apples, and cook, covered, for 5 minutes. Remove cover and cook 5 to 10 minutes longer, until apples are cooked through, turning them to glaze. Remove apples from pan and cool. Stir brandy into syrup. Arrange cooled apples over chilled cream and spoon apricot-brandy syrup over them. Chill 2 hours.

Serves 8.

CHOCOLATE MOUSSE AUX LIQUEURS

¾ cup scalded milk
2 eggs
3 tablespoons orange, mint, or
  coffee liqueur

1 cup (6 oz.) semi-sweet
  chocolate chips

Put milk into blender and turn on low. Add eggs one at a time, then add liqueur. Add chocolate chips about an eighth of a cup at a time and allow to blend well between additions. When all chips have been added, blend at high speed for 1 minute. Pour into individual ¾-cup ramekins. Chill 3 hours.
Serves 4.

COINTREAU LOG

6 egg yolks
½ cup sugar
½ cup sifted flour
2 cups hot milk
2 tablespoons butter
2 tablespoons Cointreau

4 eggs, separated
¾ cup sugar
½ teaspoon salt
1 teaspoon vanilla
¾ cup sifted flour
powdered sugar

In 3-quart saucepan beat egg yolks with a wire whisk until very thick. Gradually beat in sugar; beat for 2 to 3 minutes, until mixture is lemon yellow in color and forms a ribbon when whisk is lifted out. Beat in flour gradually. Beat in milk, a few drops at a time. Bring mixture to a boil over moderate heat, stirring constantly, and allow to boil and thicken for about 5 minutes. Remove from heat and beat in butter. Continue to beat as mixture cools, then stir in Cointreau. Cover surface with waxed paper to prevent skin from forming, and chill in refrigerator overnight.

Preheat oven to 400°. Butter sides and bottom of 15×10-inch jelly-roll pan; line with waxed paper and butter again. Beat egg yolks until thick; gradually beat in sugar and continue beating until mixture is lemon yellow in color and forms a ribbon when whisk is lifted out. Beat egg whites with salt until they form stiff peaks; beat in vanilla. Pour egg-yolk mixture over egg whites and fold gently a few times. Sift flour over mixture and fold together until blended. Pour into prepared pan and spread evenly with spatula. Bake for 10 to 12 minutes, until lightly browned. Turn out onto tea towel sprinkled with powdered sugar and allow to cool 4 hours. Remove waxed paper. Spread chilled cream mixture evenly over cake, and roll, rolling from narrow end. Sprinkle well with powdered sugar, and chill in refrigerator for 4 hours.

Serves 8.

CRÊPES

1¼ cups flour	2 tablespoons Cointreau
3 eggs	½ teaspoon salt
1 cup milk	3 tablespoons butter, melted

In a blender jar combine flour, eggs, milk, Cointreau, salt, and melted butter, and blend at low speed for 10 seconds. Scrape down sides of jar and blend at low speed for 30 seconds, then high speed for 10 seconds. Refrigerate two hours before using.

Heat a crêpe pan over medium-high heat until a drop of water will skitter around on it. (If crêpe pan has not been seasoned, it may be necessary to melt butter in the pan for the first few crêpes.) Holding crêpe pan in left hand, pour 3 tablespoons batter into pan and quickly tip pan so that batter spreads over entire bottom. Cook for two minutes, until crêpe is firm and no longer shiny. Flip over with long, thin spatula and cook for one minute on other side. Remove to plate in oven to keep warm until ready to serve.

Makes 18 crêpes.

Crêpes may be served at breakfast, brunch, lunch, dinner, or dessert. For breakfast, brunch, or dessert, serve with melted butter, powdered sugar, fresh berries, and preserves. Guests may fill crêpes with whatever they choose, then roll them up, sprinkle with powdered sugar, and eat. For lunch or dinner, crêpes may be served filled with creamed chicken, or with ham and melted cheese, and rolled. For an elegant dessert, crêpes may be served with a flaming sauce of brandy and Cointreau (*Crêpes Suzette*).

CRÊPES SUZETTE

4 tablespoons butter	6 tablespoons Cointreau
¼ cup granulated sugar	18 crêpes
juice of 2 oranges	4 tablespoons cognac
1 tablespoon lemon juice	

In a large chafing dish or skillet melt butter, add sugar, and heat until very slightly browned. Add orange juice, lemon juice, and Cointreau. Fold crêpes in fourths and place in sauce. Heat for 1 to 2 minutes. Pour brandy over the crêpes, warm for one minute, and ignite. Serve immediately.

Serves 6.

GRAND MARNIER SOUFFLÉ

24 ladyfingers	½ tablespoon vanilla
½ cup Grand Marnier	5 egg yolks
¼ cup butter	⅓ cup sugar
¼ cup flour	5 egg whites
1½ cups light cream, scalded	*Grand Marnier Sauce* (optional)

Preheat oven to 350°. Soak ladyfingers in liqueur. Butter a 2-quart soufflé dish and dust lightly with sugar. Arrange 12 ladyfingers on bottom of dish. Melt butter in saucepan. Add flour, mix to a smooth paste with wire whisk, and cook for 3 to 4 minutes. Gradually beat in cream. Cook over low heat for 5 minutes, stirring constantly. Add vanilla and let cool for 5 minutes. Beat egg yolks in a bowl and gradually beat in sugar. Continue beating until mixture is lemon yellow in color and forms a ribbon when whisk is lifted out. Add yolks to cream in a thin stream, beating constantly. Cool 10 minutes. Beat egg whites until stiff but not dry, and fold into cream mixture. Pour half the mixture into the prepared soufflé dish; arrange ladyfingers over mixture and cover with remaining soufflé. Bake for 40 to 45 minutes. Serve immediately with *Grand Marnier Sauce.* Serves 6 to 8.

Any liqueur may be substituted for Grand Marnier, and the sauce may be omitted.

GRAND MARNIER SAUCE

5 egg yolks	½ tablespoon vanilla
½ cup sugar	¼ cup Grand Marnier
2 cups milk, scalded	½ cup whipped cream

In top of double boiler beat egg yolks until thick. Gradually beat in sugar with a wire whisk and continue beating until mixture is lemon yellow in color and forms a ribbon when whisk is lifted out. Gradually beat in hot milk. Cook over boiling water, stirring constantly, until mixture thickens and coats spoon. Let cool. Stir in vanilla, liqueur, and cream just before serving. Serve with *Grand Marnier Soufflé.*

This may be made with any liqueur. Makes about 3 cups.

ORANGE CHEESE CAKE

1½ cups graham-cracker crumbs
3 tablespoons sugar
⅓ cup butter, melted
8 ounces cream cheese
½ cup sugar
1 teaspoon freshly grated orange
  peel

1 tablespoon Cointreau or triple
  sec
2 eggs
2 cups sour cream
2 tablespoons sugar
1 teaspoon vanilla

Mix graham-cracker crumbs and sugar in 10-inch pie plate. Add melted butter and mix well. Press flat on bottom of plate. Chill 15 minutes.

Preheat oven to 325°. Soften cream cheese and beat until fluffy. Blend in sugar, orange peel, and liqueur. Add eggs one at a time and beat well after each addition. Pour over chilled crust and bake for 25 to 30 minutes. Chill one hour.

Preheat oven to 425°. Combine sour cream, sugar, and vanilla. Pour over chilled pie. Bake 5 minutes, until it starts to bubble and turn brown. Chill one hour.

Serves 8 to 10.

FROZEN ORANGE SOUFFLÉ

24 ladyfingers
1 cup sugar
⅓ cup water
2 tablespoons grated orange rind

6 egg yolks
¼ cup orange-flavored liqueur
2 cups heavy cream

Fit a 4-cup soufflé dish with a 6-inch-high collar of two thicknesses of waxed paper, and line with 12 ladyfingers. Bring to a boil over moderate heat the sugar, water, and grated orange rind. Cook the syrup to 220° on a candy thermometer. Beat the egg yolks until thick and lemon-colored. Spoon a little syrup into yolks to keep from cooking them, then pour remaining syrup over yolks and beat until thick. Let cool, and beat in liqueur. Beat heavy cream until lightly whipped and fold into egg-yolk mixture. Pour into prepared soufflé dish, alternating with remaining ladyfingers. Freeze at least 6 hours.

Serves 6 to 8.

MRS. OLSEN'S FRUITCAKE

¼ pound preserved citron
¼ pound orange peel
¼ pound lemon peel
¼ pound candied pineapple
½ pound candied cherries
¼ pound California walnuts,
   chopped
½ pound whole almonds
½ pound whole Brazil nuts
½ pound dark raisins
½ pound whole dates
¼ cup sifted flour
1 cup shortening

2 cups brown sugar
4 large eggs
½ cup grape jelly
½ cup grape juice
2¾ cups sifted flour
1 teaspoon baking powder
1 teaspoon salt
1 teaspoon cinnamon
1 teaspoon allspice
½ teaspoon cloves
½ teaspoon nutmeg
⅓ cup brandy

Preheat oven to 250°. Slice finely the citron, orange and lemon peel, and pineapple; cut cherries in half. Add nuts, raisins, and dates. Dredge in ¼ cup flour and set aside. Stir shortening to soften, gradually add sugar, and cream until light. Add eggs, one at a time, beating well after each. Soften jelly and combine with grape juice. Sift flour, baking powder, salt, and spices together 3 times and add to creamed mixture alternating with grape juice. Beat until smooth. Pour over fruit and mix well. Grease tube pan and line with 2 layers of waxed paper cut to size, allowing it to extend ½ inch above all sides. Prepare a 7×3-inch bread-loaf pan in the same fashion. Pour batter into pans. Do not flatten. Bake in a very slow oven (250°) for 3 to 4 hours. Place pan containing 2 cups of water on bottom shelf of oven during baking to get greater volume, moist texture, and shiny glaze. After cake has cooled, wrap in 2 layers of cheese cloth soaked in brandy, then in heavy aluminum foil. Let rest for two months, checking cheese cloth weekly for moisture. If cloth is dry, pour ⅓ cup brandy over it. May be held and will improve up to a year.

Makes 7 pounds.

STRAWBERRY TART

2¼ cups flour
½ teaspoon salt
¾ cup shortening
¼ cup chilled water
kirsch
3 tablespoons butter
¼ cup sugar
1 tablespoon cornstarch
2 tablespoons flour
1 cup milk

2 egg yolks, beaten well
1 teaspoon almond extract
2 egg whites, stiffly beaten
½ cup heavy cream, whipped
2 tablespoons kirsch
1 quart fresh strawberries, washed
    and capped
3 tablespoons red currant jelly
2 tablespoons brandy

Mix flour and salt with a fork. Add shortening and mix with fingers until mixture has a uniform crumbly consistency. Add chilled water, a little at a time, until entire dough forms a large ball. Chill two hours. Preheat oven to 425°. Roll out on lightly floured board, then fit into bottom and sides of fluted flan pan. Trim edges and bake in 425° oven 20 to 25 minutes, until light golden brown. Remove from oven, let cool, and brush lightly with kirsch.

Melt butter in top of double boiler. Blend in sugar, cornstarch, and flour with wire whisk. Gradually beat in milk. Cook over boiling water for five minutes, stirring constantly until thickened. Add a small amount of the hot mixture to the beaten egg yolks, beating constantly, then add the yolks to the hot mixture, beating constantly. Cook over hot water 2 minutes, still beating constantly. Stir in almond extract. Put top of double boiler into bowl of crushed ice and stir cream to cool. Fold in beaten egg whites, then whipped cream, then kirsch. Turn into pastry shell brushed with kirsch. Chill 2 hours.

Arrange strawberries on top of chilled cream. Melt jelly in a saucepan and add brandy. Spoon glaze over strawberries. Chill 2 hours.

Serves 8.

APPENDIXES

APPELLATIONS D'ORIGINE FOR FRENCH EAUX-DE-VIE

There are essentially three categories under which French *eaux-de-vie* are classified. In ascending order of prestige they are as follows:

Appellation d'origine simple: Established by decrees of May 6, 1919, and August 19, 1921. A producer need only declare his use of this *appellation* in an official journal. There is no control or regulation; however, by definition, the eau-de-vie must come exclusively from the designated area.

Appellation réglementée: Established by decree of January 13, 1941. Specific requirements are included for geographical area, grape or fruit varieties that may be used in distillation, methods of distillation, maximum alcohol, and congener levels.

Appellation contrôlée: Established by decree of July 30, 1935. Requirements are established for geographical area, method of distillation, etc., as with *appellation réglementée*, but this category is reserved only for *eaux-de-vie* of "quality and notoriety."

FRENCH *EAUX-DE-VIE* BY *APPELLATIONS D'ORIGINE*

APPELLATION D'ORIGINE CONTRÔLÉE

Cognac
  Grande Champagne
  Petite Champagne
  Borderies
  Fins Bois
  Bons Bois
  Bois Ordinaires
  Bois à Terroir, or Bois Communs

Eau-de-Vie des Charentes

Esprit de Cognac

Armagnac
  Bas-Armagnac
  Haut-Armagnac
  Ténarèze

Calvados du Pays d'Auge

APPELLATION D'ORIGINE RÉGLEMENTÉE

Calvados
Calvados de l'Avranchin
Calvados du Calvados
Calvados du Cotentin
Calvados du Domfrontais
Calvados du Pays de Bray
Calvados du Pays du Merlerault
Calvados du Pays de la Risle
Calvados de la Vallée de l'Orne
Calvados du Mortainais
Calvados du Perche

Eaux-de-vie de cidre originaires de Bretagne
Eaux-de-vie de cidre originaires de Normandie
Eaux-de-vie de cidre originaires du Maine

Marc d'Alsace Gewürztraminer
Eaux-de-vie de marc originaires d'Aquitaine
Eaux-de-vie de marc d'Auvergne
Marc de Bourgogne
Eaux-de-vie de marc originaires du Bugey
Eaux-de-vie de marc originaires du Centre-Est
Marc de Champagne
Eaux-de-vie de marc originaires des côteaux de la Loire
Eaux-de-vie de marc des Côtes-du-Rhône
Eaux-de-vie de marc originaires de la Franche-Comté
Eaux-de-vie de marc originaires du Languedoc
Eaux-de-vie de marc originaires de Provence
Eaux-de-vie de marc originaires de Savoie

Eaux-de-vie de vin originaires d'Aquitaine
Eaux-de-vie de vin de Bourgogne
Eaux-de-vie de vin originaires de Bugey
Eaux-de-vie de vin originaires du Centre-Est
Eaux-de-vie de vin originaires des côteaux de la Loire
Eaux-de-vie de vin des Côtes-du-Rhône
Eaux-de-vie de vin de Faugères
Eaux-de-vie de vin originaires de la Franche-Comté
Eaux-de-vie de vin originaires du Languedoc
Eaux-de-vie de vin de la Marne
Eaux-de-vie de vin originaires de la Provence

Mirabelle de Lorraine

GROWTH OF THE VINEYARD AREA AND PRODUCTION OF COGNAC,
1850–1974

	Date	Total Vineyard Area[1] (in hectares)	Alcohol entitled to the appellation of "cognac" (in hectoliters of pure alcohol)
	1850	209,944	
	1860	216,580	
	1870	242,689	688,671
	1875	281,558	1,114,112
(Phylloxera)	1876	266,318	385,492
	1877	282,667	887,988
	1878	255,615	573,108
	1879	255,283	159,115
	1880	233,110	232,200
	1881	201,219	
	1882	171,001	
	1883	153,623	
	1884	116,217	
	1885	85,240	120,133
	1890	53,963	77,534
	1900	60,158	
	1910	47,415	
	1920	67,368	
	1930	70,851	
	1940–41	59,389	120,643
	1945–46	62,250	24,241
	1950–51	59,832	208,598
	1955–56	64,544	167,624
	1960–61	68,693	256,560
(new plantings authorized)	1961–62	69,608	234,693
	1962–63	70,646	340,239
	1963–64	72,616	263,336
	1964–65	75,452	339,914
	1965–66	78,491	299,110
	1966–67	81,058	350,181
	1967–68	81,187	357,485
	1968–69	82,372	399,650
	1969–70	82,500	325,873
	1970–71	82,734	634,315
	1971–72	86,243	421,942
	1972–73	91,483	406,708
	1973–74	98,543	740,355

[1] Includes red-grape vineyards not used in distillation.

COMPARISON OF AREA AND PRODUCTION
OF THE SIX COGNAC GROWTHS (1973)

Growth	Total area (hectares)	Cultivable area (hectares)	"Cognac" vineyards (hectares)	Percentage of "cognac" vineyards in relation to cultivable area	Production of cognac (in hectoliters of pure alcohol)	Percentage of total cognac production
Gr. Champagne	35,700	25,078	11,939	47.61%	114,369	15.45%
P. Champagne	68,400	54,368	14,152	26.03%	121,745	16.44%
Borderies	13,440	8,758	3,793	43.31%	34,690	4.69%
Total of 1st 3 growths	117,540	88,204	29,884	33.88%	270,804	36.58%
Fins Bois	354,200	250,686	33,765	13.47%	293,533	39.64%
Bons Bois	386,600	242,234	18,540	7.65%	138,295	18.68%
Bois Ordinaires	274,176	190,104	3,592	1.89%	37,723	5.08%
Total of last 2 growths	660,776	432,338	22,132	5.12%	176,018	23.76%
Total for all growths	1,132,516	771,228	85,781	11.12%	740,355	100.00%

ARMAGNAC: GENERAL STATISTICS

Year	Area of vines in the Armagnac region (in hectares)	Production of white wine (in hl)	Wine distilled into armagnac (in hl)	Production of armagnac in hl of pure alcohol	Sales of armagnac in hl of pure alcohol	Stock at end of season in hl of pure alcohol
1944–45	53,000	693,027		45,275	32,059	71,190
1945–46	54,000	613,166		39,890	35,365	75,715
1946–47	53,000	882,219		49,429	32,269	92,873
1947–48	53,500	838,584		14,732	31,835	75,772
1948–49	52,600	950,654		2,307	15,869	62,210
1949–50	52,800	891,745		1,745	6,780	57,175
1950–51	54,600	1,287,017		14,518	10,562	61,131
1951–52	52,826	1,053,739		4,364	9,269	56,226
1952–53	53,786	979,318		8,830	9,742	55,315
1953–54	53,685	1,145,032		10,436	19,498	46,968
1954–55	—	862,280		8,624	14,596	40,894
1955–56	52,353	1,466,002		14,370	17,927	40,673
1956–57	50,145	1,263,581		11,435	11,871	39,090
1957–58	46,636	665,161		3,129	9,216	33,003
1958–59	46,988	1,033,575		5,512	6,783	31,732
1959–60	46,705	822,371		12,450	10,102	34,080
1960–61	47,296	1,022,932		21,015	20,452	34,643
1961–62	45,279	638,951		8,856	10,312	33,187
1962–63	45,398	1,252,054	424,000	40,025	9,204	64,008
1963–64	47,784	1,043,850	516,000	36,642	22,239	78,411
1964–65	51,780	1,076,788	265,000	25,390	12,890	85,302
1965–66	41,608	1,001,019	280,000	23,362	15,321	91,581
1966–67	41,227	1,345,242	295,114	27,375	13,458	105,424
1967–68	40,986	1,245,577	187,139	18,232	14,695	101,738
1968–69	40,201	1,282,140	213,521	17,211	18,322	94,579
1969–70	39,662	925,182	213,446	19,127	21,663	95,445
1970–71	38,560	1,436,330	436,169	41,792	22,791	109,438
1971–72	37,037	656,011	387,181	37,306		

BRANDY PRODUCTION IN THE UNITED STATES[1]

Year	Sales (1000 proof gallons)	Inventory at year end (1000 proof gallons)	Inventory/sales ratio
1958	3,347	17,950	5.36
1959	3,556	20,468	5.76
1960	3,811	22,630	5.94
1961	4,271	22,278	5.22
1962	4,481	23,317	5.20
1963	4,931	25,118	5.09
1964	5,427	27,221	5.02
1965	6,143	33,422	5.44
1966	6,754	41,001	6.07
1967	7,471	43,589	5.83
1968	7,805	47,679	6.11
1969	8,721	48,255	5.53
1970	8,864	48,997	5.53
1971	9,197	45,715	4.97
1972	10,160	41,080	4.04
1973	10,573	40,628	3.84
1974	10,820	45,316	4.19

American spirit production is measured in proof gallons (1 gallon at 100 American proof). 1000 proof gallons yields 6250 bottles of 80 proof brandy.

[1] Essentially all California brandy

A List of Common Ingredients in Liqueurs

Ingredient	Form	Major sources
Almond (bitter)	Apricot kernel	France, California
Aloes	Wood, resin	Africa
Angelica	Root	Belgium
Aniseed	Seed	Spain, Morocco, Italy, Mexico
Apricot	Fruit (fresh & dried)	France, South Africa, California
Arnica	Rootstock	North America, northern & central Europe
Artemisia	Herb, flower	Asia, South America
Balsamite	Resin	South and Central America
Banana	Fruit, skin	Guatemala, Venezuela
Bilberry	Fruit	Central Europe
Blackberry	Fruit	Europe, western U.S.A., New York
Black currant	Fruit	France
Blueberry	Fruit	U.S.A.
Caraway	Seed	Holland, Poland
Cardamom	Seed pod	India, Sri Lanka, Guatemala
Cherry	Fruit	Denmark, western U.S.A., New York
Cherry blossom	Flower	Japan
Cherry (gean)	Fruit	France
Cherry (marasca)	Fruit, kernel	Italy, Yugoslavia, France
Cinchona	Bark	South American Andes, Java
Cinnamon	Bark	Sri Lanka
Cloudberry	Fruit	Finland
Clove	Flower	Madagascar
Cocoa	Bean	Venezuela, Ivory Coast
Coffee	Bean	Brazil, Guatemala
Coriander	Seed	Morocco
Cranberry	Fruit	U.S.A., Finland
Cumin	Seed	North Africa
Dill	Seed	Mediterranean Europe
Fennel	Seed	France, Italy
Gentian	Root	Mountains of France, central Europe
Ginger	Root	Jamaica, Nigeria
Ginseng	Root	China
Grapefruit	Peel	Israel, U.S.A.
Hyssop	Leaf	Southern Europe
Juniper	Berry	Italy, France, Yugoslavia, Hungary
Lemon	Peel	Algeria, California
Licorice	Root	Mediterranean
Macadamia	Nut	Hawaii
Mace	Nutmeg peel	East Indies
Maidenhair	Fern	Central and South America
Mandarin	Peel	Algeria, South Africa
Melissa	Plant	Europe

Ingredient	Form	Major sources
Mint	Leaf	United Kingdom, France, north-western U.S.A.
Myrrh	Resin	Eastern Africa, Arabia
Nutmeg	Kernel	East Indies, Molucca Islands
Orange	Peel	Spain, Algeria, Israel, U.S.A.
Orange (bitter)	Peel	Curaçao, Haiti, Italy, Spain
Orris	Root	Italy
Peach	Fruit	Georgia, Virginia
Pear	Fruit	France, Switzerland
Pimento	Berry	Jamaica
Pineapple	Fruit	Hawaii
Pine nut	Seed	Europe, Asia
Raspberry	Fruit	France, western U.S.A., Germany
Rose	Flower, fruit (hips)	Europe, England, Asia
Rosemary	Herb	Spain, Portugal, France, California
Saffron	Flower	Southern Europe, Asia
Sage	Herb	South-central Europe, western U.S.A.
Shaddock	Peel	Southern U.S.A.
Sloe	Fruit, kernel	France, Hungary
Strawberry	Fruit	Europe, U.S.A.
Strawberry (fraise des bois)	Fruit	Alsace
Tea	Leaf	Sri Lanka, India, China
Thyme	Herb	France, California
Vanilla	Pod	Réunion, Madagascar
Verbena	Leaf	France

ALCOHOLIC STRENGTH

°Gay Lussac	Proof (American)	Proof (British, or Sykes)
10	20	17.50
20	40	35.00
30	60	52.50
40	80	70.00
41	82	71.75
42	84	73.50
43	86	75.25
44	88	77.00
45	90	78.75
46	92	80.50
47	94	82.25
48	96	84.00
49	98	85.75
50	100	87.50
57.14	114.28	100.00
60	120	105.00
70	140	122.50
80	160	140.00
90	180	157.50
100	200	175.00

The British sometimes refer to spirits as "over" or "under" 100 proof. Thus a spirit at 70 British proof (40° G.L.) may also be referred to as "30 under proof."

European spirit production is statistically measured in hectoliters of pure alcohol (100° G.L.)

1 hectoliter of pure alcohol equals:
26.4 American gallons of pure alcohol
22.0 Imperial gallons of pure alcohol

Most brandies are bottled at 40° G.L. (80 American or 70 British proof). One hectoliter of pure alcohol will yield 333 bottles of brandy.

TABLE OF LIQUID MEASURES

Metric

10 milliliters (ml)	=	1 centiliter (cl)
100 centiliters	=	1 liter (l)
100 liters	=	1 hectoliter (hl)

United States

16 fluid ounces (fl. oz.)	=	1 pint (pt.)
2 pints	=	1 quart (qt.)
4 quarts	=	1 gallon (gal.)

British

20 fluid ounces (fl. oz.)	=	1 imperial pint (imp. pt.)
2 imperial pints	=	1 imperial quart (imp. qt.)
4 imperial quarts	=	1 imperial gallon (imp. gal.)

U.S		British		Metric
1 fl. oz.	=	1.04 fl. oz.	=	29.6 ml
1 pt.	=	16.65 fl. oz.	=	473.2 ml
1 qt.	=	1 imp. pt. 13.31 fl. oz.	=	946.4 ml
1 gal.	=	.833 imp. gal.	=	3.79 liters

British		U.S.		Metric
1 fl. oz.	=	.96 fl. oz.	=	28.4 ml
1 imp. pt.	=	1 pt. 3.22 fl. oz.	=	568.3 ml
1 imp. qt.	=	1 qt. 6.43 fl. oz.	=	1.14 liters
1 imp. gal.	=	1 gal. 25.7 fl. oz.	=	4.56 liters

Bottle Sizes

187 ml	=	6.32 fl. oz. U.S.	=	6.58 fl. oz. British
375 ml	=	12.68 fl. oz. U.S.	=	13.20 fl. oz. British
700 ml	=	23.67 fl. oz. U.S.	=	24.64 fl. oz. British
750 ml	=	25.36 fl. oz. U.S.	=	26.40 fl. oz. British
1 liter	=	33.81 fl. oz. U.S.	=	35.20 fl. oz. British

1 fifth U.S. (⅕ gallon) = 25.6 fl. oz. U.S. = 26.65 fl. oz. British = 75.7 cl
1 quart U.S. = 32 fl. oz. U.S. = 33.31 fl. oz. British = 94.6 cl

MEASUREMENTS OF LENGTH

$$
\begin{array}{rcl}
10 \text{ mm} & = & 1 \text{ cm} \\
100 \text{ cm} & = & 1 \text{ meter} \\
1000 \text{ meters} & = & 1 \text{ km}
\end{array}
$$

$$
\begin{array}{rcl}
1 \text{ cm} & = & .3937 \text{ inch} \\
10 \text{ cm} & = & 3.937 \text{ inches} \\
100 \text{ cm} = 1 \text{ meter} & = & 39.37 \text{ inches}
\end{array}
$$

$$
\begin{array}{rcl}
1 \text{ km} & = & .621 \text{ mile} \\
100 \text{ km} & = & 62.1 \text{ miles}
\end{array}
$$

$$
\begin{array}{rcl}
1 \text{ mile} & = & 1.609 \text{ km} \\
100 \text{ miles} & = & 160.9 \text{ km}
\end{array}
$$

MEASUREMENTS OF AREA

1 acre = 0.405 hectare
640 acres = 1 square mile = 2.59 square kilometers
1 hectare = 2.47 acres
100 hectares = 1 square kilometer = 0.39 square mile

TEMPERATURE

$$^\circ\text{Celsius} = \tfrac{5}{9}\,(^\circ\text{Fahrenheit}-32)$$
$$^\circ\text{Fahrenheit} = (\tfrac{9}{5}\,^\circ\text{Celsius})+32$$

°C	°F	°F	°C
0	32	0	−17.78
10	50	20	−6.67
20	68	40	4.44
30	86	60	15.56
40	104	80	26.67
50	122	100	37.78
60	140	120	48.89
70	158	140	60.00
80	176	160	71.11
90	194	180	82.22
100	212	200	93.33
		212	100.00

ACKNOWLEDGMENTS

In addition to those mentioned in the Preface, many other individuals and firms provided us with information without which the writing of this book would have been impossible. We personally visited the great majority of those organizations and producers listed below, and we would like to take this opportunity to thank those who gave up their time and responded to our countless questions with courtesy and frankness.

AUSTRALIA
Australian Wine Board (Adelaide)

FRANCE

Alsace
Adrian Frères (Albé)
Cusenier (Mulhouse)
Dolfi (Strasbourg)
Jacobert (Colmar)
A. Legoll (Neubois)
G. E. Massenez (Bassemberg)
Meyblum (Albé)
F. Meyer (Hohwarth)
Gilbert Miclo (Lapoutroie)
Jos. Nusbaumer (Steige)

Armagnac
Bureau National Interprofessionnel de l'Armagnac (Éauze)
Janneau (Condom)
Sempé (Aignan)
L'Union des Coopératives Viticoles de l'Armagnac (Éauze)

Calvados
Bureau National des Calvados et Eaux-de-vie de Cidre et de Poiré (Caen)
Busnel (Pont-l'Évêque)
Cidrerie de Montgomery (St. Foy de Montgomery)
Distilleries Réunies (Cormeilles)
Roger Groult (St. Cyr du Ronceray)
Établissements Lecompte (Lisieux)

Cognac
Bureau National Interprofessionnel du Cognac (Cognac)
Bisquit-Dubouché (Jarnac)
Camus (Cognac)
Comandon (Jarnac)
Georges Courant (Cognac)
Courvoisier (Jarnac)
Delamain (Jarnac)

Denis-Mounié (Cognac)
A. E. Dor (Jarnac)
Hennessy (Cognac)
Hine (Jarnac)
Martell (Cognac)
Monnet (Cognac)
Otard (Cognac)
Rémy Martin (Cognac)
Salignac (Cognac)
Tonnellerie Taransaud (Cognac)
Union Coopérative de Viticulteurs Charentais (Cognac)

Other
Institut National des Appellations d'Origine (Paris)
Syndicat National des Fabricants de Liqueurs (Paris)
Bénédictine (Fécamp)
Chartreuse (Voiron)
Cointreau (St. Barthélémy d'Anjou and Paris)
Cusenier (Paris)
Garnier (Enghien-les-Bains)
Get Frères (Revel)
Jean Goyard (Ay-Champagne)
Intermarque (Cenon)
Izarra (Bayonne)
Lejay-Lagoute (Dijon)
Marie Brizard (Bordeaux)
Marnier-Lapostelle (Paris)
Pagès (Le Puy-en-Velay)
Rocher Frères (La Côte St. André)

GERMANY
Asbach & Co. (Rüdesheim am Rhein)
Eckes (Nieder Olm)
Adolf Huber (Achern/Baden)
Kammer-Kirsch (Karlsruhe)
3-Tannen Brennerei KG R. Herr (Rastatt)

ITALY
Italian Commercial Consulate (San Francisco)
Buton (Bologna)
Distillerie Grappa Valbrenta (Bessano del Grappa)
Distillerie Riunite di Liquori (Milan)
Distillerie Stock (Trieste)
Gruppo Grandi Marche Associate (Milan)
Industria Lombarda Liquori Vini Affini (Saronno)
Girolamo Luxardo (Torreglia)
Tuoni & Canepa (Livorno)

IRELAND (EIRE)
Irish Mist Liqueur Co. Ltd. (Tullamore)
Waterford Liqueurs Ltd. (Waterford)

NETHERLANDS
Erven Lucas Bols (Nieuw-Vennep)

SOUTH AFRICA
South African Consulate-General (San Francisco)
Oenological and Viticultural Research Institute (Stellenbosch)
Ko-Operatieve Wijnbouwers Vereniging (Suider-Paarl)

SPAIN
Torres (Vilafranca del Panadés)

SWITZERLAND
Verband des Schweiz. Spirituosengewerbes (Bern)
A. Dettling (Brunnen)

UNITED KINGDOM
Drambuie Liqueur Co. Ltd. (Edinburgh)
Ronald Morrison & Co. Ltd. (Edinburgh)

UNITED STATES
California Brandy Advisory Board (San Francisco, California)
California Wine Association (Delano, California)
The Christian Brothers of California (Reedley, California)
Cointreau Ltd. (Lawrenceville, New Jersey)
East-Side Winery (Lodi, California)
Franzia Brothers (Ripon, California)
Guild Winery (Lodi and Fresno, California)
Heublein, Inc. (Hartford, Connecticut)
Italian Swiss Colony (Asti, California)
John de Kuyper & Son (Cincinnati, Ohio)
Munson Shaw (New York, New York)
Nan Yang Trading Company, Inc. (Palo Alto, California)
National Wine & Spirits Co. (New York, New York)
Park Avenue Imports (New York, New York)
Paul Masson (Saratoga, California)
Schenley Affiliated Brands Corp. (New York, New York)
Suntory Ltd. (New York, New York)
United Vintners (San Francisco, California)

INDEX